The Horse in Celtic Culture

The Horse in Celtic Culture

Medieval Welsh Perspectives

edited by

Sioned Davies and Nerys Ann Jones

UNIVERSITY OF WALES PRESS
CARDIFF
1997

936.4
HOR

British Library Cataloguing-in-Publication Data
A catalogue record for this book is available from the British Library.

ISBN 0–7083–1414–7

Published with the financial support of the Arts Council of Wales

Cover design by Olwen Fowler
Front cover illustration: sculpture of the goddess Epona, reproduced by permission of Musée Luxembourgeois, Arlon, Belgium; horseman frieze based on the decoration on an early Iron Age sword scabbard from Hallstatt, Austria.

Typeset at the University of Wales Press
Printed in Great Britain by Bookcraft Ltd., Midsomer Norton, Avon

Contents

Illustrations

Acknowledgements

This volume grew out of two conferences held at University of Wales, Cardiff (1993) and the University of Edinburgh (1994). We are grateful to all those who participated in the conferences, and to both institutions for their support, especially the Department of Welsh at Cardiff, the Departments of Celtic and Scottish History and the School of Scottish Studies at Edinburgh. Special thanks go to Dauvit Broun for constructive criticism and general encouragement. We should also like to acknowledge the valuable comments we have received from D. Ellis Evans, Colin Williams, Marged Haycock, Mark Redknap and Catrin Redknap. Our thanks, too, to Susan Jenkins and Ceinwen Jones at the University of Wales Press for their help and advice in preparing the work for publication. Finally, as editors, we would like to express our gratitude to the contributors, without whom the volume would not have been possible. Diolch yn fawr.

The Contributors

Miranda Aldhouse Green, Head of Research in the Humanities, University of Wales College, Newport

Rachel Bromwich, Emeritus Reader in Celtic Languages and Literature, University of Cambridge

Sioned Davies, Senior Lecturer, Department of Welsh, University of Wales, Cardiff

Irene Hughson, Tutor in Archaeology, Department of Adult and Continuing Education, University of Glasgow

Bleddyn Owen Huws, Lecturer, Department of Welsh, University of Wales, Aberystwyth

Dafydd Jenkins, Emeritus Professor of Legal History and Welsh Law, University of Wales, Aberystwyth

Nerys Ann Jones, Honorary Research Fellow, Faculty of Arts, University of Edinburgh

Patricia Kelly, College Lecturer, Department of Early Irish, University College Dublin

Juliette Wood, Honorary Lecturer, Department of Welsh, University of Wales, Cardiff

Introduction

Sioned Davies and Nerys Ann Jones

Ever since its domestication, the horse has played a central role in the history of mankind. This multifunctional animal was responsible for the revolutionizing of transport infrastructures and fighting techniques which led ultimately to significant social, economic and cultural changes. The aim of this volume is to open up a topic which has hitherto received little attention from historians and literary specialists, namely the study of horses in Celtic culture, with the emphasis firmly on medieval Welsh perspectives. Over the past ten years historians have shown an increased interest in horses and horsemanship in medieval Europe in general, as witnessed, for example, in the work of R. H. C. Davis (1989), while English war-horses have received rigorous scrutiny by scholars such as Andrew Ayton (1994). Little use, however, has been made of Welsh sources in such studies. This collection of essays is, therefore, not only important *per se*, but also in the wider context of the development of horsemanship and military tactics in medieval Britain and Europe.

In the present volume, the contributors present in-depth analyses of the horse as reflected in their own specialist field of inquiry. It should be stressed at the outset that the intention is not to present a comprehensive collection, but rather to sample current research. A little is already known from historical sources about the significance of the horse in medieval Wales. It would seem, for example, that the horses of eastern Wales, in particular, enjoyed a good reputation, as attested by Gerald of Wales's reference to excellent stud-farms in Powys, owing to the importation of Spanish horses by Robert de Belesme, earl of Shrewsbury (Thorpe 1978, 201; Davis 1989, 81–2). Indeed, the roll of horse drawn up for Edward I at the Battle of Falkirk reveals that one-third are Powys horses (Giffin 1958, 34). There is also plenty of evidence to confirm that 'monasticism and horse-breeding often went hand in hand' (Davis 1989, 57): for example, Llywelyn ap Gruffudd (d. 1282) 'proved generous in his bestowal of foals from his own stud and others rendered to him by the monasteries of the Cistercian order' (Smith 1984, 172; see also Cowley 1977, 68, 83, 124). We know, too, that there was an active trade in horses between Ireland and Wales before the Norman Conquest, and that Welsh horses were highly valued by the Irish (Ó Corráin 1972, 58). Visual evidence from medieval Wales can, of course, be extremely useful. A carved figure of a horseman, for example, found on the late tenth- or early eleventh-century pillar-cross at St Dochdwy's churchyard, Llandough, Glamorgan, reaffirms the close bond between the rider and his steed (Redknap 1991, 67), as do the seals of the medieval Welsh lords and princes, which normally carry an image of a knight on horseback, following the same design as their Norman counterparts (Siddons 1983; Williams 1993). In spite of accessible data, such as those outlined above, there has been little extensive research on the horse in medieval Wales. F. C. Suppe's analysis of military institutions on the Welsh Marches (1994) is an exception, as is Jenny Rowland's recent article (1995) on warfare and horses in the sixth-century Welsh poem, the *Gododdin*, in which she examines the plausibility of mounted fighting, and Jane Ryan's unpublished dissertation (1993) on horses in early and medieval Welsh literature. Since the horse plays such a key role in medieval society, it was felt that a volume such as this was not only long overdue but also had exciting potential in that the topic crosses disciplines. This is clearly reflected in the diversity of the essays commissioned, which draw on folklore, pagan Celtic religion, archaeology, iconography, legal tracts, linguistics and literary sources. Another important consideration in compiling this collection was to make data in the Welsh language accessible to those who lack the relevant linguistic background.

The first chapter examines the horse's symbolism in pagan Celtic religion from around 600 BC to AD 400. Miranda Aldhouse Green's evidence is threefold: the ritual associated with the sacrificial deposition of horse remains; the images of horses and horsemen in the pre-Roman Iron Age; and finally the deities and horses in Romano-Celtic Europe, including the cult of Epona, the goddess of horses. Such evidence emphasizes the close relationship between horse and human in early European society, and may well enhance our understanding of medieval Welsh (and Irish) narrative. Irene Hughson, too, makes use of visual evidence in her discussion of horses on Pictish sculptured stones. She combines the evidence of the stones, dated from the late sixth or early seventh century to the ninth century, with information regarding the practicalities of keeping horses, to give an insight into the complex military activities of the Picts and their neighbours. This may help to throw light on some of the references to horses in our earliest Welsh poetry which, geographically, belong to the area known as the Old North (the Welsh-speaking areas of southern Scotland and northern England), and not to Wales. Two poets in particular are associated with this region, namely Taliesin, who is regarded as the founding father of the Welsh praise tradition, and Aneirin, who in his long poem, the *Gododdin*, commemorates the defeat of the war-band of the Gododdin by the Anglians of Deira and Bernicia at Catraeth (possibly Richmond near modern Catterick). Questions have been raised regarding the references to mounted fighting in the *Gododdin* (Higham 1991), and the evidence of the Pictish stones is crucial to the debate (Rowland 1995).

One important source for any study of horses is the law. Medieval Welsh law texts, unlike those of England and Ireland, have a great deal to say about horses. The body of law is generally known as the 'law of Hywel' – according to tradition, the various versions of the law operating in the Welsh kingdoms were brought together by Hywel ap Cadell, 'Hywel the Good', who became king over nearly all Wales in 942. However, it must be emphasized that these texts cannot be cited as evidence for conditions in tenth-century Wales, for the earliest manuscripts derive from the thirteenth century and show signs of development and adaptation to changing circumstances. Dafydd Jenkins examines two tractates within the corpus, namely the tractate on the Value of Wild and Tame, which gives information about the different kinds of horses, and the Laws of Court, with their illustration of the life-style of the local ruler and his entourage, including officers such as the Groom of the Rein and the Chief Groom. An interesting and sometimes problematic feature of the legal – and literary – material is the terminology used for horses. Patricia Kelly's chapter focuses on such linguistic data, and examines the various words for 'horse' in the Celtic languages, together with their derivation. The discussion is mainly confined to an investigation of the oldest words, primarily in Irish and Welsh, with a brief coverage of the changes brought about by Anglo-Norman influence, where new terms may well reflect technological developments and highlight intercultural exchange in the period.

The fact that horses played a central role in medieval Welsh life and society is clearly reflected in the poetry and prose narratives of the period. An index to the knowledge of the poets and story-tellers is preserved in the catalogue of characters and episodes arranged in threes, and known collectively as the 'Triads of the Island of Britain' (Bromwich 1978). The 'Triads of the Horses' (the earliest versions are found in two thirteenth-century manuscripts) form a distinct group within the corpus. These, together with an obscure poem in the fourteenth-century Book of Taliesin (NLW Peniarth MS 2), entitled *Canu y Meirch* ('The Song of the Horses'), list the individual names of horses and often give the names of their owners. The material is analysed here by Rachel Bromwich. Her discussion also examines the allusions in Welsh literary sources and French poems to the horses named in the Triads. It is perhaps surprising that so few of these proper names occur in medieval Welsh narrative, for horses play a significant role in the tales, especially in the later romances. The eleven native prose tales, dated between the end of the eleventh and the beginning of the fourteenth centuries, and known collectively as the *Mabinogion*, are the focus of Sioned Davies's chapter. Her discussion centres on the descriptions of horses as a stylistic element within the corpus. She argues for the existence of an established narrative technique for describing horses, and draws particular attention to the use of compound adjectives resulting in a rhythmic pattern which in itself echoes the movement of the animal. The essay also makes some reference to the role of horses within the narrative, including the mutilation of the Irish horses in the Second Branch of the *Mabinogi*.

Two chapters draw directly on the poetic tradition of Wales. Nerys Ann Jones examines the horse as depicted by the court poets of the twelfth and thirteenth centuries. These professional poets, known generally as the Poets of the Princes, were associated with the royal families of the independent kingdoms of Wales, and their main function was to sing the praises of such families. The ideal patron is praised for two major reasons – his ferocity in battle and his generosity at court in times of peace. Horses feature prominently in both themes, for they are ridden in battle and distributed to suppliants at court as a symbol of the patron's largesse. Care must be taken, however, when using this corpus as a historical source, owing to the conservative tendencies in Welsh court poetry. As emphasized by Jones, these *Gogynfeirdd* (literally 'the fairly early poets') echo themes, imagery and vocabulary of the earlier *Cynfeirdd* ('the early poets'), such as Taliesin and Aneirin. With the demise of the independent princes by the end of the thirteenth century, poets sought new patrons, and turned to the native *uchelwyr* ('gentry'). The professional poet now had to be mobile to make his living – the gentry could not afford to support him on a permanent basis, and he was forced to travel the country, moving from one patron to another. A sturdy horse was therefore essential. As a result, a large number of the surviving poems from the fourteenth to the mid-sixteenth century request and offer thanks for horses, which is the theme of Bleddyn Owen Huws's chapter. In this context, the ideal horse is described in great detail, its characteristics conforming to those of the perfect horse as evinced in the sixteenth-century *Llyfr Marchwriaeth* ('Book of Horsemanship'), a translation of an English treatise by Leonard Mascall (O'Rahilly 1960). As well as being an important source for historical evidence, Huws shows that these poems are polished literary productions, demanding great skill and craft on the part of the poet, as exemplified by Tudur Aled. Towards the end of the period, the traditional *cywydd march* ('horse poem') becomes an object of parody, although it would seem that the genre itself continued to be popular until the later seventeenth century, when patronage declined and the professional bardic order ceased to exist.

The volume opens with a discussion of horses in pagan Celtic religion. The final chapter takes us back to this early period to examine the theory that medieval – and modern – folklore consists of fragments or survivals of ancient beliefs and myths. Juliette Wood questions this model of cultural survival, and argues that the links between the ancient Celtic past and modern Celtic cultures should be expressed as continuity of structure and symbolic meaning, rather than continuity of culture. She focuses on three examples – the Mari Lwyd (a winter custom involving a horse skull draped in a sheet); the character Rhiannon from the medieval 'Four Branches of the *Mabinogi*', whose equine associations have suggested to many scholars a link with the Celtic horse goddess Epona; and thirdly, supernatural-experience narratives in contemporary Welsh folk tradition which feature horses, both real and ghostly. She concludes that, although some of the examples may echo earlier Celtic material, one should not underestimate the importance of boundary images in the three examples – they all involve temporal, geographical or social transition.

Many other aspects of the horse in medieval Wales remain to be investigated. We hope that this volume will not only be of use as a work of reference, but will also encourage others working in the field, be it history (social and economic), linguistics, folklore, religion, literary or, indeed, veterinary studies. The importance of interdisciplinary research, and the pooling of information and knowledge, cannot be overestimated

– it is only through specialist, diverse approaches, such as those presented here, that the general picture of the horse in medieval Welsh life and society, and indeed in a wider Celtic context, can begin to emerge.

References

Ayton, Andrew. 1994. *Knights and Warhorses: Military Service and the English Aristocracy under Edward III* (Woodbridge, Boydell Press).

Bromwich, Rachel (ed.). 1978. *Trioedd Ynys Prydein: The Welsh Triads*, 2nd edn. (Cardiff, University of Wales Press).

Cowley, F. G. 1977. *The Monastic Order in South Wales, 1066–1349* (Cardiff, University of Wales Press).

Davis, R. H. C. 1989. *The Medieval Warhorse: Origin, Development and Redevelopment* (London, Thames & Hudson).

Giffin, Mary. 1958. 'The Date of the *Dream of Rhonabwy*', *Transactions of the Honourable Society of Cymmrodorion*, 33–40.

Higham, N. J. 1991. 'Cavalry in Early Bernicia?', *Northern History*, 27, 236–41.

Ó Corráin, Donncha. 1972. *Ireland Before the Normans* (Dublin, Gill & Macmillan).

O'Rahilly, Cecile. 1960. 'A Welsh Treatise on Horses', *Celtica*, 5, 145–60.

Redknap, Mark. 1991. *The Christian Celts: Treasures of Late Celtic Wales* (Cardiff, National Museum of Wales).

Rowland, Jenny. 1995. 'Warfare and Horses in the *Gododdin* and the Problem of Catraeth', *Cambrian Medieval Celtic Studies*, 30, 13–40.

Ryan, Jane. 1993. 'A Study of Horses in Early and Medieval Welsh Literature, *c*.600–*c*.1300 A.D.' (University of Wales M.Phil. thesis).

Siddons, Michael Powell. 1983. 'Welsh Equestrian Seals', *National Library of Wales Journal*, 23, 292–318.

Smith, Llinos Beverley. 1984. 'The *Gravamina* of the Community of Gwynedd against Llywelyn ap Gruffudd', *Bulletin of the Board of Celtic Studies*, 31, 158–73.

Suppe, F. C. 1994. *Military Institutions on the Welsh Marches: Shropshire A.D. 1066–1300* (Woodbridge, Boydell Press).

Thorpe, Lewis (tr.). 1978. *Gerald of Wales: The Journey through Wales and The Description of Wales* (Harmondsworth, Penguin Books).

Williams, David H. 1993. *Catalogue of Seals in the National Museum of Wales*, i (Cardiff, National Museum of Wales).

Further Reading

Rachel Bromwich, *Dafydd ap Gwilym: A Selection of Poems* (Harmondsworth, Penguin Books, 1985).

Rachel Bromwich, A. O. H. Jarman and Brynley F. Roberts (eds.), *The Arthur of the Welsh* (Cardiff, University of Wales Press, 1991).

A. D. Carr, *Medieval Wales* (London and New York, Macmillan Press and St Martin's Press, 1995).

T. M. Charles-Edwards, *The Welsh Laws* (Cardiff, University of Wales Press, 1989).

Joseph P. Clancy, *The Earliest Welsh Poetry* (London, Macmillan, 1970).

Tony Conran, *Welsh Verse* (Bridgend, Poetry Wales Press, 1986).

John Davies, *A History of Wales* (Harmondsworth, Penguin Books, 1994).

R. R. Davies, *Conquest, Coexistence, and Change: Wales 1063–1415* (Oxford University Press, 1987).

Sioned Davies, *The Four Branches of the Mabinogi* (Llandysul, Gomer Press, 1993).

Miranda J. Green (ed.), *The Celtic World* (London and New York, Routledge, 1995).

K. H. Jackson (ed.), *The Gododdin: The Oldest Scottish Poem* (Edinburgh University Press, 1969).

A. O. H. Jarman, *The Cynfeirdd: Early Welsh Poets and Poetry* (Cardiff, University of Wales Press, 1981).

A. O. H. Jarman (ed.), *Aneirin: Y Gododdin, Britain's Oldest Heroic Poem* (Llandysul, Gomer Press, 1988).

A. O. H. Jarman and G. R. Hughes (eds.), *A Guide to Welsh Literature*, i (revised edn., Cardiff, University of Wales Press, 1992).

A. O. H. Jarman and G. R. Hughes (eds.), *A Guide to Welsh Literature*, ii (Swansea, Christopher Davies, 2nd edn. 1984).

Dafydd Jenkins. *The Law of Hywel Dda* (Llandysul, Gomer Press, 1986).

Dafydd Johnston, *The Literature of Wales: A Pocket Guide* (Cardiff, University of Wales Press, 1994).

Richard M. Loomis and Dafydd Johnston, *Medieval Welsh Poems* (Binghampton, New York, Medieval and Renaissance Texts and Studies, 1992).

Proinsias Mac Cana, *The Mabinogi* (Cardiff, University of Wales Press, revised edn., 1992).

Eric H. Nicoll (ed.), *A Pictish Panorama* (Balgavie, Angus, The Pinkfoot Press, 1995).

Trefor M. Owen, *Welsh Folk Customs* (Llandysul, Gomer Press, 1994).

Glanville Price, *The Languages of Britain* (London, Edward Arnold, 1984).

Brynley F. Roberts (ed.), *Early Welsh Poetry: Studies in the Book of Aneirin* (Aberystwyth, National Library of Wales, 1988).

Jenny Rowland, *Early Welsh Saga Poetry: A Study and Edition of the Englynion* (Cambridge, D. S. Brewer, 1990).

Meic Stephens (ed.), *The Oxford Companion to the Literature of Wales* (Oxford University Press, 1986).

David Walker, *Medieval Wales* (Cambridge University Press, 1990).

Ifor Williams (ed.), *The Poems of Taliesin*, English version by J. E. Caerwyn Williams (Dublin Institute for Advanced Studies, 1975).

J. E. C. Williams, *The Poets of the Welsh Princes* (Cardiff, University of Wales Press, revised edn. 1994).

The Symbolic Horse in Pagan Celtic Europe: An Archaeological Perspective

Miranda Aldhouse Green

Introduction

The term 'Celtic' means different things to different people. Present-day archaeologists, in particular, often recoil from the term as used to describe the Iron Age communities of non-Mediterranean Europe (Collis 1993; 1996; Hill 1996, 96). But Graeco-Roman historians from as early as 500 BC recorded the customs and activities of a group of peoples whom they recognized as having certain common cultural elements: these they called *Keltoi* (e.g., Herodotus IV. 48, Rawlinson 1862, iii. 37; Green 1992b, 9). In addition, the material culture of much of Europe during the later first millennium BC appears to have possessed shared features: weapon types, jewellery, art and evidence for religious practices exemplify this apparent commonality of tradition. From the third century BC onwards, there is Celtic linguistic evidence in the form of personal and place-names (Evans 1995; Meid 1992). Clearly, academic rigour can demand the use of the term 'Iron Age' rather than 'Celtic' to describe the material culture of this period. However, 'Celtic' is convenient partly because the term may be used to embrace not only the last 500 years or so before the Roman era but also the cultural traditions of central and western Europe which continued alongside new Mediterranean influences during and after the Roman occupation. As long as the term is defined in any given context, the use of 'Celt' and 'Celtic' is, to my mind, perfectly acceptable and is at least as valid as the labels 'Greek' and 'Roman' (Green 1995b).

My intention in this chapter is to explore the role of the horse in the religious beliefs and practices of Celtic Europe from around 600 BC to AD 400, a time-span which includes both the Iron Age and Roman periods.

The geographical scope ranges from Britain and Spain in the west to Hungary, the Czech Republic and Slovenia in the east; from Scotland in the north to northern Italy and Croatia in the south.

The Iron Age Celts were, to all intents and purposes, non-literate, so all the evidence pertaining to this period is necessarily in the form of material culture. In the Roman period, inscriptions give us names for divinities, and there is some scattered documentary evidence from the Mediterranean world which alludes to Celtic religious practices, but we are still almost wholly dependent upon archaeological evidence. Thus any information concerning the role of horses in the pagan religious tradition comes from examination of the remains of horses themselves and from depictions of the animals in art and iconography. Because all this evidence is indirect and non-explicit and since belief-systems belong to the realm of thought, it is necessary to exercise extreme caution in making inferences about ancient perceptions of the supernatural.

Before progressing to an exploration of the horse's symbolism within the pagan Celtic tradition, two initial questions need cursory consideration: one concerns the fundamental character of Celtic religion, as far as we can perceive it; the other relates to the secular significance of the horse within early Celtic society. Both these issues are highly relevant to our understanding of the horse in religious thought and practice. The evidence at our disposal points to a religious system based upon recognition of the numinous in all aspects of the natural world, an animistic perception in which each tree, lake, mountain and spring contained a spiritual presence, as did the sky, sun and thunder. As part of this belief in the all-pervading presence of the supernatural, animals were recognized as having a sacred dimension; both wild and domestic beasts were strongly associated with symbolism which was frequently based upon observation of their particular qualities. Thus the stag was revered for its speed and virility, the dog for its usefulness to humans and for its ability to heal itself, and the horse for its power, beauty, swiftness and bravery in warfare (Green 1986, 17–38; 1992a; 1992b, 22).

During the eighth century BC, the horse was adopted in Europe for riding as well as traction (for plough or cart). The importance of horses in warfare, hunting and the economy was recognized, and the animal became a symbol of an aristocratic warrior élite: it was prestigious to own a horse, which was relatively expensive to feed and maintain, and Celtic cavalry was renowned throughout Europe by the first century BC (Hyland 1990; Green 1992a, 66–87; Megaw 1970, 13). The horse-drawn chariot, obsolete in Gaul by Caesar's time but used in Britain at least until the late first century AD, was a formidable Celtic war-machine described by Roman observers with great respect (e.g., Caesar, *De Bello Gallico* VII. 66, Wiseman and Wiseman 1980, 162). In addition, the sexual vigour of the horse endowed it with symbolism associated with fertility and prosperity.

Horses, Ritual and Sacrifice

All over the Celtic world there is evidence of recurring ritual associated with the sacrificial deposition of horse remains. This cult activity took place mainly during the Iron Age and occurred in shrines, settlements and graves. The sacrifice of such valuable animals as horses and cattle must have been undertaken as a response to great crises or some other momentous event. In the sixth century BC, a cave at Býčiskála in Moravia, at the eastern edge of Celtic Europe, was the focus of ritual behaviour which included the disposal of forty women, perhaps the victims of ritual murder, and two horses which had been slaughtered and then quartered. In an associated cauldron was a human skull and another had been made into a drinking-cup (Megaw 1970, no. 35). Two later pre-Roman sanctuaries in Gaul have revealed evidence of elaborate ritual activity involving the sacrifice of horses: at Gournay-sur-Aronde (Oise) which was established as a shrine in the fourth century BC, seven horses of mature years were deposited in specific positions in the enclosure ditch. Their bodies had been subjected to excarnation (exposure) after death so that decomposition was sufficiently advanced to allow the manipulation and anatomical grouping of the bones to take place prior to deposition. A significant feature of this horse ritual is that the animals were deposited in association with a great many weapons, many ritually bent or broken, and the inference is that this cult behaviour may have been related to war rites (Brunaux 1988; Meniel 1987). At the Battle of Orange in 105 BC, the Teutonic tribe of the Cimbri dedicated all the spoil, including sacrificed enemies, horses and weapons, to the gods. In view of the fact that men, too, were interred in the ditch at the Gournay sanctuary, we may be witnessing a similar rite to that chronicled by Livy (*Periocha* XIV. 79, Rivet 1988, 46). The association of men and horses in ritual deposition can be clearly seen at the pre-Roman shrine of Ribemont-sur-Ancre (Somme), where a curious 'ossuary' or bone-house was constructed, consisting of the limb-bones of people and horses, carefully selected so as to be of appropriate length for maximum stability and symmetry. Again, the bodies had been allowed to decompose to separate the long bones and again the remains were associated with weapons which were arranged to form a circle around the ossuary. Other sanctuaries also bear witness to horse ritual: the hillfort of South Cadbury (Somerset) contains a number of small rectangular buildings which have been identified as shrines, and associated with one of these were pits containing the skulls of cattle and horses, carefully deposited the right way up (Alcock 1972, 136–53; Wait 1985, 166–90). The late Iron Age fortified town or *oppidum* at Liptovska Mara in Bohemia contained a sacred area in the centre of which was a pit; inside were the burnt remains of horses, dogs and other animals (Brunaux 1988, 40; Green 1992a, 114). At a basilical shrine of third-century AD date at Bourton Grounds in Buckinghamshire, associated with a temple of traditional Romano-Celtic type (an inner *cella* surrounded by a concentric ambulatory), a horse skull was buried beneath the threshold, perhaps as a foundation offering (Green 1976, 179; Lewis 1966; C. Green 1965, 356–66), showing that horse ritual continued among the Romano-British Celts. Of similar date is the curious sunken shrine at Cambridge at which a complete horse, bull and hunting dogs were carefully interred (anon. 1978, 57–60).

Iron Age graves were the focus of recurrent and elaborate animal ritual, where creatures were buried entire in order to accompany deceased humans into the Otherworld, or as joints symbolizing the cult feast. The chariot burial known as the 'King's Barrow' in East Yorkshire is rare among this grave type in that the horse team itself was slaughtered and interred along with the chariot and its owner (Green 1986, 124–6; Stead 1979). Generally, the horse harness only was buried to represent the presence of the animals. This dead warrior must have been of high status for such valuable beasts to have been taken out of circulation for sacrificial purposes: it is unlikely that the two horses were both killed simultaneously in battle. At Soissons, two cart burials were accompanied by veritable funerary cortèges, each consisting of whole horses, goats, sheep, pigs and dogs (Green 1992a, 105, fig. 5.8; Meniel 1987, 101–43). A recent discovery, made during excavations for the extension to the London Underground system at Stratford, East London, consists of the burial of a horse and a man, dating to the third century BC (Green 1992a, 99, fig. 5.5). Sometimes the interment of a single horse bone in a tomb symbolized the entire animal: this happened in the Gaulish cemeteries of Rouliers in the Ardennes, Epiais-Rhus (Aisne) and Tartigny (Oise) (Meniel 1987, 33–46, 101–43; 1989).

Pits, particularly in Britain, were closely associated with animal ritual, whether or not a cult purpose was their primary function. A ritual pit at Bekesbourne in Kent contained an idiosyncratic deposit consisting of some complete pots, and underneath them a flat stone on which a circle of horse teeth had been carefully arranged (Green 1976, 230; Ross 1968, 260). In central southern England, a recurring religious tradition during the Iron Age was the use of disused grain storage pits for ritual purposes, perhaps in thanksgiving to the infernal spirits for keeping the seed-corn fresh and in propitiation for the penetration of their territory (Wait 1985; Cunliffe 1986, 155–71; 1992). The animals involved include all the main domestic species (cattle, sheep, pigs, horses and dogs), and may consist of complete or partial bodies. Some pits contain multiple animal burials: in a number of instances, horses and dogs were interred together, perhaps in reflection of the particularly close relationship with humans enjoyed by both these animals. Indeed, the combination of these two creatures as sacrificial deposits may represent rituals involved with hunting, an activity which employed both dogs and horses. It is the grain silos of Danebury in Hampshire which have revealed the most complex cult practice associated with horses. Here the recurrent custom of interring horses and dogs together was observed: in one pit where this occurred, one fore- and one hind-leg of the horse were deliberately repositioned and the animal's head had been placed behind the torso and close to the body of its canine companion. In another multiple burial, only part of the horse was present and heavy lumps of flint had been carefully positioned inside the thoracic cavity. The body bore evidence of its evisceration prior to burial, and two young pigs were deposited with the horse remains. Associated with the beasts were other objects whose presence must have been the result of complicated ritual behaviour: burnt flints, blocks of chalk, slingstones, pottery and a whetstone (Green 1992a, 115–16; Grant 1989; Cunliffe 1986, 155–71). In many of the Danebury pits, only the skulls of horses had been buried and the inference has to be that the heads were of specific significance. We would do well to remember the emphasis placed by the ancient Celts on the human head (Lambrechts 1954). It may be that the head could represent the entire body, *pars pro toto*.

It is open to debate how we should interpret these pit burials of horses: they could have been sacrificial deposits, the result of rituals whereby a prestigious and useful animal was perceived as an appropriate offering to the infernal deities. Alternatively, these animals and the dogs sometimes associated with them may have represented the much-loved companions of humans which were dispatched at the same time as their owners died, in order to transfer with them to the Otherworld.

Current rethinking of certain British Iron Age issues involves the construction of new models for the interpretation of some animal deposits, including those of horses. The frequent discovery of horse remains, especially in Wessex, in situations which can be described as liminal (associated with boundaries or thresholds) has led some scholars to argue for their possible association with liminal perceptions of horses as creatures that straddled the two worlds of the 'civilized' order connected with settlement, on the one hand, and the areas outside enclosed habitations and shrines (Hill 1996; Parker Pearson 1996). Horses were domesticated, but they enjoyed a special relationship with humankind which included a particular respect, and their management as animals which were rounded up and broken in at need (Cunliffe 1993, 84), rather than kept in herds like cattle, may support the notion that horses were regarded as belonging both to the wild and the settled worlds.

The hypotheses proposed in the above discussion can be nothing more than that. J. D. Hill has given a timely warning against glib interpretations based upon perceptions which are intelligible to the modern mind. The possibly fundamental 'otherness' of the Iron Age should not be underestimated (Hill 1989, 16–24) and it may therefore never be possible fully to comprehend the nature of such ritual behaviour.

Images of Horses in the Pre-Roman Iron Age

The European Iron Age covers a period from around the early seventh century BC to the Roman conquest (first century BC to first century AD depending on region). Religious iconography is relatively rare during this period but certain images of horses and indeed horsemen indicate that the animal was of considerable symbolic importance both to artists and to their patrons.

During the earliest Iron Age, the so-called 'Hallstatt' phase (from the great cemetery at Hallstatt in Austria), the influences of the knightly élite made themselves felt in the artistic themes of their metalwork. Sheet-bronze vessels bear images of horsemen and horses: the seventh–sixth century BC bucket lid from Kleinklein in Austria is decorated with friezes of solar wheel symbols, foot soldiers and cavalry (Green 1991, fig. 18; anon. 1980a, 3.58). This is some of the earliest Iron

A horseman frieze on an early Iron Age sword scabbard from Hallstatt, Austria
(Natürhistorisches Museum, Vienna).

Age evidence for a symbolic link between horses and the sun, which recurred throughout the Iron Age and which had its roots in the preceding Bronze Age. The horses on the Kleinklein piece have radiate manes, as if in imitation of the sun's rays, and they are ithyphallic in reflection of their symbolism of virile fecundity. In about 400 BC one of the martial aristocracy was buried at Hallstatt with a sword whose scabbard was ornamented with a frieze of horsemen riding to battle, spears at the ready; the leading cavalryman tramples an enemy beneath his mount's hoofs (Green 1992a, fig. 4.2; anon. 1980b, 260–1, no. 115). The bronze model cult wagon from Strettweg in Austria dates to the seventh century BC: it comes from the tomb of a warrior or hunter who was cremated and his remains interred with his weapons, and the model is often interpreted as representing a ritual stag-hunt. The wagon supports two model stags accompanied by infantry and cavalry; at the centre of the group is a goddess who raises a basin above her head as if in acceptance of sacrificial gifts (Megaw and Megaw 1989: 33–4; anon. 1980a, 3.50; Green 1989, fig. 56). What is interesting here is the inference of the horse's use in hunting. This is confirmed in other iconography, such as the Iron Age rock art of Camonica Valley in north Italy, where men are depicted on horseback hunting deer (Green 1992a, 49; Anati 1965, 1, 29, 89–90). Pots from the seventh–sixth century BC tombs at Sopron-Varhély in Hungary depict horsemen, sometimes associated with stag-hunting (Green 1992a, 78, fig. 4.10; Megaw and Megaw 1989, 30–2). The Greek historian Arrian, writing in the second century AD, remarks on the hunting practices of the Celts, for whom it was a sport of nobles rather than a means of acquiring food (*Cynegeticus* XXIII, Hercher 1884, 72) and it was thus appropriate to use horses in such an élite pastime.

A group of Iron Age shrines and *oppida* in the lower Rhône Valley region of southern Gaul contain carved stones which demonstrate the importance of the horse as a war symbol. The sanctuary at Roquepertuse was decorated with a stone on which a frieze of four horse heads had been incised, perhaps as early as the sixth century BC. The shrine may well have been dedicated to a god of war, since the columns of the portico contained a number of niches within each of which the skull of a young man killed in battle had been placed. Roquepertuse also produced stone figures of warrior gods wearing armour (Benoit 1969). A stone lintel from a shrine within the *oppidum* of Nages (Gard) is carved with images of trotting horses which alternate with severed human heads, reinforcing the war associations of these horse depictions. A number of classical commentators on the Celts speak of their custom of collecting the heads of their dead enemies as battle trophies (Livy X. 26, Weissenborn 1886, 175–7; Diodorus V. 29.4, Tierney 1960; Strabo IV. 4.5, Tierney 1960). A stone at the nearby town of Entremont shows a horseman with a severed head slung from his horse's neck. The chest of the stone warrior-figure from Sainte-Anastasie is decorated with a frieze of incised horses. The sanctuary at Mouriès, also in the lower Rhône Valley, was decorated with incised stones depicting stylized figures of horses and horsemen; one of the animals has three horns, a feature which clearly marks him as a supernatural creature (bulls and even boars with three horns are recorded in Romano-Celtic iconography) (Benoit 1969, pls. VIII, IX, XI; Benoit 1981, Bémont 1984, nos. 152–4, 160; Pobé and Roubier 1961, no. 13; Green 1989, 146, fig. 62). The warrior-horse–severed-head connection may be seen again at Saint-Michel de Valbonne (Var), where an Iron Age stone shaped like a menhir depicts a schematized figure of a horseman, his head of exaggerated size, riding over five severed heads (Espérandieu, no. 38; Thevenot 1968, 56–7).

Horses form part of the imagery of the later Iron Age: one of the plates of the great silver-gilt cauldron from Gundestrup in Jutland depicts a procession of warriors with battle-gear which is of recognizably late La Tène type: swords, helmets, shields and carnyxes (boar-head trumpets). The upper group consists of cavalrymen who ride into battle wearing spurs (Green 1992a, fig. 4.5; Olmsted 1979). A number of Iron Age coins depict horses either ridden or harnessed to chariots. On coins of the Breton tribe of the Redones, a female charioteer controls a large galloping horse with a human head, a common image on coins of north-west Gaul (Green 1992a, fig. 4.13; 1992c; Duval 1987) and one which, like the Mouriès triple-horned horse,

A horse on an early Iron Age silver coin from Bratislava, Slovakia
(Slovenské Národné Múzeum).

betrays its supernatural status. A great many Celtic coins are decorated
on the reverse with horses associated with unequivocal solar symbols,
echoing the later Bronze Age and Hallstatt links between horses and the
sun alluded to above. The prototypes of this Iron Age currency were
fourth-century BC coins of Philip II of Macedon on the reverse of which
is the image of Apollo as a sun god driving the solar chariot. The Celtic
artist took this original and transformed it according to local taste which
favoured abstract, schematized designs: the chariot was reduced to a
single horse sometimes with an isolated wheel beneath, but the solar
symbolism is intensified and must reflect local cult tradition. Indeed,
wheel and sun may be virtually interchangeable and the solar disc may
be represented by a great wheel hanging in the sky.

Communities in European prehistory often depicted the sun as a
spoked wheel, presumably because of perceptions of a resemblance
between the spokes and the solar rays and because the moving wheel
symbolized the daily rotation of the sun across the sky (Green 1991,
117–18; Allen 1980, 141–2). A silver coin from Bratislava depicts a horse
accompanied by a huge wheel-like sun symbol (Zachar 1987, pl. 201):

9

the beast is, once again, presented as belonging to the supernatural dimension, being portrayed with a triple phallus, a fertility symbol which appears on horse images of the Hallstatt Iron Age and at Camonica Valley, and which presumably serves to emphasize the role of the animal as an emblem of sexual vigour and the fecundity of the herd.

Of the fourteen or so hill-figures of white horses carved in the chalk of the Wessex downlands, only one, the Uffington White Horse, has a genuine claim to Celtic antiquity. The elegant, attenuated figure was carved high up on the escarpment just beneath the Iron Age hill-fort of Uffington Castle in Oxfordshire. The animal is highly schematic, with a long body, disjointed legs and a curious beaked head. It has been difficult to posit an accurate chronology for the horse, but it pre-dates the twelfth century since it is mentioned in references going back to 1084. Stylistically, the horse appears to belong to the later Iron Age, bearing close resemblances to Celtic horse images on coins and to a bronze horse model from Silchester, not far from Uffington. Recent investigations by the Oxford Archaeological Unit support an early date for the Uffington White Horse. Whilst the traditional view is that it was perhaps carved by the Atrebates in about 50 BC as a tribal emblem designed to protect the tribe and its territory (Woolner 1965; Petrie 1926; Grinsell 1958, 149–50, pl. VIII; Palmer 1990; Green 1995a), it should be noted that the latest research on the Uffington Horse (Miles and Palmer 1995) suggests that the image may have been carved as early as the Late Bronze Age (*c.* 900 BC).

The hoard of bronzes from Neuvy-en-Sullias (Loiret) was buried just at the time of the Roman conquest of Gaul, in the mid first-century BC. It probably came from a nearby sanctuary at Fleury and may have been buried to safeguard the temple treasures from looting at the hands of the invading Roman forces. The hoard consisted of a number of figurines including those of female dancers, three boars (one nearly life-size), a stag and a horse (Megaw and Megaw 1989, no. 238; Espérandieu, no. 2978; Green 1989, figs. 55, 59, 63). Roman influence is indicated by the inscription accompanying the horse which dedicates the image to a Celtic deity Rudiobus. We have no clue as to the identity or function of Rudiobus, but we can take it that a horse statuette was deemed an appropriate offering to him. With the Neuvy-en-Sullias horse, we have reached the Romano-Celtic period where, for the first time, inscriptions give us names of people and divinities, and where imagery begins to illuminate the roles and functions of Celtic horses.

Deities and Horses in Romano-Celtic Europe

The physical expression of the sacred blossomed in Celtic Europe under the influence of Graeco-Roman artistic tradition, in which the gods were represented mimetically as humans and epigraphic dedications gave them names. Now images of divinities were given accompanying emblems or attributes which symbolically represented their functions and concerns. What happened in the Celtic world is that pre-existing belief-systems were for the first time given fully tangible expression. That this expression reflects a pre-Roman system is indicated by their foreignness to the Mediterranean world: a complex pantheon seems to have been venerated, particularly in the Rhineland, Gaul and Britain, which conceptually had little to do with the religious structures of the classical world, although such indigenous divine beings may reflect certain influences from Graeco-Roman tradition in their representation or in the use of dedications using Latin written forms.

The importance of horses to early Celtic societies is reflected in the many Romano-Celtic cults for which this animal was a central focus. It is interesting that some of the symbolism attributable to horses during the pre-Roman Iron Age – notably fertility, warfare and the sun – continued very strongly during the Roman period.

Epona: goddess of horses

Epona's name derives from *epos*, a Celtic word meaning 'horse'. The image of the goddess, which is frequently associated with dedications to her, shows her extremely close link with her cult animal, without which she is never represented. There are two main forms by which Epona was depicted: one type consists of a figure of a woman seated side-saddle on a mare, a foal frequently shown suckling or lying asleep beneath its mother; on the second type, Epona is depicted seated or standing between two or more horses. The goddess was venerated over wide areas of Celtic Europe, but her cult was particularly popular in the Rhineland and in eastern parts of Gaul, especially among the Burgundian tribes. She was worshipped as far afield as Scotland and North Africa, and she was invoked in Rome itself, where she enjoyed sufficiently high status to merit an official festival within the Roman religious calendar, on 18 December. Several Classical writers allude to her cult (for example, Minucius Felix, *Octavianus* XXVIII. 7, Holden 1853, 151; Apuleius *Metamorphoses* III. 27, van der Paardt 1971, 21) and it is clear that

A representation of Epona from near Meursault, Burgundy
(Beaune, Musée des Beaux Arts)

Epona was respected even among the educated middle classes of Roman society.

Epona appears to have been a multifunctional goddess, and her horse symbolizes the diversity of her concerns. To the soldiers serving in the Roman army on the Rhine frontier (many of whom were recruited from the Celtic provinces), Epona was worshipped as a goddess who was perceived as a protectress of both themselves and their horses. The calibre of a cavalryman's mount on the battlefield was crucial both to his personal safety and to the outcome of a campaign, and these Romano-

Celtic horsemen were probably often the descendants of the warrior aristocracy who were at the apex of free (pre-Roman) Celtic society. At Kastel near Bonn, Epona is represented on a stone relief riding side-saddle on a proud, well-bred horse whose high-stepping walk resembles that of an animal taking part in a military parade (Green 1989, 22, fig. 8; Espérandieu, no. 5863). On a stone from Beihingen near Stuttgart, Epona sits between two groups of three and four horses which walk towards her in formation as if to do her homage (Espérandieu, *German* vol., no. 404).

The Burgundian images of Epona show her to have been venerated above all as a divinity of domestic prosperity and well-being. The evidence for this lies both in the images and dedications themselves and in their context. Most of the evidence for Epona's cult comes from houses in which there must have been private shrines. Only at Entrains (Nièvre) have the remains of an official temple to Epona been found, together with two inscriptions, one of which records the dedication of the sanctuary to the goddess (Magnen and Thevenot 1953, nos. 2–3). The Burgundian images from the tribal territories of the Aedui and the Lingones emphasize the link between Epona and fertile abundance: their most distinctive characteristic is the presence of a foal which suckles his mother, trots behind her or lies asleep between her hoofs. The relief found between Puligny and Meursault depicts Epona seated on a high-stepping mare whose foal walks behind her front legs (Magnen and Thevenot 1953, no. 181); on the carving from Mellecy near Châlon-sur-Saône, the foal trots behind his mother, his head raised towards the goddess as though hoping she will feed him (Green 1989, 19, fig. 7). Indeed on many depictions, Epona offers corn or fruit to the foal on an offering-dish. A bronze group from an unprovenanced site in Wiltshire displays the goddess seated between two ponies, one male and one female, which eat from a *patera* (offering-plate) filled with corn resting on her lap (Johns 1971–2, 37–41). Sometimes Epona rests her feet on the back of the foal, a curious gesture but one which Drioux (1934, 78–82) suggests has healing symbolism associated with the curing of injuries to feet or hoofs. Certainly Epona's presence at such healing sanctuaries as Sainte-Fontaine de Freyming (Moselle) and Allerey (Côte d'Or) (Thevenot 1968, 187–91; Espérandieu, no. 8235) indicates that her functions could embrace healing as well as plenty.

Epona's cult could also be associated with the passage of life and death: she is depicted several times at the great Metz cemetery of La Horgne-au-Sablon, and one of these images shows the goddess seated on her mare accompanied by a figure who follows close behind (Espérandieu, no. 4355). The suggested interpretation is of Epona as a guardian of the dead, leading the human soul to the Otherworld. This chthonic (underworld) symbolism is apparent from some of Epona's attributes, notably the key and the *mappa*. At Grand (Vosges) and Gannat (Allier), the goddess holds a large key which, at one level, may represent the stable door but, at another, the key to the Otherworld (Espérandieu, nos. 4894, 1618). On the relief at Mussig-Vicenz near Strasbourg (Espérandieu, no. 7290), Epona carries a *mappa* or napkin, an object which was used in Roman sport as the signal for the start of horse races (Suetonius, *Nero* 22, Graves 1962, 197–8). Graham Webster (1986: 70–2) has suggested that the presence of the *mappa* as Epona's symbol may link the horse theme with the goddess's role as presider over the beginning of life just as the key may symbolize the end. Other possible chthonic attributes include the dog and the raven, both of which accompany Epona at Altrier in Luxemburg (Espérandieu, no. 4219).

Epona was clearly a complex deity with many concerns, but we have to start with the premise of her fundamental horse symbolism. At the most basic level, Epona may have been a goddess of horse breeding: the tribes of Burgundy, where she enjoyed such popularity, were renowned both for their horses and for the skill of their cavalry. Among the Romano-Celtic soldiers who guarded the frontier provinces, the goddess was their patron and protector. In a civilian context, Epona was a divinity of plenty, healing and death, and in this respect she shared many of the functions of the mother goddesses. Epona may have been, in a sense, a goddess of sovereignty, a guardian of territory and of tribal boundaries, a role in which her symbolism as purveyor of abundance and fertility would accord well with her concern as presider of cavalrymen and, by implication, war (Linduff 1979; Oaks 1986).

The Horseman Cults

In an earlier section, reference was made to some early Iron Age representations of horsemen. In Romano-Celtic Europe, especially in Britain, there is evidence of a horseman cult which has an outward military symbolism but which may, within the context of a peaceful Roman province, have had connotations of benevolent protection. A glance at the cult of Mars in Britain and Gaul serves to explain this kind of transmutation. Here the Roman war god turns his martial prowess into the power to guard and protect humans against such evils as

*A bronze horseman from Westwood Bridge, Peterborough
(Peterborough City Museum).*

barrenness and disease. This is why he appears – albeit sometimes in full
military regalia – as presider over healing shrines, such as that at Mavilly
in Burgundy (Espérandieu, no. 2067; Deyts 1976, no. 284), or as a
peaceful provider of plenty, as at Custom Scrubs in Gloucestershire,
where he appears carrying *cornucopiae* (Green 1986, fig. 14). The cult of
the horseman, especially popular among the tribes of eastern Britain,
may similarly have had a peaceful, protective dimension. In the
territories of the Catuvellauni, Coritani (sometimes called the
Corieltauvi) and Iceni (roughly between Essex and Lincolnshire), the

divine horseman was depicted on stone reliefs and small bronze figurines, mention of a few of which will suffice. A complex of small shrines at Brigstock (Northants) yielded several small statuettes of an armed, mounted warrior (Greenfield 1963). At Martlesham in Suffolk, a bronze horseman figure was dedicated to a native version of the Roman war god, Mars Corotiacus, who is depicted riding down a prostrate foe, perhaps an allegory of good triumphing over evil (Green 1976, 218); a similar image occurs in stone at Stragglethorpe in Lincolnshire (except that here the enemy takes the form of a serpent) (Ambrose and Henig 1980).

Horseman cults are also discernible in Gaul where, at the healing shrine of Bolards (Nuits-Saint-Georges) in Burgundy, a bronze horse or mule was dedicated to Segomo ('Victorious') and where suppliants brought gifts of clay horses and horsemen (Thevenot 1955). Mars Segomo was venerated among the Sequani of eastern Gaul. Mars Mullo was an important Gaulish mule god who had sanctuaries in north-west Gaul, at Rennes and Allonnes (Marache 1979, 3; Térouanne 1960, 185–9; Thevenot 1968, 65–9). His high status is indicated by dedications which link his cult with that of the emperor. Both Mullo at Allonnes and the horseman god of Bolards demonstrate links with curative cults. There is evidence also that the Celtic Apollo, worshipped particularly as a healer in the Gaulish provinces, had horse associations: at Sainte-Sabine in Burgundy, for example, Apollo Belenus ('Bright Apollo') was venerated with votive offerings of horse and horseman figurines (Thevenot 1951, 129–41). In both classical and Celtic contexts, Apollo was a solar deity as well as a healer; the cult of the Gaulish Apollo seems to link horses with the sun, an association which we have already noted as occurring in late European prehistory and one which is considered further in the section below, which discusses the Celtic sky/sun god as a horseman.

The Celestial Horseman

Celtic communities in Gaul and the Rhineland venerated a celestial god who was a deity of both sky and sun, and who was perceived as a warrior, a conqueror of evil, darkness and death. The cult appears to have been a dualistic one, where positive and negative forces such as summer and winter, day and night, life and death, were seen as interdependent. This Celtic sky god was conflated with the Roman Jupiter but the two divinities did not have precisely similar functions:

A bronze horse from Neuvy-en-Sullias (Loiret)
(Musée Historique et Archéologique de l'Orléanais, Orléans).

only the Celtic god was also a solar deity. As a celestial warrior, the indigenous Gaulish sky/sun god was represented on horseback. His mount is depicted riding down and subjugating the chthonic forces which are symbolized by the image of a monstrous giant, with a huge head and lower limbs in the form of snakes. These sculptures form the summit group of so-called 'Jupiter-Giant Columns', high pillars which, by their carved decoration, appear to represent trees (Bauchhenss 1976; Bauchhenss and Noelke 1981). Sometimes the sky warrior is also demonstrably solar: on a number of depictions, he is represented on a galloping horse, armed with a thunderbolt as a weapon and a solar wheel as a shield, turned against the dark enemy. Stone images such as those at Butterstadt and Obernburg in Germany (Espérandieu, *German* vol., no. 76; Kellner 1971, pl. 85) and Meaux and Luxeuil in France

(Espérandieu, nos. 3207, 5357) depict the celestial god thus. An interesting feature of this imagery is that it is the horse which is in physical contact with the chthonic giant. A variant of the solar horseman theme occurs at Mouhet (Indre) where the giant carries the sun on his back as a monstrous burden, like Atlas holding up the world (Lelong 1970, figs. 1–2; Green 1991, 135). It is clear from the Mouhet imagery that horse and sun could be interchangeable and that the horse is a fundamental solar image, just as it appears to be on earlier Celtic coinage. The link between the horse and the sun may reflect a very ancient Indo-European religious tradition, where the solar disc was perceived as travelling across the sky in a *biga* or *quadriga* (a two- or four-horse chariot). This belief in the chariot of the sun is reflected in the Bronze Age of northern Europe, its most well-known image being the Danish Trundholm chariot which dates to about 1300 BC. The model vehicle carried a great sun-disc, gilded on one surface (to represent the daytime and night-time sun), and was drawn by an elegant horse. It was buried, deliberately broken, as a votive offering in a marsh. It was probably used in cult ceremonies, perhaps in magical imitation of the sun moving across the sky, and maybe in invocation of the sun in the hope that it would return to warm and fertilize the earth after the dark cold of a northern winter (Green 1991, 112–16, pl. 45). Northern Europe, the Mediterranean world, India and Persia all had cults associated with solar chariots drawn by horses which were acknowledged as the swiftest and most prestigious animals to convey the vehicle of the divine sun. This close and long-established relationship between the horse and the sun seems to have manifested itself in Romano-Celtic Europe as the image of a solar horseman, conqueror of evil, darkness and death, and promoter of life and seasonal fecundity.

Conclusion

The veneration of the horse by early Celtic communities appears to have had a direct correlation with the secular attitude to the animal which appears to have been present. The acknowledgement of the horse's qualities, which made it an invaluable creature in so many aspects of daily life, was transmuted into a profound reverence for horses as sacred beasts whose image enhanced that of the deities with whom they were associated. Moreover, the involvement of horses in sacrificial ceremonies and ritual again reflects their centrality to Celtic life. The power, speed, courage, beauty and intelligence of the animal gave it tremendous prestige value in a highly ranked, proud, élitist and honour-conscious society. The horse was crucial in warfare and hunting, and this is reflected in many of the cults with which it was associated. Its high secular status may have led to its link with the high gods of the sky and sun. In addition, the horse's vigorous sexuality perhaps caused it to become part of the imagery of deities like Epona, who was concerned with domestic fertility and abundance. Guardianship and protection may have been an important element in cults associated with horses. We have seen that Epona's military role may have been that of a protectress of territory, and it may be that the horse's link with both warfare and healing may lie partly in its symbolism as a guardian not only against human enemies but also against the less tangible enemies of disease and barrenness. It was noted earlier that animals in general played a major role in Celtic religion. It may be that the particularly powerful and multifaceted nature of horse symbolism within this belief-system resulted from the especially close relationship between horse and human in early European society.

References

Alcock, Leslie. 1972. *'By South Cadbury, is that Camelot . . .'* Excavations at Cadbury Castle 1966–70 (London, Thames & Hudson).

Allen, Derek. 1980. *The Coins of the Ancient Celts* (Edinburgh University Press).

Ambrose, Timothy and Henig, Martin. 1980. 'A New Roman rider-Relief from Stragglethorpe, Lincolnshire', *Britannia*, 11, 135–8.

Anati, Emanuel. 1965. *Camonica Valley* (London, Jonathan Cape).

Anon. 1978. 'The Cambridge Shrine', *Current Archaeology*, 61, 57–60.

Anon. 1980a. *Die Hallstattkultur* (Steier, Schloss Lamberg).

Anon. 1980b. *Die Kelten in Mitteleuropa* (Salzburg, Keltenmuseum Hallein).

Bauchhenss, Gerhard. 1976. *Jupitergigantensäulen* (Stuttgart, Württemberg- isches Landesmuseum).

Bauchhenss, Gerhard and Noelke, Peter. 1981. *Die Iupitersäulen in den germanischen Provinzen* (Cologne and Bonn, Rheinland Verlag).

Bémont, Colette. 1984. *L'Art celtique en Gaule 1983–1984* (Paris, Direction des Musées de France).

Benoit, Ferdinand. 1969. *L'Art primitif méditérranéen de la vallée du Rhône* (Aix-en-Provence, Annales de la Faculté des Lettres).

Benoit, Ferdinand. 1981. *Entremont* (Paris, Ophrys).

Brunaux, Jean-Louis. 1988. *The Celtic Gauls: Gods, Rites and Sanctuaries*, tr. D. Nash (London, Seaby).

Collis, John. 1993. 'Los Celtas en Europe' in *Los Celtas: Hispania y Europa*, ed. M. Almagro-Gorbea (Madrid, ACTAS de El Escorial), 63–76.

Collis, John. 1996. 'The Origin and Spread of the Celts', *Studia Celtica*, 30, 17–33.

Cunliffe, Barry. 1986. *Danebury: Anatomy of an Iron Age Hillfort* (London, Batsford).

Cunliffe, Barry. 1992. 'Pits, Preconceptions and Propitiation in the British Iron Age', *Oxford Journal of Archaeology*, 11, 69–84.

Cunliffe, Barry. 1993. *Danebury* (London, Batsford and English Heritage).

Deyts, Simone. 1976. *Dijon, Musée Archéologique: sculptures gallo-romaines mythologiques et religieuses* (Paris, Éditions de la Réunion des Musées Nationaux).

Drioux, Georges. 1934. *Cultes indigènes des Lingons* (Paris, Picard/Langres, Imprimerie Champenoise).

Duval, Paul-Marie. 1987. *Monnaies gauloises et mythes celtiques* (Paris, Hermann).

Espérandieu, Émile. 1907–66. *Recueil général des bas-reliefs de la Gaule romaine et pré-romaine* (Paris, Leroux).

Evans, David Ellis. 1995. 'The Early Celts: The Evidence of Language' in *The Celtic World*, ed. M. Green (London and New York, Routledge), 8–20.

Grant, Annie. 1989. 'Animals and Rituals in Early Britain: The Visible and the Invisible' in *L'Animal dans les pratiques religieuses: les manifestations matérielles*, ed. J.-D. Vigne (Paris, Anthropozoologica troisième numéro spécial), 79–86.

Graves, Robert (tr.). 1962. *Suetonius: The Twelve Caesars* (London, Cassell).

Green, Chris. 1965. 'A Romano-Celtic Temple at Bourton Grounds, Buckingham', *Records of Buckinghamshire*, 17, 356ff.

Green, Miranda. 1976. *A Corpus of Religious Material from the Civilian Areas of Roman Britain* (Oxford, British Archaeological Reports, British Series, no. 24).

Green, Miranda. 1986. *The Gods of the Celts* (Gloucester, Alan Sutton).

Green, Miranda. 1989. *Symbol and Image in Celtic Religious Art* (London, Routledge).

Green, Miranda. 1991. *The Sun-Gods of Ancient Europe* (London, Batsford).

Green, Miranda. 1992a. *Animals in Celtic Life and Myth* (London, Routledge).

Green, Miranda. 1992b. *Dictionary of Celtic Myth and Legend* (London, Thames & Hudson).

Green, Miranda. 1992c. 'The Iconography of Celtic Coins' in *Celtic Coinage in Britain and Beyond*, ed. M. Mays (Oxford, 11th Symposium on Coinage and Monetary History), 151–63.

Green, Miranda. 1993. *Celtic Myths* (London, British Museum Press).

Green, Miranda. 1995a. 'British Hill-Figures: A Celtic Interpretation', *Cosmos*, 11, 125–38.

Green, Miranda. 1995b. 'Introduction: Who were the Celts?' in *The Celtic World*, ed. M. Green (London and New York, Routledge), 3–7.

Greenfield, Ernest. 1963. 'The Romano-British Shrines at Brigstock, Northants', *Antiquaries Journal*, 43, 228–68.

Grinsell, Leslie. 1958. *The Archaeology of Wessex* (London, Methuen).

Hercher, Rudolfus (ed.). 1884. *Arriani Nicomediensis Scripta Minora* (Leipzig and Berlin, B. G. Teubner).

Hill, J. D. 1989. 'Rethinking the Iron Age', *Scottish Archaeological Review*, 6, 16–24.

Hill, J. D. 1996. 'Hillforts and the Iron Age of Wessex' in *The Iron Age in Britain and Ireland: Recent Trends*, ed. T. Champion and J. Collis (Sheffield, J. R. Collis Publications), 95–116.

Holden, Hubert Ashton (ed.). 1853. *M. Minucii Felicis Octavius* (Cambridge University Press).

Hyland, Ann. 1990. *Equus: The Horse in the Roman World* (London, Batsford).

Johns, Catherine. 1971–2. 'A Roman Bronze Statuette of Epona', *British Museum Quarterly*, 36, 37–41.

Kellner, H. J. 1971. *Die Römer in Bayern* (Munich, Süddeutscher Verlag).

Lambrechts, Pierre. 1954. *L'Exaltation de la tête dans la pensée et dans l'art des Celtes* (Bruges, Dissertationes Archaeologicae Gandenses, 2).

Lelong, Charles. 1970. 'Note sur une sculpture gallo-romaine de Mouhet (Indre)', *Revue Archéologique du Centre*, 9, 123–6.

Lewis, Michael. 1966. *Temples in Roman Britain* (Cambridge University Press).

Linduff, Kathryn. 1979. 'Epona: A Celt among the Romans', *Collections Latomus,* 38, 817–37.

Magnen, R. and Thevenot, Émile. 1953. *Epona* (Bordeaux, Delmas).

Marache, Roger. 1979. *Les Romains en Bretagne* (Rennes, Ouest France).

Megaw, Vincent. 1970. *Art of the European Iron Age* (New York, Harper & Row).

Megaw, Ruth and Megaw, Vincent. 1989. *Celtic Art, from its Beginnings to the Book of Kells* (London, Thames & Hudson).

Meid, Wolfgang. 1992. *Gaulish Inscriptions* (Budapest, Archaeolingua).

Meniel, Patrice. 1987. *Chasse et élevage chez les Gaulois (450–2 av. JC)* (Paris, Errance).

Meniel, Patrice. 1989. 'Les Animaux dans les pratiques religieuses des Gaulois' in *L'Animal dans les pratiques religieuses: les manifestations materielles,* ed. J-D. Vigne (Paris, Anthropozoologica, troisième numéro spécial), 87–97.

Miles, David and Palmer, Simon. 1995. 'White Horse Hill', *Current Archaeology*, 142, 372–8.

Oaks, Laura. 1986. 'The Goddess Epona: Concepts of Sovereignty in a Changing Landscape' in *Pagan Gods and Shrines of the Roman Empire*, ed. M.

Henig and A. King (Oxford University Committee for Archaeology, no. 8), 77–84.

Olmsted, Garrett. 1979. *The Gundestrup Cauldron* (Brussels, Latomus).

Palmer, Susanne. 1990. 'Uffington: White Horse Hill Project', *Archaeological News: The Quarterly Newsletter of the Oxford Archaeological Unit*, 18, 28–32.

Parker Pearson, Michael. 1996. 'Food, Fertility and Front Doors in the First Millennium BC' in *The Iron Age in Britain and Ireland: Recent Trends*, ed. T. Champion and J. Collis (Sheffield, J. R. Collis Publications), 117–32.

Petrie, Francis. 1926. *The Hill Figures of England* (London, Royal Anthropological Institute).

Pobé, Marcel and Roubier, Jean. 1961. *The Art of Roman Gaul* (London, Galley Press).

Rawlinson, George (tr.). 1862. *History of Herodotus* (London, John Murray).

Rivet, A. L. F. 1988. *Gallia Narbonensis* (London, Batsford).

Ross, Anne. 1968. 'Shafts, Pits, Wells (Sanctuaries of the Belgic Britons)' in *Studies in Ancient Europe,* ed. John Coles and Derek Simpson (Leicester University Press), 255–85.

Stead, Ian. 1979. *The Arras Culture* (York, Yorkshire Philosophical Society).

Térouanne, Paul. 1960. 'Dédicaces à Mars Mullo. Découvertes à Allonnes (Sarthe)', *Gallia,* 18, 185–9.

Thevenot, Émile. 1951. 'Le Cheval sacré dans la Gaule de l'est', *Revue Archéologique de l'Est et du Centre-Est*, 2, 129–41.

Thevenot, Émile. 1955. *Sur les traces des Mars celtiques* (Bruges, Dissertationes Archaeologicae Gandenses, 3).

Thevenot, Émile. 1968. *Divinités et sanctuaires de la Gaule* (Paris, Fayard).

Tierney, J. J. 1960. 'The Celtic Ethnography of Posidonius', *Proceedings of the Royal Irish Academy*, 60 (1959–60), 189–275.

van der Paardt, R. (ed.). 1971. *L. Apuleius Madaurensis. The Metamorphoses. A Commentary on Book III with Text and Introduction* (Amsterdam, Adolf M. Habbert).

Wait, Gerald. 1985. *Ritual and Religion in Iron Age Britain* (Oxford, British Archaeological Reports, British Series, no. 149).

Webster, Graham. 1986. *The British Celts and their Gods under Rome* (London, Batsford).

Weissenborn, Wilhelm (ed.). 1886. *Titi Livi Ab Urbe Condita Libri, Pars II, Libri VII–XXIII* (Berlin, Weidmannsche Buchlandlung).

Wiseman Anne and Wiseman, Peter (ed.). 1980. *Julius Caesar: The Battle for Gaul* (London, Chatto & Windus).

Woolner, Susan. 1965. 'The White Horse, Uffington', *Transactions of the Newbury and District Field Club*, 11, 27–44.

Zachar, Lev. 1987. *Keltische Kunst in der Slowakei* (Bratislava, Tatran).

2

Horses in the Early Historic Period: Evidence from the Pictish Sculptured Stones

Irene Hughson

Studies of the development of equines in prehistory and early history have depended on two types of material, horse bones and horse trappings brought to light by archaeological investigation, and representations of horses in art beginning with cave paintings. In the previous chapter, Miranda Aldhouse Green has alluded to examples of the archaeological evidence of equines in Celtic society. That evidence can be fleshed out by looking at the horses and ponies carved on the sculptured stones, the characteristic monument of the Picts, a Celtic people who flourished in Scotland north of the Forth–Clyde line in the Early Historic Period.

The sculptured stones have been the subject of much work by art historians. Debate has centred on the distinctive Pictish symbols carved on the stones with various suggestions being made as to their significance. While that remains obscure, out of the vigour of the debate has emerged a growing consensus of opinion concerning the dating of the stones and their outstanding merit as works of art (Laing and Laing 1985).

They are widely distributed in the eastern part of Scotland from north of the Forth to Shetland. There are concentrations in Perthshire, Angus, Aberdeenshire and the area round the Moray Firth; others are scattered on the western seaboard, the Western Isles, in Galloway and East Lothian. In their classic work, *The Early Christian Monuments of Scotland* (1903), Romilly Allen and Joseph Anderson listed and described the stones, dividing them into two categories. The Class I stones are the earliest. They are unshaped blocks with a range of

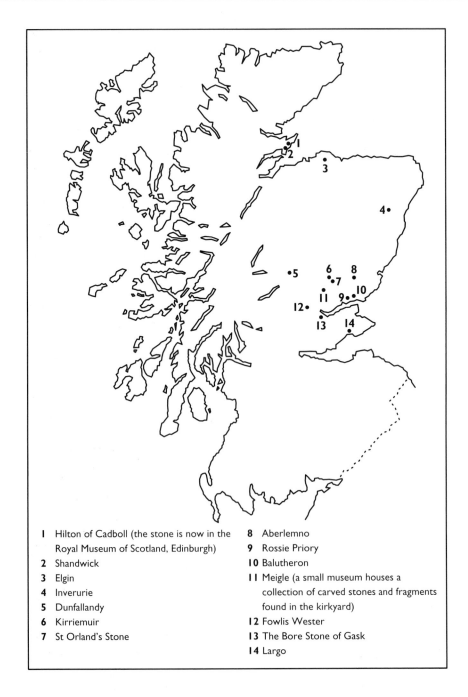

1	Hilton of Cadboll (the stone is now in the Royal Museum of Scotland, Edinburgh)	8	Aberlemno
2	Shandwick	9	Rossie Priory
3	Elgin	10	Balutheron
4	Inverurie	11	Meigle (a small museum houses a collection of carved stones and fragments found in the kirkyard)
5	Dunfallandy		
6	Kirriemuir	12	Fowlis Wester
7	St Orland's Stone	13	The Bore Stone of Gask
		14	Largo

A distribution map of Pictish stones depicting horses discussed in Chapter 2.

symbols or pictures of animals, birds or fish incised in outline upon them. They have been dated to the late fifth and the sixth centuries. The Class II stones are regular in shape and are carved in low relief. On one side there is a cross, usually highly ornate with panels of interlace and geometric patterns. As the symbols continued to be shown, it seems that whatever they signified did not conflict with the Christian iconography. Biblical scenes, such as Daniel in the lions' den, and scenes which are not overtly religious are carved on them. They are dated from the late sixth/early seventh century to the ninth century. Allen and Anderson also list a large number of stones which they designate Class III. It is a much more heterogeneous group, which includes grave slabs and crosses. Some are very fine works; others are derivative and inferior in execution. What they have in common is the absence of the distinctive Pictish symbols. Because of this they are dated after 843, when the kingdoms of Pictland and Dalriada were united under Kenneth mac Alpin, and the Picts ceased to have a separate political identity. The vagueness of the dating of Class III stones and, in some cases, the mediocrity of their workmanship make them unsuitable for consideration here. In contrast, the excellence in design and execution of the Class I and Class II stones means that we have 'snapshots in stone' of several aspects of Pictish society. Horses and ponies figure on many of them. Amongst the best known and most accessible of these are The Bore Stone of Gask, St Orland's Stone and stones from Mortlach, Dunfallandy, Scoonie, Elgin, Migvie, Kirriemuir (no. 3), St. Madoes, Rossie Priory, Hilton of Cadboll, Shandwick, Edderton, Fowlis Wester, Meigle (nos. 1 and 4), Fordoun, Largo, Aberlemno (roadside), Aberlemno (kirkyard).

There has been wide-ranging discussion about where exactly Pictish art belongs in the wider tradition of Insular art, and controversy about suggested chronological progressions. A measure of agreement seems now to have been reached on relative dating and on who borrowed what from whom (Henderson 1995). It is now generally accepted that Pictish art was a vibrant, flourishing, indigenous phenomenon capable of influencing, and being influenced by, other related northern artistic traditions, and that the particular Pictish contribution to the totality of Insular art was vigorous, naturalistic animal portrayal. It is not appropriate to think of the Pictish horses as having been copied from Roman coins or from pieces of Roman sculpture such as the Bridgeness Distance Slab from the Antonine Wall. Nor need we think of them as being derived from the creatures of manuscript or from Saxon jewellery (Finlay 1973). There are considerable differences in conformation

Shetland pony

Exmoor pony

Horse on the Class I Inverurie Stone

between the horses carved on the Pictish stones and the images that have been suggested as prototypes for them. Differences in conformation are crucial when judging living horses. When the experience of evaluating living horses is brought to bear on the Pictish horses and the others it soon becomes clear that the extent of the differences in conformation rules out direct copying. A glance at the stones themselves will confirm Isabel Henderson's statement, 'The naturalism of the Pictish animals is particularly striking' (1990, 4). It is safe to assume that Pictish artists drew their inspiration from life and modelled their work on the animals that they saw around them. They had immense artistic skill and were able to carve what they observed in the difficult medium of stone. In the words, once again, of Dr Henderson: 'The bull, bear, stag, wolf, deer, horse, eagle and salmon, depicted in strict profile, take their place amongst the greatest works of art in contemporary Europe' (1990, 4).

The earliest stone on which a horse is depicted is the Class I stone from Inverurie. Though details of the hindquarters have worn away, what is left reveals a clean-limbed, high-stepping, well-proportioned animal with a slightly dished face and a suggestion of flaring nostrils. There is some indication of musculature and the stifle-joint of the off-hind-leg is shown with a lobe-ended scroll characteristic of animal carving of this date. (It is, for example, used in the series of bull carvings associated with Burghead.) The neck is arched and slopes down to muscular shoulders. The rump is rounded and the tail appears to be carried out from the quarters. The position of the legs shows that the horse is moving forward vigorously at a walk. The overall impression is of a fine, well-fed animal in the peak of condition. There is nothing to give any clue to its height but its whole appearance is at variance with the idea that the only horses available in Britain in the Early Historic Period were 'little shaggy creatures, like Exmoors or large Shetlands' (Thomas 1971, 124). Exmoors and Shetlands, which look very different from each other in most respects, do indeed have thick winter coats, which could certainly be described as shaggy. They look sleeker in the summer, but they always have fetlocks which neither the Inverurie horse nor any of the later Pictish horses have. Shetland ponies have particularly thick manes and forelocks – another characteristic not shared by any of the sculpted horses or ponies.

There is always a temptation to think of horses and ponies in the past as resembling one or other of the so-called native breeds of Britain, as if somehow they represent equines at a more 'primitive' level. There are difficulties in doing that, however, because there is a lack of hard information about how far back the native breeds go or what their status, if any, was in the past. Aficionados claim great antiquity for particular breeds, but, as the breed society records go back only just over a hundred years, the claims are unsubstantiated. In fact, knowledge of how the hundreds of different breeds and types of horses that exist in the modern world developed is limited, although growing all the time, and one thing seems clear: man had a hand in that development from very early on. It seems much more likely that our native breeds are the descendants of types of horses and ponies that were developed for particular purposes in the past. There are, after all, nine different breeds that are regarded as native within the relatively small confines of the British Isles.

The true wild horse (*equus ferus*) had a wide natural range in the mid-latitudes of Europe and Asia at the end of the last Ice Age. Work done by the Swedish zoologist Bengt Lundholm, first published in 1949 (quoted in Groves 1974, 167), concluded from the study of equine skulls from variously dated archaeological contexts in Sweden, that the species *equus ferus* could be divided into four ancestral types, differentiated in the fossil record by differences in dentition. A similar conclusion was arrived at quite independently by Hermann Ebbardt, who was himself a horse-breeder and student of equine behaviour. His intensive studies of group horse behaviour identified four basic patterns (Groves 1974, 170). The existence of four ancestral types has now been verified by studies of skulls from other parts of Europe. The territories of the four types overlapped, yet no bones indicating mixed breeding have been found in early contexts where the horses were living in the wild. Evidence of interbreeding occurs later, in circumstances where the horses were domesticated. Diversification and distribution, then, seems to have been rapid. In fact, in the words of John Clabby (1976, 5), 'their story becomes largely one of the diversification of the species into breeds to suit man's varied requirements for work and recreation.'

A very early centre of horse domestication was identified by the Ukrainian zoologist Bibikava at a Neolithic site excavated in 1967 at Dereivka on the banks of the Dnieper about thirty miles from the modern town of Krementchug in the south of the Ukraine. There, excavators recovered over 2,000 horse bones which showed signs of domestication, including complete skulls and bones of the foot (Bökönyi 1974). The settlement site was dated to the second half of the fourth millennium BC. Claims that horses were domesticated early in China have not been supported by archaeological evidence. Though domestication may have taken place independently at other places,

Dereivka is the earliest known, and its location in an area where the natural vegetation and conditions favour the horse makes its pre-eminence likely. Bones of non-domesticated horses are numerous in other Ukrainian Neolithic sites and show that there were plenty of horses around. Unlike other animals, horses did not become smaller in stature in the early stages of domestication. Their human herders must have been able to ensure that they were well fed. The herding practices may have resembled those of much later Lapp reindeer herders which allowed the animals enough freedom within limits to choose the grazing best suited to their needs. The maintenance of their natural size has important implications for the study of how horses developed. Right from the start, people were dealing with animals around fourteen hands high rather than with diminutive creatures. The breeds of small ponies that exist today have been 'bred down', either through deliberate selection or through inadequacy of feeding regimes in geographical areas beyond the equine's natural range.

The interval between domestication, probably as a food resource in the first instance, and the use of horses as pack-animals is not known for certain. The use of horses to pull war-chariots is attested by their appearance on relief sculpture from the late Hittite period and on Mycenaean gravestones of about 1600 BC, though the four-wheeled cart may very well have been developed earlier. Representations of horses with riders appear around 1200 BC (Renfrew 1987). Horses had important functions in the Bronze Age cultures in all parts of Europe, including areas such as Britain and Greece where the wild horse was totally absent.

Visual evidence from Egyptian, Assyrian, Chinese and Classical art testifies to the various uses of horses and to there being a variety of different types available. From Classical and Chinese sources it emerges that there was a decided preference for fine, showy horses as riding animals. These have been labelled Bactrian horses, taking their name from Bactria, the place where it appears they were first bred. Bactria corresponds roughly in extent to the modern state of Uzbekistan (Azzaroli 1985). They were probably the ancestors of modern breeds, widely separated geographically, like the Akhal Teke, the Karabakh and the Arab. Remains of Bactrian horses have been found hundreds of miles to the east, in the Pazyryk area of the Altai Mountains in *kurgans* which are the burial monuments of first-millennium BC Scythian chieftains. As these particular *kurgans* occur at altitudes where the subsoil is permanently frozen, the bodies of horses and ponies have been preserved alongside those of their riders. The *kurgans* so far investigated have contained one Bactrian type horse in each case and one or more smaller, coarser ponies of three other distinct types. The Bactrian horses were probably the prized riding horses of the chiefs, used on grand occasions, when creating an impression was important, while the smaller ponies were the ones used at other times and for other purposes. The majority of the horses and ponies recovered from the *kurgans* have been chestnut – light-coloured horses are rare.

It is the contention of John Clabby that the Bactrian horse was brought into central Europe by migrating groups of Battle-Axe people (Clabby 1976). It is from the fusion of the Battle-Axe people and the people identified by their Urn-field culture that the Celtic culture emerged. Current archaeological evidence no longer supports the idea of successive waves of migrants sweeping across Europe in the Bronze and Iron Ages. Instead, the development of similar cultural traits observable in the archaeological record over a wide area is attributed to peer polity interaction and the effects of trade. Limited demographic change brought about by the movement of élite groups is not ruled out. The emergence of élite groups is attributed to some technological advantage or linked to their control of valued resources (Renfrew 1987). The ability to ride is just such a technological advantage. Control of the supply of elegant, fast-moving, spirited horses is likely to have been of some significance. There can be little doubt that horses were involved in the process that Christopher Hawkes called 'cumulative Celticity' (Hawkes 1973).

Finds of horse and pony trappings decorated in Celtic style are not rare in Britain. Their existence is an indication of the status value of equines. Archaeological evidence of horses and ponies that can be securely dated to the same period as the Pictish sculptured stones is much less plentiful. However, there is no compelling reason to believe that the range of equines found on the Pictish stones was different from the range of equines found in other parts of Britain at the same time.

An examination of the horses carved on the stones reveals that there are several different types of equines shown. One of the best-known and most photographed of the stones is the one from Hilton of Cadboll in Easter Ross which is now in the National Museum of Scotland in Edinburgh. It shows a lively hunting scene on one panel of one side. The central figure in the scene is 'a fine lady upon a fine horse'. To the left is the mirror and comb symbol. It occurs frequently along with other symbols on the stones and has been interpreted as relating to femininity

The Hilton of Cadboll Stone (Photograph: Robert Taylor).

(though it has been pointed out that it is not unknown for men to comb their hair!). The mirror is of the type that has been recovered from various archaeological contexts in England (e.g. the Desborough mirror), and its presence on the stones testifies to the continuity in cultural terms from the pre-Roman Iron Age to the Early Historic Period. To the right are two musicians possibly blowing a fanfare on bronze instruments or, possibly, playing on the Pictish triple pipes which are shown more clearly on other stones, notably the Lethendy stone. Below are two horsemen and two hounds in hot pursuit of a fleeing hind. To some viewers the lady is the embodiment of the horse goddess Epona (Dent and Goodall 1962, 72). To others she is a Pictish queen or princess escorted by a groom (Black 1993). His head can be seen in profile to the left of her head and the outline of his horse can also be made out. The figures of the people in the hunting scene help to give an idea of the relative size of the horses. The lady's horse looks as if it is around 14 hands high. To a generation used to seeing 16- and 17-hand racehorses and show jumpers, 14 hands may not seem very big, but it is perfectly adequate. A fit horse of this size will carry an adult easily and will be comfortable for an average-sized adult to ride. In purely practical terms, it was probably high enough for a rider to mount without assistance in the era before the development of stirrups. Her horse has a very erect head carriage (an indication, perhaps, of a spirited animal being kept in check), a long body and a high-set tail. It is different from the horse below and to the right which is smaller, closer coupled with sloping hindquarters, and has long, light limbs and small hoofs. Horses on the Aberlemno Kirkyard stone resemble the latter with their sloping hindquarters, but they are altogether stockier animals with bigger, heavier hoofs. Just as stocky is the horse on the Meigle (no. 4) stone but it is a small animal with a powerful neck, a good deep chest and a tail carried low from well-rounded quarters. It, however, is fine-limbed. In short, there is ample evidence for a range of good riding-horses in Pictland in the Early Historic Period. The likelihood is that similar types existed all over Celtic Britain. Some of our British native breeds may very well be the descendants of various types of Celtic horse and pony.

There are one or two examples of small, rough ponies in Pictish art as well, such as that found on the Fowlis Wester stone. As it has a fine horse and a coarse pony both present on the one stone, it is not just a case of difference in artistic techniques. In practice, there may very well have been more small, rough ponies around than showy riding-horses. They would have been easier to keep and to feed then, just as they are now, and they would have had their uses. They would have made excellent pack-animals, especially over rough terrain.

There are deductions that can be made about Pictish society from the horses on the stones, for as Andrew Fraser (1987, 5) has written, 'Horses and ponies might not at first glance seem to offer great assistance in studying historical sociology, but they can provide many clues.'

First of all we can rule out any notion that the Picts, or any of their Celtic relations for that matter, relied on capturing wild horses for their mounts. There were no truly wild horses in Britain, although it is possible that there were groups of feral horses and ponies, free-living descendants of domesticated horses that had strayed or been lost. The cattle-raiding of the times, so well attested in the literature, would have created opportunities for that to happen. Given the homing instincts of horses, it is unlikely that the feral groups were big or numerous, and they would not have been an important source of riding-horses. In a society that depended on horses for moving goods and people about, all horses and ponies, whatever their size and looks, must have been regarded as a valuable resource. Basing her conclusion on an extensive study of pre-Roman Iron Age material relating to horses in southern Britain, Natalie Palk has stressed the importance of horses in Iron Age economies, and shown the absurdity of the notion of great herds of wild horses being present in Britain. As she puts it,

> The idea of wild ponies roaming the countryside with one or two being 'picked off' as and when required, should be nipped in the bud. With the development of large scale land management programmes required by later Iron Age societies it is unlikely that the resources provided by equines would be allowed to take a lower position on the scale of exploitation than other domestic livestock. (1984, 98)

Producing a reliable riding-horse or draught animal requires investment in feeding and training. It takes time and a proper diet to build up the physique that enables a horse to carry or pull a weight, and it takes time and patience to build up a trusting relationship between horse and handler. There are no short-cuts; rodeo-style treatment and shows of force are counter-productive. Bringing on young horses and ponies is a job for full-time experts. The households of the Pictish aristocracy and those of their southern neighbours must surely have included grooms whose time was devoted to the care and management of their four-footed status symbols. Knowledge and expertise are necessary, not just in early training but throughout the lifetime of the horse if it is to be kept fit and in good condition, as the horses on the sculptured stones undoubtedly are.

All horses have a fast metabolic rate, though it differs from type to type and, indeed, from animal to animal. Food intake has to be adjusted according to the season and according to what work is required of the horse. Horses in work, lactating mares and mares in foal would have required hard feed (cereals) and hay during a Scottish winter; they would not have thriven left to graze with no additional feed. Studies carried out on the location of Pictish settlements (Cottam and Small 1974; Alcock 1989) have shown that land with good potential for arable crops was preferred for settlements. If the condition of the Pictish horses is anything to go by, Pictish farming methods allowed the potential to be realized so that there was grain available for horses to consume. Oats are the favoured grain for feeding horses because they are rapidly converted to energy. Barley can be fed but tends to produce fatty tissue if used constantly. A mixture of the two, varying the proportions according to the season, the type of horse and the type of work, is best. Both barley and oats would have been available in Pictish times (Findlay 1956). Further south, where winters are slightly less harsh and spring comes earlier, less feeding might have been required, but it is totally unreasonable to think that fine riding-horses could have survived, even in the extreme south, without some feeding.

The Pictish horses would have required access to grass, but that access would have had to be regulated, particularly in the summer, or the horses would have become 'soft', i.e. overweight and lethargic. In extreme cases they would have foundered completely. At best they would have been unfit for sustained work. Grazing can be regulated by dividing pasture into units of different sizes with different carrying capacities and moving the animals around as appropriate. In May and June it might have been necessary to take smaller ponies off grass completely for a few hours each day. Surveys show that Pictish territory is criss-crossed by networks of field-banks, mostly undated and possibly undatable. There is every likelihood that some of them were in use during the Pictish era for controlling the movements of horses and other livestock.

The time and expertise needed in the day-to-day management of equines is a further argument for the presence in Pictish and British aristocratic households of full-time 'stable managers'. The groom on the Hilton of Cadboll stone is probably the most persuasive piece of evidence for their existence. He has the unenviable task of controlling two horses in the excitement of a hunt. The lady rider is often described as riding side-saddle (e.g. Black 1993). This is an anachronism. The development of the side-saddle, which allowed the rider to face forward and exercise control through the lower leg and through shifting weight forwards or backwards, came much later. This lady rider is merely sitting on sideways, an unsteady position with little scope for real control; it is the groom who is in charge. The ability to control two horses in such a situation argues for considerable skill in equitation, and for the existence of well-trained reliable horses.

The Hilton of Cadboll stone is one of many that depicts a hunting scene. Hunting on horseback is the classic high-status activity, rarely, if ever, undertaken to provide food. There have always been far more efficient ways of bringing down game. Hunting on horseback, however, provided opportunities to display martial qualities – boldness and daring, good horsemanship, expertise with the spear and bow – without as many risks as a real military encounter. It allowed men to display their good horses, decorated harness and personal finery, again without the risk of losing them all. The organizer of the hunt could strengthen the bonds of clientship through inviting others to join in and through hospitality before and after. Hunting displayed the extent of a chieftain's domination of an area. It was a chance to reinforce or enhance standing in the community.

There is only one portrayal of actual fighting on horseback on a Class II Pictish stone and that is on the Aberlemno Kirkyard stone. It has been suggested that the battle scene may allude to the Battle of Dunnichen (or Nechtansmere) at which the Picts, under the leadership of Bridei (or Bruide), halted the advance of the Angles, commanded by Ecfrith of Northumbria, into Pictish territory. Some of the combatants are wearing helmets with prominent nose-guards like the Sutton Hoo and the York helmets (Cruickshank 1991). Whether or not it is possible to differentiate between Pict and Angle by the presence or absence of helmets, it is certainly possible to see that some of the combatants are fighting on horseback with spears and swords. They carry, as protection, round shields with central protruding bosses. Doubts have been cast on the effectiveness of spears used on horseback by riders with no stirrups (White 1962; Higham 1991). But it should be remembered that while stirrups provide support for the feet, they by no means guarantee a secure seat. The use of stirrups in Europe is first attested in Western art in an illustration of the Four Horsemen of the Apocalypse dated to the late eighth century AD (Hyland 1994, 11–12). It was a technological

The Aberlemno Stone.

advance that led to the development of other weapons such as the mace, because riders could stand up in the stirrups and gain advantage in height over their adversaries, but it did not prevent riders from falling off or from being unseated. Modern training in equitation involves a great deal of flat work and jumping without stirrups so that riders develop a good, deep, safe seat. Riders at the Spanish Riding School in Vienna perform 'Airs above the Ground' such as the Capriole and the Courbette without stirrups. Staying on is a matter of sitting deeply and making small adjustments to the position of the upper part of the body in keeping with the horse's movements so that balance is maintained at all times. Inability to do that cannot be compensated for by the use of stirrups (Podhajsky 1973). Ann Hyland has shown, through her experiments with replicas of the saddlery known to have been used by riders of various ethnic origins serving in the Roman cavalry, that riders were much more secure in the saddles of the time than was previously thought to be the case (Hyland 1990). The rider's weight on the padded leather seat pulled the angled corners or 'horns' of the saddle around the rider's thighs, giving added security. Competent riders would have been able to use spears, swords, javelins and bows as effectively without stirrups as later riders did with stirrups. Jenny Rowland has cited a great number of references in early Welsh literature to fighting on horseback which serve to show that using weapons while mounted was an accepted practice in the Early Historic Period (Rowland 1995).

None of the carved horses is shown in a static position. They are all depicted in motion, some of them pacing (i.e. with the legs at either side moving forward together) rather than trotting, where the near-fore and off-hind and the off-fore and near-hind move together. Though pacing is a natural gait, it is rarely found in British-bred horses today (Smythe 1993). It is, however, one of the natural gaits found in Icelandic ponies, which must be the descendants of ponies and horses taken to Iceland from Scandinavia, Britain and Ireland during the Viking settlement. It is also found in some American horses whose ancestors were the strays of the Conquistadores and included a breed known as the Asturión, which was a pacer.

Pacing has advantages for riders without stirrups. In the diagonal movement of trotting the rider is bumped up and down. The strategy for overcoming the bumpiness is to 'post', to rise up slightly off the horse's back on one of the diagonals. Novice riders use the stirrups to 'post'. With more experienced riders, the rising movement is from the knee. It can be done without stirrups, but that is tiring over a long distance.

Though cantering is a comfortable gait for stirrupless or bare-back riders, there is a limit to how long even a fit horse can stay in canter. Over a long distance, varying the gaits – walking, trotting, pacing and cantering according to the terrain – is best for horse and rider. When pacing was regarded as an advantage, horses and ponies that paced naturally would be valuable. The natural tendency for them to pace would have been encouraged in their early training and, presumably, they would have been selected for breeding purposes.

As well as horsemen shown on the sculptured stones as part of a hunting or battle scene, a horseman armed with a spear appears frequently as a sort of motif, perhaps indicating that high-status individuals regularly appeared on horseback on ceremonial occasions, when the horse and its accoutrements would have been indications of social standing. The mounted warrior would have been recognized as a symbol of authority.

Whatever activity a horse was required for at any particular time, it would have had to be kept fit through regular exercise. While the aristocratic owner of the horse must have done some of that exercising in order to keep himself fit and his equestrian skills up to the mark, in instances where the owner had political and administrative duties to perform, some of the regular exercising would most likely have been done by grooms. The necessity for having horses fit and ready for action at all times has implications for the layout of settlement sites. Some provision would have had to be made so that horses were readily accessible at need; a wet and muddy horse roaming around at grass half a mile away is not a great deal of use in an emergency!

It has been established that several so-called nuclear forts were in use during the Early Historic Period (Alcock *et al.* 1989). Nuclear forts have a well-defended citadel with adjoining enclosures whose size and position are more or less dictated by the topography of the site. One or two of the small enclosures could have functioned as holding areas for horses kept ready for use. Some sort of enclosure or picketing facility would have been required in a horse-owning household whatever type of site they inhabited – a fact that excavators of such sites could bear in mind.

An obvious answer to the readiness problem is stabling. For some of the very fine horses shown on the stones, winter stabling might well have been a necessity. While horses are equipped by nature to withstand cold and frost, prolonged rain can cause loss of condition. The elaborate stable blocks of, for example, the Georgian period – highly pleasing as they are in aesthetic and architectural terms – are far in excess of what is required for the comfort and well-being of the horses. Adequate room to go down and to rise up again without getting cast, and protection from the rain is all that is necessary, and that can be provided in the most basic of buildings. In the archaeological record such buildings might be indicated by nothing more than a few post holes and there could be no evidence at all to show that they were used as stabling. Buildings could have been used as stabling during what are the worst months for horses, January to April, when the weather is at its wettest and the grass has next to no nutritional value. The same buildings could have been used for other purposes, such as food and fodder storage, at other times. It is unlikely that such uses would show in the archaeological record either. It cannot be proved that stabling existed in the Pictish period, but it is possible to deduce that, given the nature of some of the horses portrayed on the stones and the value attached to them as status symbols, and given the knowledge of horses' requirements gained from experience of horses in our own times, the provision of stabling is probable. It should be borne in mind in the interpretation of sites of the period.

Some consideration of the practicalities of keeping and using horses should also form a part of discussions of military activity in the early historic period. The deployment of mounted men has potentials, but it would also have imposed some restraints. Speed over short distances is an obvious advantage. Over longer distances the advantage is less. Average speed for horses ridden purposefully forward for a whole day is about seven miles per hour, roughly twice average walking speed. In terms of distance covered, riders would have had an advantage over those on foot. The amount of advantage would, however, have depended on the terrain and the 'going'. Weather conditions would also have played a part. On heavy going horses would have had to slow down. They would have tired more quickly and consequently covered less ground. Dry, stony ground and rocky areas would have slowed them down, too. Riding is not significantly less tiring than walking, and so mounted warriors would not have been very much fresher than foot soldiers at the end of a day's journey. In cold or wet weather they would probably have been a lot stiffer and had numb hands and feet into the bargain.

In the Golden Horseshoe Ride, which is the British Horse Society's supreme test of extremely fit and well-trained endurance horses and riders, the participants are asked to complete a course of 100 miles in two days. Each horse and rider has a back-up crew which, at resting places on the course, can provide the rider with sustenance and the horse with high-energy food and preparations to prevent dehydration. Dehydration is a very real problem when horses are ridden hard over several miles and, once it has set in, it cannot be overcome by allowing the horse to drink out of the nearest burn. Riders in the past would probably have been satisfied with covering much shorter daily distances. Horses can work day in, day out provided they are adequately fed. Nightly access to grass would have kept them going for a day or two, but their condition would have begun to deteriorate after that unless they were given hard feeding.

The need to carry rations for the horses, as well as for the men, would have had to be considered in the tactical planning of any expedition. More ambitious undertakings such as the Gododdin's ill-fated expedition, immortalized in a poem attributed to sixth-century Aneirin (Jackson 1969; Jarman 1988), must have been the culmination of weeks, if not months, of planning. Roughly a thousand years later, when the Regent Moray sent an expedition south it consisted of 5,000 fighting men, 4,000 of whom were mounted and there were '4,000 carriage horse with victuals and 3,000 boys and young men to look after the horses' (Caldwell 1988, 56). Half the total number of horses were there to carry supplies both for the human and equine components of the army, and a high proportion of support staff was required. The Gododdin war-band was much smaller and the conditions were different, but horses and men needed to be fed just as surely in the sixth century as they did in the sixteenth. Kenneth Jackson (1969, 14–15) has suggested that each mounted warrior probably led his own retinue of foot soldiers, though they are not mentioned in the poem. If the war-band was, as Professor Jackson maintained, an expeditionary force it would have needed a good number of sumpter-horses to carry supplies. The strategic skills and the organizational abilities of the Gododdin's leaders should not be underestimated.

Studying the horses on the stones leads to several conclusions. It is possible to see that the Picts had several types of horses and ponies, including good-quality riding-horses, which were well fed, well cared for and well trained. The evidence of well-fed horses implies that Pictish agriculture, based in areas of land recognized as having good arable potential, was successful and capable of providing large quantities of grain. The evidence of good care and training implies that the Pictish economy was buoyant and capable of supporting individuals who were specialist horse-masters.

Combining the evidence of the stones with knowledge of the practicalities of keeping horses suggests ways of interpreting the field remains and excavated sites of the period, as well as giving an insight into the complexities of the military activities of the Picts and their neighbours.

References

Alcock, Elizabeth A. 1989. 'Pictish Stones Class I: Where and How?', *Glasgow Archaeological Journal*, 15, 1–21.

Alcock, Leslie, Alcock, Elizabeth A. and Driscoll, Stephen T. 1989. 'Reconnaissance Excavations on Early Historic Fortifications and other Royal Sites in Scotland 1974–84, 3, Excavations at Dundurn, Strathearn, Perthshire, 1976–77', *Proceedings of the Society of Antiquaries of Scotland*, 119, 189–226.

Allen, J. Romilly and Anderson, Joseph. 1903. *The Early Christian Monuments of Scotland* (Edinburgh, Society of Antiquaries of Scotland).

Azzaroli, A. 1985. *An Early History of Horsemanship* (Leiden, E. J. Brill).

Black, Catriona. 1993. 'Hilton of Cadboll: A Mysterious Woman', *Pictish Arts Society Journal*, 4, 37–43.

Bökönyi, Sándor. 1974. *The Przevalsky Horse*, tr. Lili Halápy (London, Souvenir Press).

Caldwell, David H. 1988. 'The Use and Effect of Weapons: The Scottish Experience', *Review of Scottish Culture*, 4, 53–62.

Clabby, J. 1976. *The Natural History of the Horse* (London, Weidenfeld & Nicolson).

Cottam, N. B. and Small, Alan. 1974. 'The Distribution of Settlement in Southern Pictland', *Mediaeval Archaeology*, 18, 43–65.

Cruickshank, Graeme. 1991. *The Battle of Dunnichen* (Balgavies, The Pinkfoot Press).

Dent, A. A. and Goodall, D. M. 1962. *The Foals of Epona: A History of British Ponies from the Bronze Age to Yesterday* (London, Galley Press).

Findlay, William M. 1956. *Oats: Their Cultivation and Use from Ancient Times to the Present Day* (Edinburgh and London, Oliver & Boyd).

Finlay, Ian. 1973. *Celtic Art: An Introduction* (London, Faber & Faber).

Fraser, A. F. 1987. *The Native Horses of Scotland: Scottish Breeds of Horses and their Folk* (Edinburgh, John Donald).

Groves, C. P. 1974. *Horses, Asses and Zebras in the Wild* (Newton Abbot, David & Charles).

Hawkes, Christopher. 1973. '"Cumulative Celticity" in Pre-Roman Britain', *Études Celtiques*, 13 (1972–3), 607–28.

Henderson, Isabel. 1990. *The Art and Function of Rosemarkie's Pictish Monuments* (Rosemarkie, Groam House Museum).

Henderson, Isabel. 1995. 'Pictish Art and its Place within the History of Insular Art' in *A Pictish Panorama: The Story of the Picts and a Pictish Bibliography,* ed. Eric H. Nicoll (Balgavies, The Pinkfoot Press), 15–19.

Higham, N. J. 1991. 'Cavalry in Early Bernicia?', *Northern History*, 27, 236–41.

Hyland, Ann. 1990. *Equus: The Horse in the Roman World* (London, Batsford).

Hyland, Ann. 1994. *The Medieval Warhorse from Byzantium to the Crusades* (Dover, Alan Sutton).

Jackson, Kenneth H. (ed.). 1969. *The Gododdin: The Oldest Scottish Poem* (Edinburgh University Press).

Jarman, A. O. H. (ed.). 1988. *Aneirin: Y Gododdin, Britain's Oldest Heroic Poem* (Llandysul, Gomer Press).

Laing, L. R. and Laing, J. 1985. 'The Date and Origin of the Pictish Symbols', *Proceedings of the Society of Antiquaries of Scotland,* 114, 261–76.

Palk, Natalie A. 1984. *Iron Age Bridle-Bits from Britain* (Occasional Paper no. 10, University of Edinburgh, Department of Archaeology).

Podhajsky, Alois. 1973. *The Riding Teacher: A Basic Guide to Correct Methods of Classical Instruction*, tr. Eva Podhajsky (London, Harrap).

Renfrew, Colin. 1987. *Archaeology and Language: The Puzzle of Indo-European Origins* (London, Jonathan Cape).

Rowland, Jenny. 1995. 'Warfare and Horses in the *Gododdin* and the Problem of Catraeth', *Cambrian Medieval Celtic Studies*, 30, 13–40.

Smythe, R. H. 1993. *Horse Structure and Movement,* 3rd edn., rev. P. Gray (London, J. A. Allen).

Thomas, Charles. 1971. *Britain and Ireland in Early Christian Times: A.D. 400–800* (London, Thames & Hudson).

White, Lynn. 1962. *Medieval Technology and Social Change* (Oxford University Press).

3

The Earliest Words for 'Horse' in the Celtic Languages

Patricia Kelly

The importance of the horse in the medieval Celtic world, as illustrated in the other chapters in this volume, finds linguistic expression in a well-stocked and richly nuanced lexicon of equine terms in the Insular Celtic languages.[1] These words in their turn – their existence, precise connotations, and sense demarcation from semantically related items – can throw light on the *realia* of the role and status of horses in the Middle Ages. Even more ancient perceptions of the horse can be uncovered, as an investigation of etymologies can reveal original meanings and sometimes also illuminate the naming process which gave rise to a particular word. In this way it will on occasion be possible to extend the chronological scope of this survey back into late antiquity and prehistory.

The three possible sources for the lexicon of a language are exemplified in this specific semantic field: etyma inherited from its parent-language, in this case proto-Indo-European (IE), new lexemes formed from inherited elements by derivation or word formation, and borrowings.[2] Both branches of Insular Celtic feature these processes, but to different degrees and with different elements.

References to horses are ubiquitous in the medieval literatures of the Insular Celts, and from these texts a variety of general terms, as well as marked terms for the male, female and young, can be gleaned. The discussion below will follow this semantic classification. The scope is confined to the oldest terms, primarily in Irish and Welsh, to their Continental Celtic predecessors, where attested, and to the subsequent history of these words in the insular languages.

Generic Terms

1. OIr *ech*

The most ancient identifiable stratum in this lexical field is represented by Early Irish *ech*, which is the Q-Celtic or Goidelic form of the proto-Indo-European word for 'horse'.[3] As the generic term it forms the basis for a large number of derivatives and compounds denoting horse-related items and concepts in Early Irish texts. Alone among the European languages which inherited this word, Scottish-Gaelic has retained it as the normal generic term down to the present day – a remarkable archaism. Modern Irish has innovated in a variety of ways, but *each* survives in literature and proverbs.

In Brittonic Celtic, the innovation had already taken place by the time of the earliest Welsh texts, in which *march* appears as the generic. Traces of the earlier state of affairs can, however, be seen. An Old Breton gloss has preserved evidence for *eb* 'horse' (Fleuriot 1964, 154, 165). The generic sense is also retained in the Middle Welsh compounds *ebran* 'horse-fodder', *ebodn* 'horse-dung', *ebediw* 'heriot'.[4] The simplex is retained, but with its meaning restricted to 'foal', in the old compound MW *cyfeb,* MBr *kenep* 'with foal'. An alternative development is the expression of 'foal' by means of a derivative: MW *ebawl,* MBr *ebeul.*

In Continental Celtic this inherited term occurs in many onomastic forms. The P-Celtic *epo-* is the most common, attested frequently as an element in personal, divinity, ethnic and place names (Evans 1967, 190–2), for example *Epona,* the name of the goddess identified as an equine figure by her iconography as well (see above, pp. 11–14). Other divine figures also have equine affinities: in Celtiberian, which is Q-Celtic, the rock inscription of Peñalba de Villastar contains *equeisui,* an adjectival derivative 'equine' (Meid 1994a, 35), applied to the god Lug. If the month-name EQUOS in the Coligny Calendar belongs here,[5] the retention of the older Q-Celtic form in a P-Celtic area may be due to the archaic religious context. The simplex is nowhere attested as a common noun in Continental sources, but is found in P-Celtic form in compounds such as *epocalium,* glossed *'ungula caballina'* ('colt's foot'), and *eporediae,* which Pliny's Natural History explains as *'boni equorum domitores'* ('good tamers of horses') (Evans 1967, 199).[6]

The reconstructed IE etymon **ek̂uo-* has played a major role in linguistic palaeontology, which seeks to establish the homeland of the Indo-Europeans on the basis of plant and animal data encoded in the lexicon. While virtually all the daughter-languages featured this word at least in their earliest attested stages,[7] a morphological analysis shows that its creation is to be assigned to a late phase in the proto-language. This suggests that the domestication of the horse did not take place until shortly before the break-up of Indo-European into individual language families. Mastery of the horse is thought to have been a powerful factor in the population movements which resulted in the linguistic conquest by the Indo-European family of languages of areas stretching from the most westerly parts of Europe to the Indian subcontinent in the east.[8] One quality of the recently domesticated animal which was surely advantageous in this development was that of rapid movement. This may also be reflected in the etymology of the IE word: despite Buck's verdict (1949, 167) that the 'root connection [is] wholly obscure', a derivation from an adjective *ōk̑ú- 'swift' (Gk. ὠκύς) is often mooted (Pokorny 1959, 775), though the precise morphological process remains unclear.[9]

2. W. *march*, OIr *marc*

British Celtic shares the general trend of European languages, apart from Goidelic, by its dislocation of the inherited Indo-European word. In Early Welsh literature the most common generic term is *march*.

This too has a Continental congener: *marco-*. Like *epo-*, it occurs in onomastic forms, but less frequently (Evans 1967, 198 n. 1). It is also attested as the common noun appellative for 'horse', and is recorded as such by the Greek traveller Pausanias, writing in the second century AD, but thought to be drawing on a description of the Galatian Celts from the third century BC (Tierney 1960, 196).[10] A further contrast is that this is a much younger word than *ek̑uo-*, with a secure attestation outside Celtic only in Germanic (OHG *marah*, a poetic word for 'horse').[11] The relative lateness of *marko-* is also reflected in the comparative lack of old compounded Celtic names containing this element (Schmidt 1957, 237).

The Continental Celtic juxtaposition of inherited *epo-/equo-* and probably younger *marco-* has been taken to reflect a semantic differentiation between 'chariot-horse' and 'riding-horse' respectively (Loth 1925). This interpretation receives some support from the derivative τριμαρκισια, recorded by Pausanias as a term of the Celtic cavalry denoting a group of three in which 'two servants of a mounted cavalry-man provide him with remounts or take his place in battle' (Tierney 1960, 196). In the late spindle-whorl inscriptions, written in a mixture of Gaulish and Latin, a verbal form *marcosior* has been explained as 'I desire to ride' (Meid 1980, 24). Birkhan (1970, 398–400) adduced archaeological evidence from La Tène sites in Germany for two types of horse, a smaller one, with a maximum withers height of 137 cm, and a larger, stronger breed, up to 150 cm in height, which may have been bred for riding. This development Birkhan attributes to the influence of a Thracian riding culture. A linguistic reflex of this connection might be perceived in allegedly Thracian personal names containing the element **mark-*, but the interpretation of these forms is disputed (Orel 1987, 8).

The phonology of the Celtic and Germanic forms does not allow conclusions about the direction of a possible borrowing between the two language families. No satisfactory etymology has been proposed.[12]

The semantic dichotomy posited for Continental Celtic may also be reflected in the distribution of the terms in Insular Celtic. Early Irish texts feature *ech,* and in the earliest tales of the Ulster Cycle this is almost exclusively applied to chariot-horses. In early Welsh literature, however, warriors are shown riding, and chariots are conspicuous by their absence. The simple contrast OIr *ech* versus MW *march* implied here must, however, be modified to accommodate an Early Irish form of **marko-,* namely *marc,* and the associated *marcach* 'rider'. Greene (1972), observing the contrast between the societies depicted in the two Insular literatures, concluded that riding, and the terms denoting it, were borrowed into Ireland from Britain. According to this theory, OIr *marc* is not inherited from Continental Celtic, but is a Welsh loan-word, and *marcach* a calque on W. *marchawc* 'rider'.

While the hypothesis of borrowing from British is supported by other borrowings to be discussed later (OIr *capall, gabor*), by Latin terms for horse-gear transmitted to Ireland via Britain, and by historical evidence that British horses were greatly prized in Ireland, two objections could be raised to Greene's argument. First, as regards the primacy of chariotry in pre-Christian Ireland, the reliance on the Ulster cycle as a guide to the material culture of Iron Age Ireland has been criticized in recent scholarship (Mallory 1992). Further, as is now well known, there is a discrepancy between the culture depicted in the texts and the objects recovered in excavations of Iron Age sites. The archaeological evidence suggests that riding was much more common than paired draught by horses (Raftery 1991).

The linguistic data from Irish also present a few puzzles. The borrowing *marc*, if such it be, does not displace *ech.* Instead it is found in the function of a poetic word even in very early texts. This is a use in which one would expect to find old obsolete forms, not newly introduced ones. On the other hand, in some texts, *marc* appears as the generic term, and in decidedly non-poetic contexts.

One possible explanation for these asymmetries is that we are dealing, in language as in material culture, with regional differences. Lexical variation, such as that suggested by the distribution of *ech* and *marc*, may be evidence for dialect differentiation (Kelly 1982).

As regards Continental Celtic, however, technological and breeding developments are very plausible explanations for the lexical innovation.[13]

3. MW *cafall, ceffyl, caffon* (pl.), OIr *capall*

Here we have another item shared by British and Irish, in a plethora of variants. That these words are in some way connected with Lat. *caballus* is evident. However, the suggestion that *capall* might be a borrowing from Latin was not adopted by Vendryes in his study of Latin loans in Irish (1902, 121); nor does Jackson include any of the Welsh forms in his list of 'the more striking examples' of Latin borrowings in British from the category of animals, birds and fish (1953, 78).

Another possibility is that both Insular branches have independently inherited from Common Celtic. On the evidence of the Gaulish personal name *Ro-cabalus*, which he interprets as 'great horse', Schmidt (1957, 58) argues that the word was already present in Continental Celtic, whence it was adopted into Latin.

The most frequent Welsh form of the word is *ceffyl*, which cannot be borrowed from either Lat. *caballus* or Celtic *caballos*. The regular reflex of either of these putative proto-forms would yield W. *cafall*, and this is indeed attested, in early poetry. The *Gododdin* contains a description of a warrior in armour and mail-coat:

> oid girth oed cuall
> ar geuin e gauall
> (Williams 1961, ll. 1202–3)

('He was fierce, he was rash, on the back of his horse.')

Another instance is *am cavall* from the early saga poetry (Williams 1935, 29), where, however, it may also be a place name. In later Welsh texts, *Cafall* functions as the name of a warrior's horse.[14]

Ceffyl has become the generic term for the horse in Modern Welsh, relegating *march* to the literary register, or to the special sense of 'stallion' in some dialects (Thomas 1973, 267).[15] It is this form which is closest to the Irish *capall*. The vowel and consonant quality of both W. *ceffyl* and OIr *capall* show that the proto-form from which these are derived must have been **cappillos*.[16] This **cappillos* differs from Lat. *caballus* firstly through the suffix *-illos,* and secondly through the double consonant *-pp-*, as against the single *-b-*. Consonant doubling ('gemination') of this kind, sometimes combined with devoicing as in this case, is a feature of affective or expressive word forms, and is frequent in kinship and animal terms, and also in short forms of originally compounded personal names.[17] Given that Irish, being Q-Celtic, cannot have inherited the medial *-p-*, the Early Irish word must be interpreted as a borrowing from British Celtic at some time before the sound change *-pp- > -ff-*.

Affective gemination is thought to develop initially in the short or abbreviated forms of words likely to be used in contexts where there is a marked expression of feeling. From these the gemination can then spread to derivatives. In the case of W. *ceffyl,* we actually have that short form. This is *kaffon* (pl.),[18] which occurs only once, in the eulogy on Urien traditionally ascribed to Taliesin. The passage describes the remnants of a defeated army:

> gwanecawr gollychynt rawn eu kaffon,
> gwelais i wyr gospeithic gospylat
> (Williams 1975, ll. 22–3)

('The waves washed the tails of their horses. I saw disheartened men pillaging (?).')

The use of *kaffon* here seems disparaging, and the image of the waves reaching up to the horses' tails could perhaps be taken as an indication that these are small, pony-like animals. There may be an implied contrast with the steeds of the victors.

A sense of disparagement is also conveyed in the earliest attested use of *ceffyl* in the *Mabinogion*. The tale of Peredur depicts his arrival at court as a rustic youth mounted on one of the farm-horses, described as *y keffyleu a gywedei gynnut udunt ac a dygei bwyt a llyn* ('the nags which carried firewood for them and brought food and drink') (Goetinck 1976, 9). This recalls the distinction implied in the early eighth-century Irish law tracts, where *capall* is used for a work-horse and juxtaposed pejoratively with *ech*, which designates a superior-quality riding-horse: *capall fognama 7 ech immrimme* (Binchy 1941, 6) 'a nag for work and a steed for riding'. The earliest poetic occurrence in Welsh is in the work of fourteenth-century Iolo Goch, where he lists the disadvantages of horses, asserting his poem to be more valuable than an animal he might receive in exchange, such as *ceffyl trymgul tremgoeg* (Johnston 1993, 12.22) ('a slow(?), skinny, blind nag').

Thus we see that the 'emotional' or 'expressive' connotation of the forms which feature the gemination (W. *kaffon/ceffyl*, OIr *capall*) is a negative one. This contrasts with the marked positive connotations of the one certain occurrence of W. *cavall* as a common noun.

The idea of a borrowing from Latin can now be reconsidered. This would match well with the considerable body of incontrovertible Latin loan words in Welsh for 'horse equipment'; some of these were borrowed further into Irish.[19] Borrowings are usually motivated by the superiority or desirability – material, ideological or whatever – of the artefact or construct in the culture of the donor language. The low status of W. *caffon* or *ceffyl* and OIr *capall*, however, belies the likelihood that these are such loans. The status of Latin *caballus*, on the other hand, must have been in the ascendant since the first century BC, when, according to the grammarian Varro (116–27 BC), it is already synonomous with *equus* in popular speech. The cluster of loans for horse-gear shows that a number of artefacts presumably of a higher technology were introduced to Britain under the Roman Empire. These would have played a major role in the equipment of the cavalry units of the army, where the term for 'horse' was more likely to be *caballus* than the high-register *equus*.

These facts can best be reconciled by seeing in W. *cavall* a borrowing of Latin *caballus*, which, by appealing to the use of *cavall* in the *Gododdin*, one might surmise denoted a horse bred for the use of mounted soldiers.[20] The native Brittonic Celtic diminutive *cappillos* had a pejorative flavour in contrast to the high status words *epo-* and *marko-*.

The need for a motivation for the borrowing of OIr *capall* from Brittonic *cappillos* still remains. In the discussion of W. *march*/OIr *marc* above, the historical evidence for the export of horses from Britain into Ireland was mentioned. The sources, mainly annalistic and legal, make it clear, however, that such references are to valuable animals, to which the derogatory *cappillos* would not have applied. One has to envisage a speech community where British and Irish speakers were in such close contact that the borrowing of everyday, low-register words was possible. This recalls T. F. O'Rahilly's controversial theory of P-Celtic communities in Ireland (O'Rahilly 1936), but the historical Irish settlements in Wales could also have been the facilitating conduit.

With regard to the ultimate origins of *caballos* and its congeners, no generally accepted theory has been advanced. A conventional etymology would attempt to link the element *cab-* with an established IE root of appropriate semantics. A possible candidate is the root *(s)kep-* etc. (Pokorny 1959, 930), where the relevant cognates in the individual languages have meanings such as 'cut' (Greek), 'scrape, rub' (Latin) and, most significantly, 'castrated' (Old Church Slavonic).[21] Evidence for an early meaning 'gelding' is no longer tangible in Celtic, and is disputed for Latin *caballus* and *cabo*. However that may be, development of the words *ceffyl* in Welsh and *capall* in Irish into generic terms in the modern languages is a belated parallel to the fate of Lat. *caballus* in the Romance languages.

4. W. *gorwydd*

This word belongs to the oldest stratum of Welsh, being found mainly in early poetry, but also in the prose of the tale 'Culhwch and Olwen', whose language agrees in many points with Old Welsh usage (Bromwich and Evans 1992, xv–xxv). In general it seems to have a highly positive connotation. It is obsolete by the later medieval period, when it requires explanation in the glossaries. A homonym *gorwydd* 'swift' occurs in the Book of Taliesin which raises the possibility that the horse term is a substantivization of this adjective.

Gorwydd is the first of the general terms to be discussed here which has no direct correspondence in Goidelic. Nevertheless, there is a close connection, in that both its component parts have cognates in Irish. *Gorwydd* is conventionally and plausibly derived from *uo-rēdos*, where *uo-* is the prefix whose Irish equivalent is *fo*, originally meaning 'under', and the second element is based on the Celtic root *rēd-*. This root is indirectly attested for Continental Celtic, and its semantic range delineated, through Latin borrowings from Celtic, viz *rēda* meaning 'a kind of car', and *veredus* the horse which pulls the *rēda*. Thus the Welsh word must have had a direct precursor in Celtic, though in the Insular sources it is used exclusively of riding-horses. The underlying verbal root *reidh-* is another Celto-Germanic isogloss (like Celtic *marko-* /Germanic *marha-* above) in this field of equine terms. The attestations in the Germanic languages reflect only the meaning 'ride' (Meid 1994b, 65), but an originally wider semantic range 'travel (with a horse)' is suggested by the frequent use of OIr *réd-* and derivatives in connection with chariotry.

The syntagms of *epo-* and *rēd-* in Continental Celtic personal names, e.g. *Eporēdorīx* (Evans 1967, 90–2, 198), attest to the collocation of these two items, but do not allow any certainty about the meaning of **reidh-* in these contexts. Here, however, Goidelic throws some light. The OIr collective *echrad* 'horses' has been analysed as a compound of *ech* and a suffix *-rad* deriving from **rēda* 'course' = OIr *ríad*: the semantic development envisaged is 'horse-course or -drive' > 'team of two chariot-horses for a drive' > 'horses (coll.)' (Thurneysen 1946, 169).

Further evidence for the semantics of **reidh-* is supplied by the passage in Pliny's Natural History which explains Gaulish *eporediae* as *boni equorum domitores* 'good tamers of horses' (Le Roux 1956, 372). This suggests a more general meaning 'tame, break in', which is confirmed by the application to oxen in Early Irish. This may, however, be a purely Celtic extension of meaning.

Whereas Loth (1925) interpreted **voreidos* as meaning 'under the *rēda*' and thus 'harnessed horse', Hamp (1982) and Lambert (1994, 197) propose 'travel swiftly' as the original meaning of the root.

The Latinized *veredus* undergoes further compounding with the Greek prefix *para* to form another noun, Low Latin *paraveredus*, which is the source of German *Pferd*. It also gives French *palefroi*, which appears in the Welsh laws as the Anglo-Norman borrowing *palffrai*. The French word is also borrowed into Early Modern Irish, where it has the form *falafraigh*.

Thus **reidh-* and its derivatives give an excellent insight into the cross-currents of language and material culture which can determine the configuration of the vocabulary of equine terms in a language.

5. W. eddystyr

As above with *gorwydd*, here we are again dealing with a word which has no direct correspondence in an equine term in Goidelic, although in this case too the base word features in Irish. *Eddystyr* is plausibly derived by *Geiriadur Prifysgol Cymru* from Celtic **adastrio-*. The closest cognate is OIr *adastar* 'halter'. Vendryes (*LEIA* 1981, 16) explains the semantic development as an instance of *pars pro toto*, i.e. 'halter' > 'horse'. One could also envisage a development from an adjectival derivative

*adastrio- 'haltered', i.e. 'haltered (horse)' > 'horse'. We have seen above the possibility that *gorwydd* is a substantivized adjective, and this explanation will be suggested for OIr *gabor* also (see section 6 below).

In Old and Middle Irish, *adastar* has a derogatory flavour, being found in satires and in an unflattering sobriquet. The Welsh derivative seems free of this pejorative aspect, being found in similar old contexts to *gorwydd*. In the *Gododdin*, for example, it occurs in a list of desirable luxuries, and is qualified by the adjective *pasg: edystrawr pasc* (Williams 1961, l. 146) 'well-fed horses'. This suggests that the word has undergone semantic amelioration in Welsh, and highlights the more archaic character of the Early Irish vocabulary in general.

6. OIr gabor[22]

The entry for this term in the Early Irish glossary of Cormac, the king-bishop of Cashel who died in 908, states that it originally denoted a white horse, or one with some white in its coat, this being the most valued colour (Meyer 1912, 55). Textual attestations confirm the high status, often royal, of the animal so designated.

Cormac's Glossary also adds that it is derived from a Welsh word which he writes *goor*,[23] meaning '*cach solus*'. The Irish gloss has generally been taken to contain the noun 'light' and to indicate that *gabor* is a borrowing from Welsh *gwawr* 'dawn'. If, however, one interprets *cach solus* as 'everything light or bright', the 'etymology' could suggest that the underlying Welsh word is a colour adjective meaning 'light-coloured'. A suitable candidate is the sparsely attested *gawr*, which occurs in the early saga poetry and in the Book of Taliesin, and is tentatively rendered 'grey' in *Geiriadur Prifysgol Cymru*. The use of substantivized colour adjectives for horses is common in early Welsh poetry. Examples are *can* ('white (horse)'), *gwineu* ('chestnut'), *gell* ('bay'), *erch* ('dappled') (see below, p. 87). The last of these has a parallel in Early Irish, in which *erc* denotes a highly valued 'white (red-eared) cow'.

7. mandu- ?

Traces of a lost equine term may perhaps be seen in the element *mandu-*. It is attested in Continental Celtic, but only in onomastic material (Evans 1967, 222–3). Evidence for its relevance for the present discussion comes mainly from Latin, where *mannus* has the meaning 'small Gaulish horse' since the first century BC, in the writings of Lucretius. This is deemed a borrowing from Gaulish by the fifth-century grammarian Consentius.

Celtic evidence for a connection with this lexical field is suggested by words in which *mandu-* is compounded with elements which clearly have equine associations. These are the Gaulish place-names *Epamanduodurum* in Gaul, and Romano-British *Manduessedum,* on the Antonine itinerary (Jackson 1948, 57). The second component of the latter is the Belgic word for a chariot recorded by Caesar.

An etymological derivation of *mandu-* from a root **mend-* 'to (give) suck' links it with words in other Indo-European languages for 'young animal', including MIr *menn,* MW *myn,* diminutive *mynnan* 'kid' (Pokorny 1959, 729).[24] While the semantics of this etymology are attractive, the vowel alternation remains a problem (*LEIA* 1960, 38). Nevertheless, this word, if its Celticity be admitted, can be assigned to the category of new Celtic formations using inherited roots. The lack of textual evidence makes it impossible to hazard a guess about why it was lost.

'Stallion'

A method common to both Irish and Welsh to signify 'stallion' is by a syntagm comprising a generic term for 'horse' with an adjective 'male'. The adjectives are OIr *caullach* (later *cullach*) and W. *ceillog.* These are derived from a Common Celtic root for 'testicle': the underlying noun appears in Irish as *caull,* and in Welsh as *caill,* which indicate the proto-forms **kallu-* and **kallio-* respectively. The syntagms are OIr *echcullach*[25] and W. *march keillawc,* both attested in early legal texts: the Welsh phrase is rendered *equus testiculatus* in the Latin redaction of the laws (Emanuel 1967, 234). The basic notion is therefore 'testicled', an immediately transparent naming construction for a male animal, and one which has a direct parallel in the Baltic words for 'stallion' (Buck 1949, 169). Thus it is not surprising that it can be applied to other males, too, as in OIr *muccullach* 'boar'. In Middle Irish the substantivized adjective *cullach* is used of either the equine or porcine kind; in the modern language it is confined to the meaning 'boar'. The Welsh laws show a wider application, in *anyueil keillawc* 'entire animal' (Owen 1841, ii. 210). These laws also feature two further syntagms: *march grewys,* literally 'stud horse' and *march gweini* 'service horse'.

In addition, Middle Irish has *midach*, for which the meaning 'stallion' was suggested by Stokes on the basis of the gloss *mo dechaib e no maith ech* ('greatest of steeds he or a good steed') (O'Donovan 1868, 118). None of the citations under this headword in *DIL* confirm this meaning, though they all show that the word has markedly positive connotations, and is an element of the literary register. Both meaning and 'poetic' flavour, however, are indicated in an onomastic *Dindshenchas* legend involving a wild young stallion: where the prose version has *fiadcullach* 'wild stallion' (Stokes 1895, 58), its (unpublished) metrical counterpart in the Book of Uí Mhaine features *fiadmhidhach*.

This word too is in origin an adjective. Vendryes's derivation (*LEIA* 1983, 49) from the rare poetic word *mid* 'honour, renown' is unconvincing. In view of the etymology of OIr *caullach*/W. *ceilliog,* a connection with Greek μέζεα, μέδεα 'male genitals' seems more attractive. Pokorny (1959, 706) books these tentatively under a root **med-* 'to swell'. On semantic grounds, they could also plausibly be derived from the better-attested root **med-* (Pokorny 1959, 705), with its connotations of 'power, ability'.[26] A parallel for the sense development is furnished by OHG *gimaht* 'testicles' (cf. ModG *Macht* 'power').

Another Early Welsh term is *amws*. This is a back-formation of *emys*, which is a borrowing from Latin *(equus) admissus*, 'a derivative of *admittere* "give access to", in the sense of "put the male to the female"' (Buck 1949, 169). The form of *emys* (with *i*-affection) being interpreted as a plural, a new analogical singular *amws* was created. While 'stallion' is the original meaning, a specialization to 'destrier' is shown by the correspondence between Welsh *amws* and Latin *dextrarius* in the Welsh and Latin version of the Laws respectively (see below, p. 71).

Elsewhere in the Welsh laws the term is *ystalwyn.* This derives ultimately from OFr *estalon*, which also gives rise to Anglo-Latin *stalonus* and ME *staloun*, first attested in Wyclif's Bible of 1388. The Welsh word may therefore be the oldest attestation of this borrowing in the vernaculars of Britain. In the modern language, *stalwyn* is characteristic of the northern dialects (Thomas 1973, 267 and fig. 7).[27]

In Irish, this borrowing does not make an appearance until the modern language. 'Stallion' in many dialects is *stail*. The palatalized final suggests that it derives from one of the English forms with *-ly/li-*[28] which is also the source of ModE *stallion*.

Like Welsh *palffrai, ystalwyn* has a heterogenous history, as its parent OFr *estalon* is itself based on the forerunner of German *Stall* 'stall': the stallion is therefore the 'stalled' animal.

It is noteworthy that the marked term for the male is highly susceptible to renewal and innovation. The material correlative for this is probably the importation and use of high-quality stallions to improve breeds.

'Gelding'

The oldest term which can be established for the castrated male in the Insular vernaculars is OIr *meile*, which is already obsolete in the earliest texts, and requires glossing. It seems reasonable, following Vendryes (*LEIA* 1960, 29), to derive this word from IE *mel-* 'grind', especially as this root is the base for the Common Celtic term for the castrated sheep: cf. OIr *molt*, W. *mollt,* Bret. *maout* 'wether', which have been explained as passive participles in *to-*, therefore originally 'ground' (Pokorny 1959, 716). This may indicate an ancient practice of castration, for which some evidence pertaining to ancient India in found in the Sanskrit *Atharvaveda* (Buck 1949, 142, 158). The morphology of the horse word is more difficult, however, as the underlying *yo-* derivative would normally have an agentive function. A meaning 'grinder' would suit if we envisage the gelding as a work-animal set to turning a mill.[29] That such mills existed in early Ireland is shown by the compound *marcmuilenn* 'horse-mill'.

The word most frequently used to gloss *meile* is *gerrán*. This is a derivative of the adjective *gerr* 'short' (Pokorny 1959, 443). The adjective also provides the base for a verb *gerraid* 'cut'. While there is no unequivocal textual evidence from the early period for the meaning 'gelding' for this word, the evidence of the majority of the modern dialects, where it does have this semantic range, can be taken as decisive. Thus the animal is named 'the short i.e. cut one'.

Welsh again shows influence from Latin. The technical term for castrating animals is *disbaddu*. This is a compound consisting of a Celtic prefix *di* and a verbal form *ysbaddu* which is a borrowing from Late Latin *spadāre*, itself a denominative from *spadō* 'impotent person or animal'. While the verb *disbaddu* occurs in a thirteenth-century law manuscript (Wiliam 1960, 87) in relation to boar and ram, the earliest instance of *march disbadd*, literally 'gelded horse', seems to be from the fifteenth century.[30]

'Mare'

In the marked terms for the female we find the greatest divergence yet encountered between the two insular branches. On the other hand, the terms remain remarkably stable throughout the history of the languages, unlike their counterparts for the male.

Here Brittonic has preserved the oldest item, and perhaps another Germano-Celtic isogloss. W. *cassec*, Corn. *cassec*, Bret. *kazek* can be derived from Celtic **kassikā*. A connection with the element *Cassic-* in Gaulish onomastic forms seems likely, and receives support from the inscription containing the word *Cassiciate* (explained as the locative of a place name), on a votive offering of a bronze horse to the Gaulish god Rudiobus (de Vries 1961, 110). The element *Cassi-* has been linked with the Germanic equine term **hangista-*, as in OHG *hengist*, OE *hangest* 'gelding'. The correspondence suggests that the original meaning is unlikely to have been 'mare'. A relation with the Baltic words for 'swift' and 'jump' has been proposed (Pokorny 1959, 522).[31] An alternative etymology is that of Marstrander (1911, 207), who explains it as a compound of **konki-* 'yoke' and the verbal root **sthā-* 'stand': the meaning would then be 'standing yoked, a yoked horse'.[32]

The Old Irish term is *láir*, for which no satisfactory etymology has appeared in print. One could envisage a derivative from the Irish verbal root *lá-* 'throw' and compare the use of Welsh *bwrw* 'throw', and German *werfen,* in the sense of 'give birth (of animals)'.

'Foal'

Here again, Welsh has preserved the older material. It denotes 'foal' by a derivative of the inherited IE etymon, W. *ebawl*, fem. *eboles*. The precise analysis of the suffix is still under discussion.[33] It is interesting to note the presence of the l-extension already in Gaulish, in the plant name *ebulcalium* (Evans 1967, 199).

Old Irish has two terms for 'foal'. One is *lurchaire*, which is used of the animal just after birth, and when its value is not reckoned independently of its dam. The analysis is unclear. If *-chaire* is an agent-noun derivative of the verbal root *car-* 'to love', meaning 'one who loves', the first element should be the word for 'mare', giving **lárchaire*.[34] Perhaps the initial syllable has been influenced by *lu-* 'small'.

The Old Irish term for the weaned animal is *serrach*. The suffix is again adjectival, but it is not clear what the base word is (*LEIA* 1974, 95).

Conclusion

The survey gives some indication of the wealth of lexical material contained in the earliest branches of Insular Celtic in general, and in particular reflects the importance of horses in the cultures of Early Britain and Ireland.

This snapshot of a restricted lexical field in the earliest attestations of the Celtic languages provides not merely linguistic access to the realm of material culture, but also a synchronic cross-section of the whole lexicon and the semantic interrelations between some of its components. The diachronic investigation can sometimes give an insight into the strategies used to describe and designate horses, and the way individual languages exploit the linguistic elements at their disposal to create and restructure a lexicon.

The degree of divergence between Goidelic and Brittonic in this section of vocabulary is noteworthy. Agreement is closest in the retention of the Indo-European word – though only residually in Brittonic. Indo-European roots have furnished new derivatives in Gaulish *mandu-*, MW *ceffyl*, OIr *caullach*/MW *keillawc*, MIr *midach*, OIr *meile*, MIr *gerrán*. Three items reveal a close correspondence with Germanic: MW *march*, *gorwydd* and possibly *casseg*. A process frequently used to create specialized terms is the substantivization of adjectives: this has been seen in MW *gorwydd* and *eddystyr*, and in OIr *gabor, midach, caullach* and *serrach*. The salient impression, however, is the extent to which the equine terms are the result of borrowing (OIr *marc, capall, gabor*, ModIr *falafraigh, stail*, MW *cafall, amws, ystalwyn, palffrai, disbadd*). This, above all, affords a glimpse of the practical aspects of the horse culture of early and medieval Britain and Ireland.

Notes

[1] The Irish material is drawn from my unpublished dissertation (Kelly 1983). Hughes 1994 was not available to me at the time of writing. Useful discussions of the Welsh terms are found in Watkin 1958, 75–6 and Jenkins 1963, 80–5.

2 The role of substratum languages is sometimes invoked, but is difficult to substantiate.

3 See Pokorny 1959, 301 for the Indo-European congeners.

4 The second element in *ebediw* 'heriot' has been explained as a form of the verb *adawaf* 'I leave, deposit' (Howells 1973–4, 48).

5 The etymology is disputed: Evans 1967, 199 n. 12; Duval and Pinault 1986, 424.

6 See also section 4 below for a discussion of the element *rēd-*.

7 To Pokorny's list (1959, 301) of attestations (in Indo-Iranian, Greek, Thracian (proper names only), Latin, Germanic, Tocharian and Baltic, as well as Celtic) more recent scholarship has added Mycenaean Greek and Hieroglyphic Hittite.

8 The most recent comprehensive treatment of the subject is Hänsel and Zimmer 1994.

9 Hamp 1990 is a recent analysis. He adduces as semantic parallels for such an etymology the pairs OE *hengest* 'gelding': Lith. *šankùs* 'nimble', and Eng. *horse*: Lat. *currō* 'run, move quickly, hasten'.

10 Pausanias' form μαρκαν suggests an ā-stem rather than an ō-stem. The implications are investigated in Birkhan 1970, 396–416.

11 Eng. *mare* is derived from this root.

12 Birkhan 1970, 393–8 summarizes the various suggestions.

13 Birkhan's suggestion (1970, 406) that the inherited word was replaced because of tabu is undermined by the strength of *ech* in Irish.

14 For a discussion of these see Ford 1983. Bromwich (1978, ci) considers the use of *Cabal* as the name of Arthur's hound to be a corruption of the original tradition, in which it designated his horse. It could also be a reference to the size of the hound. See below, p. 116, and further Bromwich and Evans 1992, 153–4. See also Bromwich and Evans 1992, ll. 336, 739 and the notes on these lines.

15 See below, pp. 45–7.

16 Thurneysen 1946, 567.

17 See Schmidt, 1979, 121 and n. 9. In the field of animal names, consonant doubling can be seen in OIr *mucc* 'pig', W. *moch* 'pigs' < *mokk- (*LEIA* 1960, 68f.). Gaulish furnishes many examples of gemination in short forms of compound names in *epo-*, such as *Eppia, Eppius, Eppo* (Evans, 1967, 182f.).

18 The geminated singular *cappō would yield Early Welsh *ceiff.

19 Note, for example: *afwyn* 'rein' < *habēna* (OIr *abann*); *cebystr* 'halter' < *capistrum* (SG *cabstar* 'bit, curb'); *ffrwyn* 'bridle' < *frēnum* (OIr *srían*); *ystrodur* 'saddle' < *strātūra* (OIr *srathar*).

20 For a recent comprehensive study of evidence for the use of cavalry by the British Celts, see Rowland 1995.

21 This root is invoked, but merely as an indirect influence on, not the direct source of, *caballus* etc., in *LEIA* 1987, 34.

[22] The word is quoted as cited in the *DIL*, though this may not be its oldest form.

[23] Russell 1995 discusses the British words in Cormac's Glossary.

[24] See also Meid 1994b, 56.

[25] The compound is of the 'univerbated' type discussed by Mac Cana (1991, 28–9).

[26] The Celtic derivatives of this root are investigated in Williams 1921 and Hamp 1976.

[27] Some modern Welsh dialects have retained the old generic term *march* in the sense of 'stallion'. Even where the 'stallion' is *ystalwyn*, however, words for 'a mare in heat' are derived from *march* (Thomas 1973, 283 and fig. 157).

[28] These are attested from the fifteenth century, and are said by the *OED* to be of obscure origin.

[29] I owe this suggestion to Ulla Remmer, Vienna.

[30] Professor Dafydd Jenkins writes (personal communication): 'The term occurs in two unpublished passages in Peniarth 259B (the Z of Owen 1841), which can be attributed to the fifteenth century, since the manuscript, though written in the sixteenth century, is clearly a copy of a fifteenth-century original, see Huws 1996, 308–9.'

[31] This is supported by Meid 1994b, 56–7.

[32] Polomé (1983, 284) cites the Celtiberian ethnic name *Concani*. On the element *konk-* in Celtic onomastic forms, see further Birkhan 1970, 426–31; Schmidt 1957, 182.

[33] Zimmer 1987, taken up by Kratz 1988 and Hamp 1988.

[34] Pedersen 1909, 340 is the only attempt known to me to analyse the relations between *láir* and *lurchaire*.

Abbreviations

DIL   *Dictionary of the Irish Language* (Dublin, Royal Irish Academy, 1913–76).

LEIA   *Lexique étymologique de l'irlandais ancien (MNOP, RS, A, C),* ed. J. Vendryes (Dublin Institute for Advanced Studies, 1960, 1974, 1981, 1987).

OED   *The Oxford English Dictionary,* 2nd edn. (Oxford University Press, 1989).

Bret.   Breton
Corn.   Cornish
Gk.   Greek

IE	Indo-European
Lat.	Latin
Lith.	Lithuanian
MBr	Middle Breton
ME	Middle English
ModE	Modern English
ModG	Modern German
ModIr	Modern Irish
MW	Middle Welsh
OE	Old English
OFr	Old French
OHG	Old High German
OIr	Old Irish
SG	Scottish-Gaelic
W.	Welsh

References

Binchy, D. A. (ed.). 1941. *Críth Gablach* (Dublin Institute for Advanced Studies).

Birkhan, Helmut. 1970. *Germanen und Kelten bis zum Ausgang der Römerzeit* (Vienna, Böhlau, Kommissionsverlag der österreichischen Akademie der Wissenschaften).

Bromwich, Rachel (ed.). 1978. *Trioedd Ynys Prydein: The Welsh Triads*, 2nd edn. (Cardiff, University of Wales Press).

Bromwich, Rachel and Evans, D. Simon (eds.). 1992. *Culhwch and Olwen* (Cardiff, University of Wales Press).

Buck, C. D. 1949. *A Dictionary of Selected Synonyms in the Principal Indo-European Languages: A Contribution to the History of Ideas* (University of Chicago Press).

de Vries, Jan. 1961. *Keltische Religion* (Stuttgart, W. Kohlhammer).

Duval, Paul-Marie and Pinault, Georges. 1986. *Recueil des inscriptions gauloises, III, Les Calendriers* (Paris, Éditions du Centre National de la Recherche Scientifique).

Emanuel, H. D. (ed.). 1967. *The Latin Texts of the Welsh Laws* (Cardiff, University of Wales Press).

Evans, D. E. 1967. *Gaulish Personal Names* (Oxford University Press).

Fleuriot, Léon. 1964. *Dictionnaire des gloses en vieux breton* (Paris, C. Klinck-sieck).

Ford, Patrick K. 1983. 'On the Significance of some Arthurian Names in Welsh', *Bulletin of the Board of Celtic Studies*, 30, 268–73.

Goetinck, G. W. 1976. *Historia Peredur vab Efrawc* (Cardiff, University of Wales Press).

Greene, D. A. 1972. 'The War Chariot as Described in Irish Literature' in *The Iron Age in the Irish Sea Province*, ed. Charles Thomas (London, Council for British Archaeology), 59–73.

Hamp, Eric P. 1976. '*Barnu Brawd*', *Celtica*, 11, 68–75.

Hamp, Eric P. 1982. 'Two uncertain IE. roots', *Folia Linguistica Historica*, 3, 127–30.

Hamp, Eric P. 1988. 'Welsh *ebol*', *Cambridge Medieval Celtic Studies*, 15, 87.

Hamp, Eric P. 1990. 'The Indo-European Horse' in *When Worlds Collide: The Indo-Europeans and the Pre-Indo-Europeans*, ed. T. L. Markey and John A. C. Greppin (Ann Arbor, Michigan University Press), 211–26.

Hänsel, Bernhard and Zimmer, Stefan (eds.). 1994. *Die Indogermanen und das Pferd* (Budapest, Archaeolingua).

Howells, Donald. 1973–4. 'The Four Exclusive Possessions of a Man', *Studia Celtica*, 8–9, 48–67.

Hughes, A. J. 1994. 'Les Mots qui désignent le cheval dans les langues gaéliques au point de vue de la géographie linguistique', *La Bretagne Linguistique*, 8, 233–59.

Huws, Daniel. 1996. 'Yr Hen Risiart Langfford' in *Beirdd a Thywysogion*, ed. B. F. Roberts and M. E. Owen (Aberystwyth and Cardiff, National Library of Wales and University of Wales Press), 302–25.

Jackson, K. H. 1948. 'On some Romano-British Place-Names', *Journal of Roman Studies*, 38, 54–8.

Jackson, K. H. 1953. *Language and History in Early Britain* (Edinburgh University Press).

Jenkins, Dafydd. 1963. *Llyfr Colan* (Cardiff, University of Wales Press).

Johnston, Dafydd (ed.). 1993. *Iolo Goch: Poems* (Llandysul, Gomer Press).

Kelly, Patricia. 1982. 'Dialekte im Altirischen?' in *Sprachwissenschaft in Innsbruck*, ed. W. Meid *et al.* (Innsbrucker Beiträge zur Kulturwissenschaft), 85–9.

Kelly, Patricia. 1983. 'Das Wortfeld PFERD im Irischen: eine semantische und etymologische Untersuchung' (University of Innsbruck D.Phil. thesis).

Kratz, Henry. 1988. 'Welsh *gellyg, ebol, buddelw*: A Reply', *Cambridge Medieval Celtic Studies*, 15, 85–6.

Lambert, Pierre-Yves. 1994. *La Langue Gauloise* (Paris, Éditions Errance).

Le Roux, Françoise. 1956. '*Voreidos, Rêda, Eporedia*. Remarques sur un nom du cheval en Celtique', *Ogam*, 8, 367–84.

Loth, Joseph. 1925. 'Les noms du cheval chez les Celtes', *Académie des Inscriptions et Belles-Lettres. Mémoires*, 43, 113–48.

Mac Cana, Proinsias. 1991. 'Irish *maccóem*, Welsh *makwyf*', *Ériu*, 42, 27–36.

Mallory, J. P. (ed.). 1992. *Aspects of the Táin* (Belfast, December Publications).

Marstrander, Carl. 1911. 'The Deaths of Lugaid and Derbforgaill', *Ériu*, 5, 207–18.

Meid, W. 1980. *Gallisch oder Lateinisch?* (Innsbrucker Beiträge zur Sprachwissenschaft).

Meid, Wolfgang. 1994a. *Celtiberian Inscriptions* (Budapest, Archaeolingua).

Meid, Wolfgang. 1994b. 'Die Terminologie von Pferd und Wagen im Indogermanischen' in *Die Indogermanen und das Pferd*, ed. Bernhard Hänsel and Stefan Zimmer (Budapest, Archaeolingua), 53–65.

Meyer, Kuno (ed.). 1912. *Sanas Cormaic, Anecdota from Irish Manuscripts*, ed. O. J. Bergin *et al.*, iv (Halle, Niemeyer).

O'Donovan, John. 1868. *Cormac's Glossary*, ed. Whitley Stokes (Calcutta, Irish Archaeological and Celtic Society).

O'Rahilly, T. F. 1936. 'The Goidels and their Predecessors', *Proceedings of the British Academy*, 21, 323–72.

Orel, Vladimir E. 1987. 'Thracian and Celtic', *Bulletin of the Board of Celtic Studies*, 34, 1–9.

Owen, Aneurin (ed.). 1841. *Ancient Laws and Institutes of Wales* (London, Record Commission).

Pedersen, Holger. 1909. *Vergleichende Grammatik der keltischen Sprachen*, I (Göttingen, Vandenhoeck and Ruprecht).

Pokorny, Julius. 1959. *Indogermanisches etymologisches Wörterbuch* (Berne, Francke).

Polomé, Edgar. 1983. 'Celto-Germanic Isoglosses (Revisited)', *Journal of Indo-European Studies*, 11, 281–98.

Raftery, Barry. 1991. 'Horse and Cart in Iron Age Ireland', *Journal of Indo-European Studies*, 19, 49–71.

Rowland, Jenny. 1995. 'Warfare and Horses in the *Gododdin* and the Problem of Catraeth', *Cambrian Medieval Celtic Studies*, 30, 13–40.

Russell, Paul. 1995. 'Brittonic words in Irish Glossaries' in *Hispano-Gallo-Brittonica*, ed. Joseph F. Eska *et al.* (Cardiff, University of Wales Press), 166–82.

Schmidt, K.-H. 1957. 'Die Komposition in gallischen Personennamen', *Zeitschrift für celtische Philologie*, 26, 33–301.

Schmidt, K.-H. 1979. 'Indogermanische Verwandtschaftsnamen im Keltischen', *Études Celtiques*, 16, 117–22.

Stokes, Whitley. 1895. 'The Prose Tales in the Rennes Dindsenchas', *Revue Celtique*, 16, 31–83, 135–67, 269–312.

Thomas, Alan. 1973. *The Linguistic Geography of Wales* (Cardiff, University of Wales Press).

Thurneysen, Rudolf. 1946. *A Grammar of Old Irish*, tr. D. A. Binchy and O. Bergin (Dublin Institute for Advanced Studies).

Tierney, J. J. 1960. 'The Celtic Ethnography of Posidonius', *Proceedings of the Royal Irish Academy*, 60, 189–275.

Vendryes, J. 1902. *De Hibernicis Vocabulis quae a Latina Lingua Originem Duxerunt* (Paris, C. Klincksieck).

Watkin, Morgan. 1958. *Ystorya Bown de Hamtwn* (Cardiff, University of Wales Press).

Wiliam, A. R. 1960. *Llyfr Iorwerth* (Cardiff, University of Wales Press).

Williams, Ifor. 1921. '*Medd, medr, armes* etc.', *Bulletin of the Board of Celtic Studies*, 1, 23–36.

Williams, Ifor (ed.). 1935. *Canu Llywarch Hen* (Cardiff, University of Wales Press).

Williams, Ifor (ed.). 1961. *Canu Aneirin*, 2nd edn. (Cardiff, University of Wales Press).

Williams, Ifor (ed.). 1975. *The Poems of Taliesin*, English version by J. E. Caerwyn Williams (Dublin Institute for Advanced Studies).

Zimmer, Stefan. 1987. 'Three Welsh Etymologies: *gellyg* "pears", *ebol* "colt", *buddelw* "cowpost"', *Cambridge Medieval Celtic Studies*, 14, 63–4.

4

The Horse in the Welsh Law Texts

Dafydd Jenkins

Students of medieval law in other lands may find it strange that the Welsh lawbooks have so much to say about horses. In the law texts from pre-Norman England there are perhaps a dozen references to horses, in such contexts as theft and heriot; they reveal little of general interest. As for Germany, Jacob Grimm could find nothing comparable to the detail of the Welsh Laws of Court except in a fifteenth-century document from Essen (Grimm 1899, i. 350). Even the early law of Ireland has few references to horses, and it may be significant that one of those is concerned with the import of horses from Britain (Kelly 1988, 7 and other references from Index 4). The Welsh lawbooks, however, have something to say about the horse in a great variety of contexts, but their references to horses can be useful only if we properly understand what the lawbooks are. For medieval Wales (and for modern scholars writing in Welsh), the indigenous law of Wales was *Cyfraith Hywel* , 'The Law of Hywel', and as no-one doubts that the Hywel in question was Hywel 'the Good', who died as ruler of a very large part of Wales in 949 or 950, Welsh law texts have too often been cited as evidence for conditions in tenth-century Wales, though our earliest manuscripts are of the thirteenth century.

These manuscripts show clear signs of development and change: in relation to horses, for instance, the occurrence of names borrowed from French for special kinds of horse means that the rules relating to them can hardly be earlier than the Norman invasions. This is not an accident: other languages show the same kind of French influence, because the Normans were largely responsible for developments in the culture of the horse in western Europe. The late Professor R. H. C. Davis made the point in a paper given at the Economic History Conference in Budapest in 1982 (Davis 1983), and developed it in greater detail in *The Medieval Warhorse* (1989).

Though nearly four centuries separate King Hywel from the oldest surviving law manuscripts, it is very likely indeed that a small core of material from Hywel's day lies hidden in them; it is more important that a fairly substantial core of material which is common to different groups of manuscripts is generally accepted as having been put together in the twelfth, or perhaps in the eleventh, century. Most of the manuscripts have a substantial core which seems to be aiming at a comprehensive presentation of the law. Three of these basic cores have been recognized since 1841 (Owen 1841, i. viii); at that time they were called 'Codes' and attributed to three regions of Wales; the less misleading name 'Redaction' is now usual. Of the three Redactions, the Cyfnerth Redaction (Owen's 'Gwentian Code') and the Blegywryd Redaction (Owen's 'Dimetian Code') are closely related through a Latin translation, and can be regarded as presenting a southern view of Welsh law, so that it is convenient to speak of features common to Cyfnerth, Latin, and Blegywryd manuscripts as 'southern', in contrast to the Iorwerth Redaction (Owen's 'Venedotian Code'), which took shape in Gwynedd in the first half of the thirteenth century and is the most sophisticated of the Redactions, though it has the earliest surviving manuscripts.[1]

If most of our manuscripts have a comprehensive core, most of them also have additional material, some pushed into the interstices of the main text, but more perhaps as a tail: in some fifteenth-century manuscripts the tail is longer than the body. Apart from additional material, the core of each Redaction is made up of *tractates* on specific subjects; these vary greatly in size, from the tractate of Laws of the Court (which falls into thirty or forty sub-tractates) to the very neat tractate on Injury to Animals, of some 200 words. The tail attached to a Redaction may take in tractates from another Redaction, but the borrowing of fragments is more noticeable, and unrelated sentences and short paragraphs are to be found also in the material inserted in gaps in the core.[2]

References to horses, some of them unimportant enough, are scattered throughout the texts, in tractates and fragments; the one exceptional tractate is that of the Law of Women, which has a solitary reference in the Iorwerth Redaction alone – and even that reference is oblique: 'The three unclaimable things of a man: his horse and arms; and what comes to him from his land, and what comes to him as wynebwerth from his wife; he is not bound to share any of those with his wife' (*HDd* 61). Horses, whether for war or for agriculture, were for males.

Of the tractates, two stand out as telling us most about the horse. The tractate on the Value of Wild and Tame gives direct information about different kinds of horse; the compound tractate on the Court gives information, through the references to horses, about the life-style of the local ruler and his entourage, and is especially revealing in the signs of development of the ruler's power which the differences between the Redactions give. In essence, the Laws of Court apply to any king, no matter how small his kingdom – and there had been kings who ruled over areas comparable with the smaller of the modern counties; but it is clear enough that the quite elaborate organization of the court of the Iorwerth Redaction could be sustained only in a realm with substantial resources.

One point in the development of the Court tractate bears on the significance of the horse. In all Redactions, the tractate lists twenty-four officers of the court, and then deals with the officers in sub-tractates. The order of the names in the list varies from text to text, and does not always correspond to the order of the sub-tractates. These irregularities are much reduced if we pick out twelve officers as being the original complement; if we make one further assumption, the remaining irregularities are small enough to be explained as scribal errors. This further assumption is that the Groom of the Rein, rather than the Chief Groom, should have a place among the twelve – for the original court officers were attendant on the king, to serve him personally in his play by day and his merry-making by night as well as in his function as father of his people: the Groom of the Rein served the king, and (as we shall see) at least one privileged courtier, leaving the rest of the followers (if any) to fend for themselves. As the king's power grew, his entourage grew and more servants were needed, not so much to serve the king as to serve his servants: thus the Chief Groom and the other grooms were needed for the care of the horses of the thirty-six on horseback who followed the king around his realm.

Like the Court tractate, the Wild and Tame tractate can be divided into sub-tractates, each dealing with a class of animal; and this tractate has prestige because aspirants to recognition as learned in the law and qualified for judicial office must know the Three Columns of Law (concerned with homicide, theft, and arson) and the Value of Wild and Tame: the Iorwerth Redaction was deliberately edited to bring this material together in *Llyfr Prawf Ynaid*, the Justices' (or perhaps Jurists')

Test Book. There is room for a detailed study of the form taken by the Wild and Tame tractate in the several Redactions, but for our purpose it is necessary only to say that it sets out values for some wild animals (particularly deer) and goes into detail about domestic animals. For horses and neat cattle in particular it details stages in the growth of the value as the animal grows.

These values are not to be taken as prices at which the animals must be bought and sold. We may indeed suspect that when anyone had a right of pre-emption he bought at these standard prices, but the main significance of the figures was as measures of the value of the animals for various purposes of the law. Compensation for harm would normally be based on the standard value, and if an animal was given in pledge it would count as having its standard value rather than any higher market value. The punishment for theft varied with the value of the stolen property, and the right to an advocate in litigation over chattels depended on their value (*HDd* 97).

For the value of horses, the Redactions vary a good deal, and there is no point in examining the variations in detail: we need only notice that the southern texts have variants on one scheme where the Iorwerth Redaction has a much simpler scheme, which probably reflects practice more closely than the southern scheme.[3] All the schemes tacitly assume a foaling in May and an initial value of four or six pence; for the Iorwerth Redaction this value applies to the pregnancy of the dam before foaling. The basis of increase varies, but the growing horse reaches a value of sixty pence on the second Mayday after its foaling. The southern scheme goes on to add twelve pence each season during the third year, with twenty pence at the end of the year 'when caught' and a further fourpence when it is bridled, making its final value six score pence, without reference to its training (Richards 1954, 89). The Iorwerth Redaction seems more practical: at the beginning of its third year, with a value of sixty pence, the colt 'should be bridle-tame, and then it is proper to give it the training which is right for it, whether it be destrier or palfrey or working horse'; the word translated 'training' is *diwyll*, from *di-wyllt*, 'un-wild', and we are told that a wild horse (*march gwyllt*) is worth sixty pence (*HDd* 171–2).

The horse's value then depends on the character given by its training, though little is said about what the training involved and we must rely on non-legal sources for the difference between the resulting products. We shall return to these specially trained horses after looking at the workaday horse, though from the husbandman's viewpoint horses were perhaps more important as products than as productive workers. Oxen were used for the most important work in agriculture, ploughing: the Joint Ploughing tractate gives no right to put horses or mares (or, for that matter, cows) into a plough-team except by special agreement. But harrowing was work for horses, as the Luttrell Psalter shows us it was in England, though the harrowing horse (*march llyfnu*), like the 'cleanser' (*carthwr*) used in preparing the ground for ploughing, did not 'belong to joint ploughing' (*HDd* 200). The 'working horse which draws a car and a harrow' is given a price in the Iorwerth Redaction (*HDd* 172): the car thus was a sledge (*car llusg*), but in the rough country of medieval Wales even the sledge had limited use, and loads were more often carried on the horse's back. In the law of theft we are told that 'a horse can carry a steer as its burden' (*HDd* 157); and the same horse might carry a rider or a load: the fueller (*cynutai*) was allowed to ride the fuel horse 'when he goes to gather fuel' (*HDd* 37).

The Welsh word *pynfarch*, 'pack-horse', does not occur in the Wild and Tame tractate, but has a striking semantic development. It is used literally in the provision that the king's villeins must provide pack-horses for his hostings (*HDd* 124): each villein townland must also provide a man with an axe and a horse to make the king's camp (*HDd* 41). The same word is also used figuratively: the eight pack-horses of a king are sources of casual income, comparable with the incidents of tenure in English land law (*HDd* 40). In modern Wales, which has neither pack-horses nor kings, the word lives for mill-leet.

Another tractate shows that, whether as working animals or as being reared for service in a wider world, there will have been horses grazing in the open in arable country, for the tractate on Corn Damage (*Llwgr Yd*, or in English law terms Cattle Trespass) envisages horses as trespassing, and one point in the rules is puzzling. We are concerned with compensation for damage done to a growing crop, and all texts agree in providing for compensation in the early stages at a flat rate of so much for each trespassing animal of a particular kind. In the Iorwerth Redaction the rate for a horse (from fifteen days old) is a penny, but in the Cyfnerth Redaction a distinction is drawn:

> For every horse which has a fetter or hobble on it, a penny by day and twopence by night; if it is unrestricted, a halfpenny by day and a penny by night. If the taker unhobbles it when he takes it on the corn, let him pay three kine camlwrw to the King; let him however put both loops on the same foot and he will lose nothing. (*HDd* 202)

We can understand the impounder's unhobbling the horse, to make it easier to lead to pound; but why is he penalized for reducing the compensation which he can claim? Indeed, why is the compensation greater for a hobbled horse? Perhaps we are to understand a legal presumption that a hobbled horse was helped on to the crop by its owner.

More illuminating than the schematism of the value tables are the specifications of the standard animal: the Welsh law of contract gave the parties freedom to set their own conditions, but in the absence of special agreement, an animal sold would be required to have certain specific characteristics, known in Welsh by the technical term *teithi*. For a cat, for instance, these properties were 'to see and hear and kill mice, and that her claws are not broken, and to rear kittens' (*HDd* 180); according to the Blegywryd Redaction she must also be 'free from caterwauling every moon' (Richards 1954, 92), and the Cyfnerth Redaction adds that she must be 'without marks of fire' (Wade-Evans 1909, 227).

For the various classes of horse the information about *teithi* is disappointing. We have seen that the working horse (*gweinyddfarch*) is explained as drawing a sledge or a harrow; for the snobbishly-named dung horse (*march tom*) or dung mare (*caseg dom*), the properties are 'to carry a load and to draw a car uphill and downhill, without irregularity' (*HDd* 172, from the Cyfnerth Redaction). These common animals have Welsh names, but the more highly regarded horses of courtly life have names borrowed from other languages, and we are not told much about their properties. 'A palfrey's value is six score pence', and we can be quite sure that the word is the French *palefroi,* probably a direct borrowing rather than one through English, where it is evidenced from *c.*1175 (*OED s.v. palfrey*) (see above, p. 51). The palfrey was an ambler: that is, it moved both legs on the same side together, and is perhaps familiar to us in literature as ridden by medieval ladies, though it had also a military function.

Six score pence is also the value of the rouncy (*rhwnsi* in the modern Welsh form implied by the manuscripts' words). The Iorwerth Redaction's provision for training the bridle-tame colt does not refer to the rouncy, and it does not seem to be defined elsewhere in the lawbooks. The name comes from the French, probably directly: the earliest English citation is *c.*1315 (*OED s.v. rouncy*); the rouncy ridden by the ordinary trooper must have been 'strong enough to bear the weight of an armoured rider, not quite so heavy as the completely iron-clad knight, and of its own horse-armour' (Morris 1901, 82–3). According to the

Iorwerth Redaction 'the value of a rouncy or sumpter horse is six score pence' (*HDd* 172); we can argue about whether 'sumpter-horse' (Welsh *swmerfarch*) is an alternative name for the rouncy or the name of a different kind. Outside Wales the *summarius* was certainly inferior to the *runcinus*: the sources from 1250 to 1350 cited by Davis show the *runcinus* costing £5–£10 or slightly more, and the *summarius* costing between 7*s.* and 8*s.* (Davis 1989, 67). The Latin Redactions, followed by the Blegywryd Redaction, give the sumpter-horse the lower value of 80*d.* (Emanuel 1967, 154; Williams and Powell 1942, 91).[4] In the Iorwerth Redaction the sumpter-horse has perhaps been assimilated to the rouncy; if so, it may be because the rouncy/sumpter-horse was not only the horse of the less heavily armed trooper, but also that of the esquire. For on the way to battle, while the knight was riding at his ease, unencumbered by armour, on an ambling palfrey, the esquire was leading the knight's destrier; the esquire could be riding a rouncy. It seems reasonable to suppose that the destrier would carry the knight's armour,[5] but perhaps a sumpter-horse may have been used for this. At the rate given by either Redaction, the sumpter-horse is a cut above the working *gweinyddfarch*, which was no doubt the type of horse supplied by villeins to serve as pack-horse.

The standard *teithi* and guarantees implied by law seem to be the same for all horses. According to the Cyfnerth Redaction, 'Whosoever shall sell a horse, let him be answerable for the horse grazing and drinking water, and that it be not restive' (Wade-Evans 1909, 216). Since the word 'restive' seems to be generally misused as a variant of 'restless', it should be emphasized that its meaning here is nearer to 'resistant'; Richards (1954, 90) conveys the right idea with 'not to jib'. For the Iorwerth Redaction the guarantee against restiveness lasted until the horse was 'ridden in a crowd of persons and horses through their midst' (*HDd* 172; some manuscripts add 'three times', Jenkins 1963, 83). The consequences of breach of this guarantee were different according to the different Redactions: the Cyfnerth Redaction allowed the seller to 'choose between taking the horse back or returning a third of the worth to the other' (Wade-Evans 1909, 216); it is rather surprising that the choice is given to the seller rather than the buyer, and more surprising that the Blegywryd and Iorwerth Redactions gave no option: 'let a third of its value be returned, leaving the transfer as before, since it is not proper to undo the transfer' (*HDd* 172).

No special qualities are named by the lawbooks for the palfrey, rouncy, and sumpter-horse, and the most valuable horse of all is not required to have particular qualities but to be managed in a particular way. The destrier (Welsh *amws*) is not only the most valuable of Welsh medieval horses, but also the most interesting – from all points of view, linguistic, legal, social and economic. Like *palffrai* and *rhwnsi, amws* is a borrowed word, but one borrowed much earlier, and from the Latin. From [*equus*] *admissus* came by normal development the Welsh *emys*, which occurs (though rarely) as a singular noun; since this form looks like a Welsh plural, a more regular-looking singular, *amws*, was formed from it. The Latin word meant 'stallion', and so at first did *amws*: in a poem of the tenth or eleventh century falsely attributed to the sixth-century Taliesin, *Bum amws ar re* means 'I have been a stallion on a herd' (Evans 1910, 22). This background explains the fact that in the printed translations of the lawbooks *amws* has usually become 'stallion', though it is clear enough that the name is applied to a special kind of stallion; the lawbooks' word for 'stallion' is the borrowed *ystalwyn* or *stalwyn,* which is still the ordinary word in some dialects.

The special meaning of *amws* is clearly revealed by the Blegywryd Redaction, which has *amws* where the closely related Latin Redaction D has *dextrarius*; and this evidence is confirmed by at least two translations from medieval French, the version of the romances concerning Charlemagne (Williams 1930, 56, 63, 139), and the version of *Le Geste de Boun de Hamtone* (Watkin 1958, 75–6).

The destrier was the war-horse which 'had to be capable of carrying the weight of a knight in armour, and had to be trained for battle' and was called *destrier* 'probably because when off duty he was not ridden but led by a groom off his right hand' (Davis 1983, 4). Though there is no clear reference in any Welsh text to the way the destrier was led, the translation of the *Chanson de Roland* shows knights transferring from palfreys to destriers (*adaw y palffreiot, a chymryt eu hemys*, Williams 1930, 139) in order to attack the enemy.

To qualify as a destrier the Welsh horse had to be specially nourished; it was not allowed to graze freely in the open. The original rule, recorded in the Cyfnerth and Blegywryd Redactions, was that a destrier grazing in the open lost its status (*HDd* 173), but the Iorwerth Redaction was more generous, allowing the destrier to graze in the open without loss of status from mid-April to mid-May and during the whole of October (*HDd* 172). On the positive side, the acquisition of destrier status depended on stall feeding, according to the Cyfnerth and Blegywryd Redactions for six weeks; here again the Iorwerth Redaction was more generous, giving the status after three nights and three days over a stall (*HDd* 173, 172).

71

The lawbooks seem to contemplate that when the horse is fully grown it may be assigned to destrier training and will then be taken into the stable for special feeding; if (as some of the texts imply) it reached its full standard value in May, it could qualify as a destrier after three days and nights and then go out to graze until the middle of the month.[6]

The expressions used indicate two ways of looking at the management of the destrier. The *ym mhennill* of some manuscripts refers to the confinement in a stall; the forms of the verb *pesgi*, 'to fatten', found in other manuscripts, emphasize the intensive feeding which was the purpose of the confinement. Stall feeding meant oats, to judge by the references from other countries (Davis 1989, 44), as well as by other passages in the lawbooks. Oats in sheaf were an important part of the renders in kind owed to the king: it seems to be significant that the summer render owed by villein townlands is specifically said to be 'without horse-fodder' (*HDd* 129). If we could rely on the highly schematic account given in the Iorwerth Redaction, we should expect the *firma unius noctis* of the commote to yield 1,088 sheaves of single-bound oats (*HDd* 128 taken with 121);[7] these were presumably to be shared among the thirty-six mounted members of the king's entourage. The thirty-six were the twenty-four officers of the court (each of whom was provided with a horse by the king or queen) and twelve guests (*HDd* 6); of the twenty-four, four, the captain of the household (*penteulu*), steward, chief groom, and court justice, were entitled to double rations for their horses. Perhaps this was because they were the only officers who rode on destriers; and it was perhaps because the *edling* (the heir apparent) might have more than one horse (a palfrey as well as a destrier?) that his horse-fodder was to be 'unstinted'. The court justice was very close to the king, for his horse was to share the stall of the king's own horse, and he was no doubt served by the groom of the rein before the chief groom was added to the household. According to the sophisticated Iorwerth Redaction, he was 'entitled to have the chief groom equip his horse from the first nail to the last, and caparison it and bring it caparisoned to him when he is to ride' (*HDd* 16), but the Cyfnerth Redaction records an earlier practice: 'A groom of the rein brings his horse to him in proper order when he shall will it' (Wade-Evans 1909, 160).

Of special training of the destrier for battle the lawbooks tell us nothing; perhaps it sufficed that the destrier should be a stallion. 'The medieval warhorse was a stallion . . . Geldings were considered to be lacking in courage' (Davis 1983, 4), but a writer in 1584 'quoted Albertus

Illustration of stallion from Peniarth MS 28 (National Library of Wales).

Magnus to the effect that castration made horses timid and therefore unsuited for war, but added that the Turks, Muscovites and Tartars did use geldings and continued to defeat the Christians' (Davis 1989, 136). Latin Redaction A indeed seems to imply that a Welsh destrier might be a gelding: 'The value of a gelding, if it be not a destrier: eighty pence' (Fletcher 1986, 78); but it must be noted that in the wording translated, *si non dextrarius sit* (Emanuel 1967, 155), *si non* is the editor's very reasonable emendation of the manuscript *si non nisi*. Nothing to correspond to this sentence has been found in any other Latin or Welsh text; and the only other reference to a gelding seems to be that in some late manuscripts, which give the gelding a value of 120*d*.[8]

Our only positive indication that the Welsh destrier was a stallion is indirect, in one of the illustrations to the thirteenth-century Latin manuscript NLW Peniarth 28 (Huws 1988, no. 20). According to Professor Davis (1983, 4), medieval artists always made it clear that their war-horses were stallions 'as can be seen in the Bayeux Tapestry'; the illustrated manuscripts of the *Sachsenspiegel*, in which the horses' legs always seem to be decorously arranged, do not bear this out (Schmidt-Wiegand 1993; Koschorrek 1976, 55; Schott 1984, 49), but there is no doubt of the virility of the Peniarth horse, which also has its tail undocked: this means more than the first sight suggests to modern eyes. There are special provisions for the horse (of any kind) whose tail hair

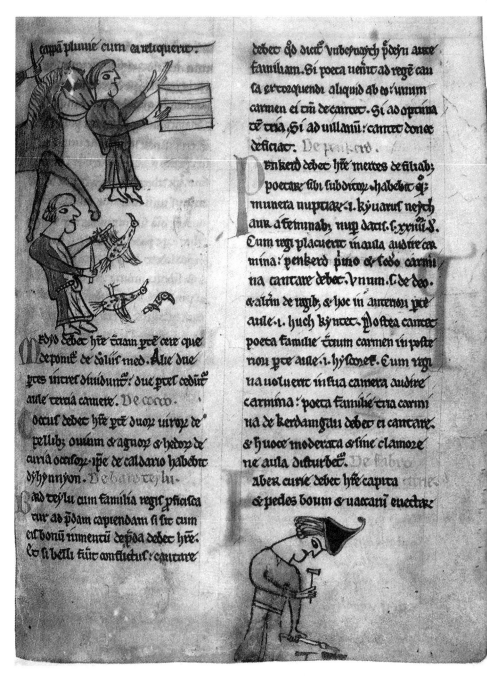

The gwastrod (groom) holding a saddle from Peniarth MS 28
(National Library of Wales).

has been cut: though the Cyfnerth Redaction gives only compensation of 24*d.*, the Iorwerth Redaction requires the culprit to 'put the horse in a place where it will not be seen, and . . . give the owner another horse to do what it would do, until the tail hair of his own horse is as it formerly was at its best' (*HDd* 173).

There is some confusion over the rather more important question of damage to the flesh of a horse's tail. The Iorwerth Redaction has the general rule 'Every harm to a horse is a third of its value, as for its ear and the flesh of its tail', but if a sumpter-horse has the flesh of its tail cut, it loses its whole value (*HDd* 172, 173); the rule of the Cyfnerth Redaction is surprising:

> A destrier's tail hair is worth twenty-four pence if it is cut outside the flesh; if however any of the flesh is cut, then the whole value of the destrier is paid and the destrier is the valid property of him who damaged it. (*HDd* 173)

The surprise in this provision is that the offender gets the victim at its value – especially since the texts give the destrier a fixed value of £1: only the Latin Redaction A provides that for a destrier stolen or killed 'compensation is to be made according to the oath of him whose it was' (Fletcher 1986, 77). The rule of the other Redactions looks like an invitation to mutilate the destrier as a way of acquiring him against the owner's will; if with docked tail he could no longer appear in good company, he would still be a desirable addition to any stud. So we would suppose; but for medieval tradition a stallion became impotent if even its mane was cut (Payne 1990, 57); and this tradition adds an economic significance to the mutilation of horses, which must in any case be seen as insult. A horse's tail-flesh does not get cut by accident: when Archbishop Thomas Becket, after his return from exile, had the tail of a sumpter-beast carrying provisions to him cut off, he knew it for a positive expression of hatred (Barlow 1986, 232). The thirteenth-century English legal writer Bracton wrote of the man convicted of rape, 'By the law of the Romans, the Franks and the English, even his horse shall to his ignominy be put to shame upon its scrotum and its tail, which shall be cut off as close as possible to the buttocks' – though the editor did not identify the source (fo. 147v; Thorne 1968, 418).

In comparison with the rules for damage to the tail, those for compensation for other kinds of damage are mundane and practical. 'The value of a horse's foot is its value in full; one third of its value for its eye, and one third for the other eye', according to the Iorwerth Redaction, but according to the Blegywryd Redaction, 'If it is wholly blinded, its whole value is paid.' 'Whosoever borrows a horse from another, and rubs the hair from his back, let him pay fourpence. If the skin is broken as far as the flesh, eightpence. If the flesh is cut to the bone, he pays sixteen pence.' To take a horse without the owner's leave was the offence of surreption (Welsh *anghyfarch*), attracting the lesser fine (*camlwrw*) of three kine payable to the ruler, with compensation to the owner: 'fourpence for mounting and fourpence for every shareland he rides, and nothing is due for dismounting, since that is proper' (*HDd* 172–4).

One brief reference to the destrier seems to have both social and economic importance. This is the triad:

> Three things a villein is not entitled to sell without his lord's leave: a destrier and honey and pigs; and if he sells them, let him be liable to dirwy [the larger fine, of twelve kine or £3], and the transfer rescinded; and if his lord does not buy them, let him sell whither he will. (*HDd* 40)

An English historian who saw this triad asked 'What is a villein doing with a destrier?' – a natural reaction, for it is clear enough that to own a destrier would not be appropriate to a villein's social status: hunting dogs and hunting birds owned by villeins would have the respective values of dunghill curs and hens (*HDd* 181,183). The answer to the historian's question must surely be in economic terms: the villein is managing the destrier for his patron-lord. When we remember the villeins' obligation to provide pack-horses for the king's hostings, we may realize that villeins were better placed than their lords to grow the fodder needed for the destrier: the contrast between the contributions of the gentry and the villeins to the support of the ruler makes it clear that villein holdings were on the lower-lying land best suited to crop husbandry (cf. Jenkins 1963, 162). But if it was technologically advantageous to concentrate the management of destriers on villein land, it seems more than probable that the villeins' lords would be economically involved in the enterprise. That is perhaps implied by their right of pre-emption, and it can be suggested that they provided the basic studs in which the horses were bred. Here three other triads may be relevant, those of the three 'nets' of king, goodman, and villein: for any strange animal found in one of these nets, the owner must pay the netsman fourpence, and for king and goodman the nets are a stud of horses, a herd of cows, and a herd of pigs. But for the villein, 'his winter-house from Mayday to August' replaces the stud of horses; and since the word for 'stud' is the relatively archaic *allwest*, these triads probably represent an early stage of society, in which it was unthinkable that a villein should have a stud of horses (*HDd* 40).

The stage of society represented by the triads must also be one in which the breeding of horses had not gained the economic significance for Wales which it certainly had by the late twelfth century. In the practical rules about the stud, the Welsh word is *gre*: we are told that a legal stud consisted of fifty mares, and that a stud mare was worth 120*d.*; as her tail and eye were each worth only sixpence, she was evidently valued only as bearing foals (*HDd* 173). If it is true that horse-breeding was increasing in importance in twelfth- and thirteenth-century Wales, we should not expect consistency in the lawbooks' references, and several passages need closer examination than they have yet had; we must rest content with a few citations. In the Iorwerth Redaction 'The value of a stallion's two testes is as much as the value of two mares, with himself as a third; that is to say, nine score pence' (*HDd* 172); this means that the stallion himself has only the value of a working horse, and is consistent with the Cyfnerth Redaction's naming of the stallion as one of the 'three animals whose properties are more than their legal value . . . for the breed is lost if they are lost' (*HDd* 178). The seriousness of loss of the breed is emphasized by Davis: it put one 'back in the position of having once again to start building up a stud from the beginning' as 'happened over and over again, not only in the Middle Ages but also in later centuries' (Davis 1989, 45).

If our law texts hint at the economic importance of horses, and perhaps of the destrier in particular, in medieval Wales, we have to venture outside them for more direct evidence, which also names the source of the excellence of the Welsh product. Giraldus Cambrensis refers to the excellent stud-farms of Powys, whose stock traced 'its descent from the Spanish horses which Robert de Belesme, Earl of Shrewsbury, had gone to some pains to have imported long ago. The horses which are sent out from Powys are greatly prized: they are extremely handsome and nature reproduces in them the same majestic proportions and incomparable speed' (Thorpe 1978, 201). It was no doubt these horses which Fulk fitz Warin III had in mind in 1210, when he offered £100 and 'j dextrarium pulchrum et talem quod non sit eo melior in Wallia' for expediting his claim to a manor (Slade 1951, 160). This Fulk was the eponym of the Anglo-Norman romance *Fouke le Fitz*

Waryn, which reads like a cross between *Robin Hood* and the *Arabian Nights*, but is accepted as having a substantial basis in the politics of the Welsh marches; the romance tells how *Morys le fitz Roger de Powys* gave King John 'un destrer gras e beal' on his visit to the marches after his coronation (Hathaway *et al.* 1975, 23), and these are not the only indications of high regard for Welsh destriers (see Davis 1989, 81). An idea of the market value of destriers is given by the 1210 Pipe Roll's reference to one valued at thirty marks (Slade 1951, 201): that figure, equal to £20, reminds us of the debtor in the Iorwerth Redaction, who owed twelve pence and had to his name nothing except a horse worth £10 (*HDd* 69). Market prices for the various horses used for war could rise very much higher than the standard values (Davis 1989, 67).

The reputation of the horses of eastern Wales continued for centuries, into a period when 'the English played little part in the development of the warhorse' (Davis 1983, 20). When George Rainsford wrote his account of Britain, *Ritratto d'Ingilterra*, in 1556, he said that *Wallia* (one of the four regions of *Ingilterra*) produced good horses for war (*buoni cavalli per la guerra*), and that while England had good horses, the best for war were in the parts on the Scottish border and the eastern part of Wales: 'Li megliore per la guerra sono nella parte di Northlandia appresso la Scotia, et nella parte orientali di Wallia' (Rainsford 1979, 72–3).[9]

Notes

[1] Cyfnerth, Blegywryd, and Iorwerth are the names of jurists named in some manuscripts of their respective Redactions: it needs to be strongly emphasized that the Redaction labels do not imply authorship. Even Iorwerth ap Madog probably had a tenuous enough connection with the Iorwerth Redaction. For more detail about the relation of the manuscripts and Redactions, see Jenkins 1987; Charles-Edwards 1989.

[2] For an idea of the wide range of borrowing in a manuscript of the Blegywryd Redaction, see the Conspectus to Richards 1990 (147–62).

[3] The southern manuscripts may well have copied obsolete material in this tractate as they certainly did in the Court tractate, where the Iorwerth Redaction has an updated version reflecting the changed conditions of the thirteenth century, The scribe Gwilym Wasta, writing in the Tywi Valley at the beginning of the fourteenth century, cut out most of the Court tractate because the law was no longer operative (Owen and Jenkins 1980).

[4] The translation 'pack-horse' (Richards 1954, 89) is misleading; elsewhere

Richards has 'pack-horses' as translation for *pynfeirch*. In the Latin Redactions *equus summarius* occurs for both *pynfarch* and *swmerfarch*.

[5] The Heidelberg manuscript of the *Sachsenspiegel* shows a knight riding to a tournament and leading a horse (larger than his own mount) which carries his armour (Koschorreck 1976, 55).

[6] Two non-legal sources hint at the importance of April for the horse. In the translation of the romance of Otinel, Charlemagne's council, meeting on Holy Innocents' Day, decides to go to war against Garsi, king of Spain, after the end of April when there would be fresh pasture for the horses (*wedy darfei vis Ebrill, a chael onadunt llyseuoed neuwyd a gwellt ir y eu meirch*, Williams 1930, 44). In an original Welsh poem by the lawyer-poet Einion ap Gwalchmai the line *Aduwyn march pennhill Ebrill ebrwyt* (Williams *et al.* 1994, 29.29) can perhaps be translated 'Pleasant for the stabled horse the swift April'.

[7] It is not certain what is meant by 'single-bound' (Welsh *unrhwym*); perhaps 'each sheaf was bound with its own straw in its natural length, i.e. not twisted so as to make a longer bond' (*HDd* 271). The term can be compared with the reference in the custom of the manor of Tudenham to a sheaf 'as large as could be bound with a bind' (Rees 1924, 167). If anyone's right to corn is expressed as a number of sheaves, there must plainly be some standard for the size of sheaf: the German *Sachsenspiegel* (roughly contemporary with the Iorwerth Redaction and with the English Bracton) lays it down that when tithe of corn is given, the bond with which the sheaf is tied shall be one ell (*dumele*) long between the two knots: *Landrecht* II.48§9, Schott 1984, 138.

[8] NLW Peniarth 259[b], fo. 50[v], col. b; the manuscript is a sixteenth-century copy of an original, probably written in the fifteenth century.

[9] I gratefully acknowledge the kindness of Dr Nerys Ann Jones in giving me references, and of Mr Malcolm Jones in sending me a copy of his paper 'Saints and other Horse-Mutilators', given at the first International Conference on Celtic Folklore at Cardiff in 1992; my understanding of several points owes much to their help.

Abbreviations

HDd   Jenkins 1990.

OED   *The Oxford English Dictionary,* 2nd edn. (Oxford University Press, 1989).

References

Barlow, Frank. 1986. *Thomas Becket* (London, Weidenfeld & Nicolson).

Charles-Edwards, T. M. 1989. *The Welsh Laws* (Cardiff, University of Wales Press).

Davis, R. H. C. 1983. 'The Medieval Warhorse' in *Horses in European Economic History: A Preliminary Canter*, ed. F. M. L. Thompson (Reading, British Agricultural History Society), 4–20.

Davis, R. H. C. 1989. *The Medieval Warhorse: Origin, Development and Redevelopment* (London, Thames & Hudson).

Emanuel, H. D. (ed.). 1967. *Latin Texts of the Welsh Laws* (Cardiff, University of Wales Press).

Evans, J. Gwenogvryn (ed.). 1910. *Facsimile and Text of the Book of Taliesin* (Llanbedrog, J. G. Evans).

Fletcher, I. F. (tr.). 1986. *Latin Redaction A* (Aberystwyth, Centre for Advanced Welsh and Celtic Studies).

Grimm, Jacob. 1899. *Deutsche Rechtsaltertümer*, ed. A. Heusler and R. Hübner, 4th edn. (Leipzig, Mayer & Müller).

Hathaway , E. J. *et al.* (eds.). 1975. *Fouke le Fitz Waryn* (Oxford, Anglo-Norman Text Society, nos. XXVI–XXVIII).

Huws, Daniel. 1988. *Peniarth 28 . . . Illustrations from a Welsh Lawbook* (Aberystwyth, National Library of Wales).

Jenkins, Dafydd. 1987. 'The Lawbooks of Medieval Wales' in *The Political Context of Law: Proceedings of the Seventh British Legal History Conference, Canterbury 1985*, ed. R. Eales and D. Sullivan (London and Ronceverte, Hambledon), 1–15.

Jenkins, Dafydd (ed.). 1963. *Llyfr Colan* (Cardiff, University of Wales Press).

Jenkins, Dafydd (ed.). 1990. *Hywel Dda: The Law,* 2nd edn. (Llandysul, Gomer Press). References equally valid for the first edition, 1986.

Kelly, Fergus. 1988. *A Guide to Early Irish Law* (Dublin Institute for Advanced Studies).

Koschorreck, W. (ed.). 1976. *Der Sachsenspiegel in Bildern* (Frankfurt am Main, Insel-Verlag).

Morris, J. E. 1901. *The Welsh Wars of Edward I* (Oxford, Clarendon Press).

Owen, Aneurin (ed.). 1841. *Ancient Laws and Institutes of Wales*, 2 vols. (London, Record Commission).

Owen, M. E. and D. Jenkins. 1980. 'Gwilym Was Da', *National Library of Wales Journal*, 21, 429–30.

Payne, Ann. 1990. *Medieval Beasts* (London, British Library).

Rainsford, G. 1979. 'George Rainsford's *Ritratto d'Ingliterra* (1556)', ed. P. S. Donaldson in *Camden Miscellany XXVII* (London, Royal Historical Society, Camden Fourth Series, 22).

Rees, William. 1924. *South Wales and the March* (Oxford University Press).

Richards, Melville (tr.). 1954. *The Laws of Hywel Dda (The Book of Blegywryd)* (Liverpool University Press).

Richards, M. (ed.). 1990. *Cyfreithiau Hywel Dda yn ôl Llawysgrif Coleg yr Iesu LVII*, rev. edn. (Cardiff, University of Wales Press).

Schmidt-Wiegand, Ruth (ed.). 1993. *Sachsenspiegel, die Wolfenbütteler Bilderhandschrift* (Berlin, Akademie-Verlag).

Schott, Clausdieter (ed.). 1984. *Der Sachsenspiegel* (Zurich, Manesse).

Slade, C. F. (ed.). 1951. *The Great Roll of the Pipe for the Twelfth Year of the Reign of King John* (London, Pipe Roll Society, New Series, 26).

Thorne, S. E. 1968. *Bracton on the Laws and Customs of England*, ed. G. E. Woodbine, tr. with revisions and notes by S. E. Thorne, ii (Cambridge, Mass., Belknap Press).

Thorpe, Lewis (tr.). 1978. *Gerald of Wales: The Journey through Wales and The Description of Wales* (Harmondsworth, Penguin Books).

Wade-Evans, A. W. (ed.). 1909. *Welsh Medieval Law* (Oxford, Clarendon Press; reprint, Aalen, Scientia Verlag, 1979).

Watkin, M. (ed.). 1958. *Ystorya Bown de Hamtwn* (Cardiff, University of Wales Press).

Williams, J. E. Caerwyn *et al.* (eds.). 1994. *Gwaith Meilyr Brydydd a'i ddisgynyddion* (Cardiff, University of Wales Press).

Williams, S. J. (ed.). 1930. *Ystorya de Carolo Magno* (Cardiff, University of Wales Press). References apply equally to the second edition, 1968.

Williams, S. J. and Powell, J. E. (eds.). 1942. *Llyfr Blegywryd* (Cardiff, University of Wales Press). References apply equally to the second edition, 1961.

5

Horses in Medieval Welsh Court Poetry

Nerys Ann Jones

My intention in this chapter is twofold: it is to survey the various ways in which horses are depicted in medieval Welsh court poetry, and also to discuss the evidence which can be gleaned from this source about the horses of medieval Wales. I will be concentrating mainly on the work of those poets who sang in the courts of the independent Welsh princes during the two centuries of strife before the Norman conquest of Wales in 1283. The Poets of the Princes, as they were later known, were almost all professional poets acting as officials in the courts of their patrons, their status defined and guaranteed by Welsh law. The work of thirty-five of them, some 12,700 lines in all, has been kept in three major manuscript collections dating from the fourteenth to the seventeenth century (Lloyd-Jones 1948; Lloyd 1992; Williams 1994; Jones 1987–8).[1]

The corpus consists of three main types of poetry: religious verse, love poems and panegyric. The small body of religious poetry can be dismissed immediately as a source of information about horses as it consists mainly of formal poems of praise to God and of meditations on the four last things: death, judgement, heaven and hell (McKenna 1991). The second genre, praise poetry to the daughters of patrons thinly disguised as love poems, does contain references to horses. Indeed horses are quite central to most of them. Some open with the poet addressing his steed and expressing his wish, either for it to carry him to the girl's home or for it to act as a love-messenger for him. In a few poems, such as that of Cynddelw Brydydd Mawr to Efa daughter of Madog ap Maredudd, prince of Powys (Jones and Parry Owen 1991, no. 5), the journey on horseback provides a dramatic framework for the whole poem. These poems are clearly the antecedents of the *llatai* poems of the fourteenth and fifteenth centuries where all kinds of birds and animals and even the elements are pressed into service as love-messengers (Bromwich 1986, 36–40). They also betray the poets' familiarity with the names of famous horses and the traditions about them, some of which have been preserved in 'The Triads of the Horses' and the poem *Canu y Meirch* from the Book of Taliesin (see below, pp. 102–20). But, however interesting the role of the horse in this type of poetry for the literary historian, it is not a particularly good source of information about the actual horses of medieval Wales. When it is described at all, the lover's horse more often than not reflects its owner's emotions, eager and passionate.

The third and final type of poem produced by the Poets of the Princes is that of praise to their patrons, sung both during their lives and shortly after their deaths. As praise was the *raison d'être* of these poets, the work for which they were paid, it is not surprising that it is to this class of poetry that most of the corpus belongs. In these poems we find horses being depicted in two roles, firstly as war-machines and secondly as prestigious objects. These two roles are closely linked to the two central themes of medieval Welsh eulogies and elegies, praise of the patron's courage and ferocity in times of war on the one hand, and praise of his wealth, nobility and generosity to his people in times of peace on the other.

During the twelfth and thirteenth centuries, the princely lines which formed the three power-blocks in Wales, the line of Gruffudd ap Cynan and his descendants in Gwynedd, the descendants of Bleddyn ap Cynfyn in Powys and the descendants of Rhys ap Tewdwr in Deheubarth, were not only constantly struggling for supremacy over one another, but were also fighting for survival against the Anglo-Normans (Lloyd 1939, ii; Davies 1987). The praise poetry of the Poets of the Princes reflects the turbulent politics of the period. Poets list their patrons' victories against both foreigners and compatriots, they extol their courageous and ferocious action in battle, praise their tenacity and qualities of leadership and revel in the death and suffering imposed on the enemy. Horses feature prominently in these, often graphic, descriptions of fighting and of carnage. We find eager, foaming steeds in the thick of battle, trampling upon the fallen enemy, the battlefield ringing with the pounding of their hoofs. Also depicted are the bowed, riderless horses of the defeated foe, blood-stained and covered in sweat. The most highly esteemed qualities in war-horses, according to the poets, seem to have been their swiftness and spiritedness. They are depicted as being ardent in battle, panting and sweating, champing at their bits, with arched necks and foaming nostrils. Adjectives such as *mwth* and *ffraeth* ('swift'), *hydaith* ('fast-moving'), *llamhir* ('leaping far') and *gosathar* ('prancing') are used to convey their movement. Their speed is commonly compared with that of stags and hawks.

The *cadfarch* ('war-horse') or *amws* ('destrier') appears to have been an essential part of a Welsh prince or nobleman's battle equipment. Patrons are referred to as *cadfarchawg* ('horseman in battle') and *marchog midlan* ('horseman on the battlefield') and are portrayed without exception as fighting from horseback, often hurling spears at the opposing army. War-horses seem to have become a symbol of their owners' military might in the poetry, and often the terms *meirch* ('horses') and *marchogaeth* ('horse-riding') are juxtaposed with *medd* ('mead') which represents the contrasting virtue of munificence (Haycock 1996, 54).

Mention of the distribution of boons by patrons to the poets themselves and to other suppliants is very common in the corpus. It is introduced by the Poets of the Princes, not only as a means of extolling their patrons' generosity, but also as an expression of the reciprocal relationship which existed between court poet and patron in this period, the poet's gift in return being his poem of praise. After gold and silver, fine horses are the gift most often named, appearing on their own and also in lists along with gold, silver, wine, beer and mead, and fine clothes of green and purple.

References to horses and to herds or studs of horses are also used by the poets in order to indicate a patron's wealth and high status. They are one of the most frequently mentioned of his possessions, and their value and quality are emphasized in a variety of ways. According to both classical and medieval sources, the four qualities to look for when judging the breeding of a horse were physique, beauty, character and colour (Marchant 1925, 297–307; O'Rahilly 1960; Payne 1990, 57, and see below, pp. 148–9). Each of these qualities are represented by the numerous adjectives employed by the poets when referring to the horses of their patrons. They are *breisgir* ('tall and strong'), *ffyrfne* ('strong in appearance'), *meingrwn* ('slender and rounded') and *pen ceirw* ('with heads like that of deer'). They are long-maned and distinctive in appearance (Davis 1989, 58–9; Salisbury 1994, 30–1), their colouring ranging from *can*, *glas*, and *llwyd* ('grey') to *melyn* ('bay'), *rhudd* ('chestnut') and *dwn* or *du* ('dun').[2] There is also mention of dappled horses, likened more than once to *gleisiaid* ('young salmon'). They are characterized as proud, spirited, playful and lively. They are *mygr* ('magnificent'), *cadr* ('fine'), *braisg* ('strong') and *dilys* ('without fault'). Their superiority is also suggested by the fact that they are often referred to as being grain-fed and kept in stables (see above, pp. 71–2). The terms used are *pasg*, *maeth* and *meithdew* ('well-fed'), *grawnfaeth* ('nurtured on grain') and *pennillfaeth* ('stall-fed'). Cynddelw's portrayal of the steeds he received from the abbot of Meifod in Powys (Jones and Parry Owen 1991, 3.213–14, 217–18) is typical of the dozen or so extended descriptions of magnificent, well-bred horses found in the corpus,

> ... rhagorfeirch gleision
> Gleisiad liw, glas ganoligion ...
> Meirch ar geirch yn garcharorion,
> Maith gerdded, mygr gydred geidron.

('Splendid grey steeds / of the colour of young salmon, grey stall-fed ones ... / Steeds fettered [and fed] on oats, / Journeying afar, fine, magnificent ones running together.')

It is clear, then, that the formal praise poetry of the twelfth and thirteenth centuries is extraordinarily rich in references to horses because of the copious use the poets made of them to represent the contrasting virtues they attributed to their patrons: but how useful is the corpus as a source of historical evidence? Using any poetry, but especially panegyric, as a quarry for historical information is a notoriously hazardous practice, and before jumping to any conclusions about what the work of the Poets of the Princes tells us about the horses of medieval Wales and their uses, a number of considerations need to be borne in mind.

Firstly, it must be remembered that the poetry presents us with an extremely limited view of life in medieval Wales. The poets were solely concerned with the members of the highest echelons of society, and with their military activities above all else (Owen 1992). There is no mention, for example, of hunting or horse-trading, agriculture or the transport of goods, and very little of travelling on horseback. Foot soldiers and the bowmen for whom Wales was famous hardly make an appearance in the corpus (Bradbury 1985, 1–16). Secondly, owing to the lack of a narrative element in the poetry, the descriptions of the military exploits of patrons are at best rather vague. Indeed, in some cases it is difficult to decide whether an incident referred to by a poet was a full-scale battle or merely a border skirmish or cattle-raid. Even when a particular battle can be identified from other sources, the poetry rarely adds to our understanding as to how it was fought. While the Poets of the Princes were extremely successful in evoking the action, blood and clamour of conflict, it is clear that there is little purpose in looking to their work for detailed evidence about the use of horses in specific incidents. Thirdly, it is quite possible that the poets in their accounts of combat would depict what was expected by their audience rather than what had actually happened. The fact that patrons are portrayed exclusively in the corpus as fighting from horseback might be an example of this, bringing to mind the Old English aphorism that a nobleman ought to be on a horse's back, *Eorl sceal on eos boge* (Shippey 1976, 66). A fourth factor is that, as horses were often referred to by the poets as a means of praising the wealth or military might of their owners or riders, it is quite possible that they were portrayed in an idealistic way and that the descriptions contain a certain measure of hyperbole. Also, poets use words very differently from historians, and their choice of a term or adjective can often be influenced by literary convention or by the constraints of metre and ornament. The verse of the Poets of the Princes is highly decorated by intricate patterns of alliteration and internal rhyme, and often, especially in the work of inferior poets, the sound of the words dominated the meaning.

The main problem for the historian, however, is that although the Poets of the Princes dealt with contemporary events and figures, the praise of patrons was often expressed by them in highly traditional terms. The alternative title used by modern scholars for these poets, *Gogynfeirdd*, literally 'the not so early poets', stresses the close relationship which exists between their work and that of the *Cynfeirdd* 'the early poets'. These are the founders of Welsh poetry, the court poets of the rulers of British kingdoms both in Wales and in the 'Old North' (the extensive Welsh-speaking areas of southern Scotland and northern England) from the late sixth century onwards. They include Taliesin, the poet of Urien, chief of the kingdom of Rheged, Aneirin, poet of Mynyddawg Mwynfawr, ruler of Din Eidyn in the vicinity of modern Edinburgh, and a host of other poets whose names have been lost to us (Jarman 1981). Some of the Poets of the Princes quote or echo famous lines and phrases of the *Cynfeirdd*. Two of them, Cynddelw and Owain Cyfeiliog, have deliberately modelled poems on the *Gododdin,* a series of elegies on the members of Mynyddawg Mwynfawr's war-band attributed to Aneirin. Most, however, seem to be recycling the ideas and expressions of their predecessors without attempting to evoke any particular poem from the past (Lewis 1992, 145–7).

If we compare the output of the twelfth and thirteenth centuries with the earlier Welsh poetry, we find that, despite the fact that five or six centuries divide them, there is great similarity, not only in the choice of themes, but also in the imagery and vocabulary used. Horses perform the same functions in the panegyric of both the *Cynfeirdd* and the *Gogynfeirdd.* The fighting techniques of both periods, when described in any detail by the poets, are identical, and the steeds distributed by the patrons of Aneirin and Taliesin seem to have been equally well bred and well cared for as those of their twelfth- and thirteenth-century successors.

Many of the expressions employed by the Poets of the Princes in their references to horses clearly derive from the work of the *Cynfeirdd*, but some seem to be even older. The phrase *meirch mai* ('horses of the plain or field'), for instance, might well have been inherited from the period before Welsh had developed from Brythonic, sometime before the sixth century (*GPC s.v.* mai[2]; Owen 1992, 9, 17–18; Koch 1988, 19–20; Hamp 1995, 50). The archaic genitive form *mai*, otherwise found only in personal and place names, probably survived as a fossil in the poetry because it alliterated with *meirch* ('steeds'). In addition to their catalogue of traditional epithets and phrases, motifs and *topoi*, the poets possessed a stock of alliterating and rhyming words of varying date and origin which they would use repeatedly. Another example commonly found in descriptions of horses from the sixth century to the thirteenth is the pair, *meirch* ('steeds') and *seirch*, a word whose exact meaning in the poetry is uncertain but which probably refers either to a horse's harness or to a warrior's armour (Williams 1961, lxii, 329). Stylistic devices were also passed down from generation to generation of poets, such as the use of adjectives to represent nouns, a common feature in descriptions of horses both in the earliest poetry and in that of the twelfth and thirteenth centuries. *Abrwysgl ei faran ar gan a glas* ('terrible his wrath on white and grey ones'), says Gwalchmai of twelfth-century prince Owain Gwynedd (Williams *et al.* 1994, 8.78), without using a noun for 'horse' at all. Similarly in the *Gododdin*, we find phrases such as *i ar feiniell fygedorth* ('upon a steaming, slender bay one') and *i ar llemenig llwybrdew* ('upon a bounding, wide-tracked one') (Jarman 1988, l. 294), again with the noun 'horse' omitted.

Sometimes the profoundly conservative tendencies of the Welsh court poets would lead to anachronisms appearing in their work. A good example of this is the way in which they continued to refer to the English enemy as *Deifr* and *Brynaich* long after the Anglian kingdoms of Deira and Bernicia had been swallowed up in Northumbria, and long after Northumbria had been engulfed in England (Owen 1992, 10). An even more striking anachronism, according to some scholars, is the use in Welsh praise poetry from the sixth century well into the thirteenth century of the term *eurdorchawg* ('wearing a gold torque') to denote high status, despite the fact that it probably represents an Iron Age custom which had disappeared many centuries before (Foster 1965, 234; Alcock 1987, 248). Could it be, then, that certain elements in the portrayal of horses by both the *Cynfeirdd* and the *Gogynfeirdd* might also be anachronistic?

Doubts have been cast recently on the historicity of the picture presented in the *Gododdin* of mounted warriors, and especially of their custom of throwing spears from horseback in combat (Higham 1991). One of the many problems with the *Gododdin* is that there is no external validation of the main event referred to in the poem, namely the defeat of the war-band of Mynyddawg Mwynfawr at the hands of the Angles at Catraeth, possibly Richmond near modern Catterick. Neither is there any dependable information in contemporary sources concerning the weaponry, fighting techniques or battle tactics of the sixth- and seventh-century Britons of the 'Old North'. Dr Jenny Rowland's comparison of the depiction of Mynyddog's war-band with other light cavalry forces such as those of the Romans and the ninth-century Bretons, however, has shown convincingly that there is no reason to see the techniques of mounted fighting alluded to in the poem as impossible or even unlikely (Rowland 1995). But were the same methods used by the Welsh five centuries later?

Historians of twelfth- and thirteenth-century Wales are more fortunate than those of the Dark Age British kingdoms in that they have to hand a wealth of contemporary documentary material in the form of chronicles, law tracts, charters and seals, accounts and extents. Reliable evidence for the methods of waging war, however, is scarce, the most useful sources being descriptive writings about Wales and the Welsh, especially those of Giraldus Cambrensis (Bartlett 1982; Richter 1972). The son of a Marcher family, born and brought up in the castle of Manorbier on the coast of Pembrokeshire, Gerald's knowledge of warfare in twelfth-century Wales was based on acute observation. His remarks accord well with the poets' descriptions of their aristocratic patrons. In his *Descriptio Kambriae* he notes that although 'most of the common people prefer to fight on foot, in view of the marshy uneven terrain . . . their leaders ride into battle on swift mettlesome horses which are bred locally' (Thorpe 1978, 234). He draws attention to the lightness of their weapons, 'small leather corselets, handfuls of arrows, long spears and round shields', and also refers to the showers of javelins which they would hurl during the initial onslaught (Thorpe 1978, 259). His observations on the speed of their attacks reminds us of the poets' emphasis on the swiftness of their patrons' steeds.

According to Gerald's testimony, then, the Poets of the Princes seem to have been describing contemporary practice. The Welsh nobility in the closing years of the twelfth century were adhering to the fighting techniques employed by their ancestors in the Old North five centuries earlier, a method which was, as Gerald points out, eminently suited to the rugged terrain of Wales. We gather from other sources, however, that Gerald did not present us with the whole picture. He had a tendency to overdraw the contrasts between the Welsh and their Norman neighbours, and this may be the reason why he did not dwell on the fact that native Welsh rulers had already begun to adopt some of the Anglo-Normans' modes of combat, including heavy cavalry (although he does mention it in passing) (Thorpe 1978, 267). By the thirteenth century the princes of Gwynedd were erecting castles and attempting to modify traditional Welsh custom by introducing a new-style 'knight-service', modelled on the Norman system (Jones 1969; Suppe 1994). In 1263, Llywelyn ap Gruffudd was reported as having a large number of armoured as well as unarmoured horses at his command during campaigns in mid-Wales, and it has been argued that his efforts to horse and equip his knights in the Norman style were partly responsible for the severe strains imposed on the Welsh economy during the final years of his reign (Williams-Jones 1976, cxxiii–cxxvii).

The Norman method of fighting involved heavily armed knights charging the enemy at high speed with lances held 'couched' (Davis 1989, 15, 19–20). There is no indication in the poetry addressed to the princes of thirteenth-century Wales that this technique had been espoused by them. To the contrary, even Llywelyn ap Gruffudd is depicted as scattering, or literally 'sowing', spears in the age old fashion (Andrews *et al.* 1996, 36.97). There are references in the corpus to the wearing of armour by horsemen but there is no suggestion that many of the war-horses would also be wearing armour by this period. This is not surprising, however, as there is hardly any mention of horse-trappings of any kind in early or medieval Welsh praise poetry, although, as in other cultures, they must have been highly prized as status symbols (Graham-Campbell 1991, 79; Owen-Crocker 1991, 229–34).

Equestrian seal of Llywelyn ap Iorwerth (National Museum of Wales).

What of the horses themselves? Although the reasons for it have long been a subject of contention, there is no doubt that the size and conformation of the best war-horses were being developed throughout the Middle Ages. According to some scholars, this is related to the increasing weight that the horses had to carry. Others argue that the more significant factor was the new technique of shock combat which called for unstoppable power rather than agility (Davis 1989, 21–4; Hyland 1994, 57–8). It is certain that the ambitious princes of Wales, wishing to keep abreast of developments in the art of warfare, would be breeding larger horses during the twelfth and thirteenth century. However, references to the size of horses both in early Welsh poetry and in the work of the Poets of the Princes are scarce.

The native ponies of the British Isles were strong and hardy, and well suited to the traditional Welsh way of fighting. Indeed, during the Viking age many Welsh horses were exported to Ireland (where similar fighting techniques were used), and were much prized there (*DIL s.n. ech bretnach,* and below, pp. 135–6). Larger mounts were probably produced through selective breeding, but this would have been an extremely costly and time-consuming business (Davis 1988, 69–72). In order to hasten the process of building up a stud, the Anglo-Normans imported stallions of Arab blood from the continent (Davis 1983, 16–17). Gerald of Wales in his *Descriptio Kambriae* refers to 'most excellent studs put apart for breeding, and deriving their origin from some fine Spanish horses which Robert de Belesme, Earl of Shrewsbury brought into this country' which he found in Powys in mid-Wales (Thorpe 1978, 201).

There is plenty of evidence in the poetry that the wealthiest members of Welsh society had been breeding horses for many centuries. As well as the references to stall feeding and stabling, we have the evidence of the archaic expression, *meirch mai*, which probably alludes to the keeping of the best stock in fields or enclosures. In the eulogies of two of the Poets of the Princes, however, we also find references to imported horses. Cynddelw Brydydd Mawr describes Madog ap Maredudd, prince of Powys (d. 1160) as *Gwesgwyn ganhymdaith* (Jones and Parry Owen 1991, 7.16) ('companion of Gascon horses'), and the mounts of Llywelyn ap Iorwerth of Gwynedd (d. 1240) are portrayed by Llywarch ap Llywelyn as *Gwasgwyn feirch goseirch gosathar* (Jones 1991, 23–58) ('horses from Gascony, harnessed and prancing'). These were not necessarily horses bred in Gascony, but were probably Spanish horses, possibly acquired by the princes themselves or given to them as diplomatic gifts, shipped at great cost to Wales from Bordeaux to be crossed with Welsh mares in the royal stables of Gwynedd and Powys (Childs 1978, 121; Davis 1989, 57–8).

As far as I know, these two references by the court poets of Powys and Gwynedd provide the only evidence of the ownership of foreign horses by Welsh princes during the twelfth and thirteenth centuries. It is a splendid example of the value of the work of the Poets of the Princes as a source which can greatly illuminate aspects of life and society in medieval Wales. I hope to have shown, however, that, especially because of its backward-looking nature, it is also a source that should be used with great care and circumspection.

Appendix: Vocabulary used for describing horses in Early and Medieval Welsh Poetry

Listed below are the adjectives and adjectival phrases, metaphors and compounds used by the *Cynfeirdd* and the *Gogynfeirdd* in their references to horses. This list is not exhaustive but includes examples from the work of early praise poets, Aneirin and Taliesin, and from early saga poetry, probably also composed by court poets, as well as from the work of about twenty of the Poets of the Princes. Apart from the *Gododdin* and those poems edited in *Early Welsh Saga Poetry* which are listed below, all other poems are referred to according to volume and number.

Poems from *Early Welsh Saga Poetry* (Rowland 1990)

'Canu Heledd', *EWSP* 429–45, 483–96.
'Canu Llywarch', *EWSP* 404–18, 468–76.
'Kyntaw Geir' *EWSP* 452–3, 499–500.
'Geraint fab Erbin', *EWSP* 457–61, 504–5.
'Llym Awel', *EWSP* 454–7, 501–3.
'Seithennin', *EWSP* 464–5, 508–9.

I Appearance and demeanour

aml eu gorne (of many colours) V 9.28
amliw (speckled) I 3.118
archfain (shapely) IV 4.90
archlun ceirw (of the appearance of deer) III 1.23
blawr (grey) III 8.25
blawr blaen eu rhawn yn ariant (the tips of their manes white with silver) 'Geraint' 27c
breichir (long-legged) *God* 519
breisgir (tall and strong) V 1.126
byr ei blew (short-haired) 'Kyntaw Geir' 9a
cain (fair) I 2.42, III 16.160
can (white) *God* 714, 'Geraint fab Erbin' 4b, I 3.150, 8.78, II 16.27, III 16.126, 26.138, V 23.65(2)
cannaid (white) V 6.18
canwelw (pale white) III 16.91
carnwelw (having pale hoofs) IV 4.228
cenedl frych (of a speckled kind) *PT* VII 35
coch (sorrel) I 7.131
cochre (a stud of sorrel steeds) *God* 559
crychrawn (having a frizzly mane or tail) III 24.127, 26.138
cyfliw (of the same colour) III 21.153
cynffun (breathing heavily) I 7.131
diffun (panting) III 8.7
du (black) I 7.133
dwn (dun) I 7.133, V 10.15, 24.42
eiliw eleirch (swan-coloured) *God* 904
eiliw pysgawd glas (of the same colour as silvery fish) III 1.24

eilon (deer) I 2.42, 9.59

erch (speckled) I 7.129, II 3.54, III 24.127, IV 4.90, 6.229, 9.21, V 26.83

erchfarch (a speckled horse) III 16.212

erchlas (dapple-grey) *God* 742

erchliw (of a speckled colour) III 24.127

erchliw gleisiad (of the speckled colour of a young salmon) V 6.19

erchlyfn (speckled and smooth) III 1.23, 24.127, V 6.19

erchrawn (having a speckled mane) IV 3.27

ffriw ddyfrig (with a foamy face) III 25.6

ffriw euraid (of splendid appearance) V 6.20

ffriw eurdo (its head adorned with gold) IV 4.170

ffroen ddyfrig (with foaming nostrils) IV 4.170

ffroenfawr (wide-nostrilled) V 6.20

ffroenwyn (white-nostrilled) III 25.6

ffrwyn ddyfrig (having a foamy bit) II 22.30

ffrwynfawr (splendid its reins) IV 6.68

ffyrfgnawd (of firm flesh) I 8.74

ffyrfne (strong in appearance) V 9.18

garhirion (long-legged) 'Geraint' 19b, 20b, 21b etc.

glas (grey) I 8.78, II 11.1, III 21.175, IV 4.169

gleisiad dylan (young salmon of the sea) III 1.24

gleisiaid gynhebig (similar to young salmon) IV 4.169

gleisiaid liw (of the colour of young salmon) III 3.214

gloywliw (of bright appearance) II 11.1

gochwys (sweating) III 8.15, V 23.189, VI 30.20

grai (grey) I 7.130

gwallt pig (spiky-haired) II 15.15

gwelw (grey, pale) *God* 725, III 21.130, 153, IV 12.4, V 10.15, VI 18.15

gwinau (chestnut) 'Kyntaw Geir' 8a, 9a, 10a, 'Seithennyn' 7a, I 7.127, III 8.10

gwisgawg (harnessed) V 24.16

llai (dun) I 7.129

llwyd (grey) I 7.129

llyfnfarch (a sleek horse) III 8.7

main (slender) *God* 16, VI 18.39

mawr (great) IV 4.168

meinddwn (slender and dark) III 26.124

meingan (white and slender) II 9.4, IV 16.217

meingrwn (slender and rounded) V 24.42

meiniell (slender and bay) *God* 298

meinllun (of slender appearance) V 16.212

meinllwyd (slender and grey) *God* 519

melyn (bay) I 7.133, II 6.36, V 6.22

mygedorth (steaming) *God* 298

myngawg (maned) I 3.67

myngdwn (with trimmed mane) I 7.133, III 16.171

myngfras (long-maned) *God* 13

myng-gan (white-maned) V 1.127

mynw eilon (of the appearance of deer) III 13.44

pen ceirw (with heads like those of deer) III 16.115

pysgawdliw eigiawn (of the colour of the fish of the sea) III 26.136

rhawngaeth (with their manes tied up) III 13.57

rhawn rhyn (rough-haired) *God* 903, 'Kyntaw Geir' 8b

rhith rhyn (erect) *God* 430

rhudd (chestnut/reddened with blood) 'Geraint' 20c, 21c, etc. III 13.57, 14.24, 16.124

rhuddfarch (chestnut horse) IV 6.261, VII 47.7

tryffun (panting) III 16.207

tu hir (with long sides) I 7.128, III 21.175

2 Movement

breisglym (fast and strong) VII 25.72

buan (fleet) *God* 16

cyngan (moving harmoniously) III 1.27, 16.160, IV 4.54

cynt nog adar (faster than birds) V 23.66

edeinfarch (a winged horse, a swift horse) V 9.12

yn ehed (flying) III 21.155

ffraeth (spirited/swift) I 7.126, IV 4.169, 6.68, V 23.61, VII 4.9, 53.23

ffysgiad (swift) VI 30.36

gosathar (prancing) V 23.58

grawthfrys (swiftly-trotting) V 26.88

gwalchfrowys (sprightly as a hawk) I 7.125

gweilch ogyfred (as swift as hawks) III 21.153

hir ei naid (long its leap) 'Kyntaw Geir' 10a

hirllam (leaping far) V 1.127

hydaith (fast-moving) III 13.43

hyddfarch (a horse as swift as a stag) V 24.16

hyweddfrys (tractable and swift) V 26.42

llamhir (leaping far) III 1.22

llemenig (a bounding horse) *God* 294, III 8.26

lluchfarch (?a horse which is like a lightning flash) IV 3.27

llwybrdew (wide-tracked) *God* 294

maith gerdded (walking far) III 3.218

mwth (swift) *God* 13, *PT* VII 9, V 1.127, 150

mythfarch (a swift horse) *God* 499

rhagfuan (swift) *God* 388, 830

rhagrygïawr (racing forward) *God* 388

rhedech hiraethawg (eager to run) 'Kyntaw Geir' 8b

rhuthr eryron glew/gwyn/brith etc (of the rush of bold/white/speckled etc. eagles) 'Geraint fab Erbin' 20c, 21c, 22c etc.

rhuthr goddaith ar ddiffaith fynydd (of the rush of a heath fire on mountain wastes) 'Geraint fab Erbin' 19c

rhuthr gwyddfoch (of the rush of wild pigs) III 16.124

rhwydd yng ngnif (free-moving in hard going) 'Kyntaw Geir' 9b, 10b

rhyging oddew (with an ambling course) 'Kyntaw Geir' 9b

rhyging woddaid (desiring to amble) 'Kyntaw Geir' 10b

rhygyngawg (ambling) I 3.82

tuthfawr (swiftly-trotting) III 21.175

3 Spirit

amgyrfod (?eager) V 26.132

anwar (savage) V 23.61

arab (playful) V 17.15

browys (spirited) *God* 924

browysfarch (spirited horse) II 16.27

brwysg (vigorous) I 7.126

campus (performing feats) I 2.44

ceinwyll (splendid and fierce) V 23.65

cynhorawr (a leading horse) *God* 429

dyrawr (eager) V 14.27

dyre (wanton) I 13.18, III 8.39, V 9.3, 14.27

erewyll (spirited) 'Canu Llywarch' 34b

ffraeth see 2

ffrawdd tywys (ardent and leading) I 7.127

ffrawddus (ardent) V 23.61

ffrwyngno (chomping at its bit) IV 4.170

ffysgiolyn (a spirited horse) *God* 947

godrudd (impetuous) *God* 875

gwâr (obedient) V 23.65

gwareus (playful) *God* 430

gwyddfarch (a lively horse) III 24.127

gwyllt (wild/fierce) III 13.44, 21.130

haerllug (proud) V 1.127

hywedd (broken in, obedient) 'Canu Heledd' 72a, V 26.42, VII 15.17

hyweddfrys see 2

llaw (tractable) III 1.22

pennawd (leading in the forefront) *God* 861

penweddawr (arching its neck) *God* 742

rhewydd (lively) II 18.42

4 Quality

anfonawg (renowned) III 14.32

arwymp (fine) VII 46.11

berthfarch (a fine horse) IV 2.49

braisg (strong) I 7.126

breisgfarch (strong horse) VII 53.23

cadr (fine, powerful) 'Seithennin' 7a, III 3.218, 25.16

ceinwiw (splendid) I 7.131

dewr (splendid) I 13.18

dilys (without fault) VII 14.26

edmig (dignified) VI 18.39

erfai (splendid) I 7.129

erfawr (magnificent) V 6.20

ffêr (strong) I 7.126, V 9.18

ffriwlwydd (prosperous in its appearance) II 22.30

ffrwythig (powerful) V 23.61

ffrwythlawn (powerful) VII 53.23

grym ddiffwys (of immense strength) I 7.130

Gwasgwynfarch (a Gascon horse) V 23.58

gweisgfarch (a fine/swift horse) II 22.29

gwellfaeth (superior in breeding) III 13.44

Gwesgwyn (Gascon) III 7.16

gwrddfarch (a sturdy horse) V 17.15

hywerth (of great value) I 7.49

maelawr (royal) *PT* VII 34

mawrydig (majestic) III 8.18

molaid (praised) V 6.22

mygr (magnificent) III 3.218, 10.26(2), 13.43

mygrfan (magnificent and noble) III 16.160

mygrfawr (magnificent and great) V 14.27

pedrongl (powerful) III 16.142

5 Feeding and stabling

canolig (nurtured in a stable) I 2.42

carcharawr (stabled) 'Llym Awel' 9b, III 3.217

carcharfarch (a stabled horse) III 25.15

carcharorion ceidron ceirch (stabled splendid ones [nurtured on] oats) III 25.16

graddfyged grawn (splendid ones [nurtured upon] grain) III 24.128

grawn addas (worthy of grain) 'Geraint' 23b

grawn anchwant (greedy for grain) 'Geraint' 27b

grawn eu bwyd (grain was their feed) 'Geraint' 25b
grawnfaeth (nurtured on grain) I 7.126
grawn fagu (nurtured on grain) 'Geraint' 26b
grawn foloch (grain-scattering) 'Geraint' 24b
grawnfyged (nurtured on grain) V 26.88
grawn gynnydd (growing sturdy on grain) 'Geraint' 19b
grawn odew (grain-nurtured) 'Geraint' 20b
grawn wehyn (grain-consuming) Geraint' 21b
grawn wenith ([fed on] wheat-grain) 'Geraint' 22b
hyganawl (stall-fed) V 1.160
lledfegin grawn (well nurtured on grain) IV 3.26
maeth (well fed) VII 53.23
mai (of the plain or field) II 22.29, III 26.34, 124, V 24.42
march pennill Ebrill (a stabled horse in April) I 29.29
meithdew (well fattened) VI 30.50
pasg (well fed) *God* 156, III 26.136, IV 2.34
pasgadur (well fed) III 16.44
pasgfarch (a well-fed horse) III 16.43, 20.48
pasgnawd (used to being fed) III 20.48
penhillfaeth (nurtured in a stable) III 16.115
uch cain ebran ([nurtured] on fine fodder) III 1.23

6 Fighting

arfawg (armed) VII 28.6
cadfarch (war-horse) II 16.41, III 26.138
cadflaen (in the van of battle) II 16.41
cochwys (bloody and sweaty) IV 6.53
crau eu cnes (whose coats are bloodstained) 'Geraint' 5b
crymrudd (bowed and bloodstained) 'Geraint' 3b, 4b
gelorfarch (a horse bearing a bier) IV 3.33
goseirch (harnessed, ?armoured) V 23.58
gweilydd (riderless) I 3.94
lluddedig (exhausted) VI 18.39
lluyddfarch (war-horse) VII 28.6
mawrthig (trained or accoutred for war) II 22.29, IV 4.168, V 23.61, VI
     18.39
pedreindor (?wearing armour on its crupper) III 16.142
rhudd see 1

Notes

[1] The whole corpus has been edited (in Welsh) by the University of Wales Centre for Advanced Welsh and Celtic Studies, and published, under the general editorship of R. Geraint Gruffydd, in a series of seven volumes. As yet, however, only a small fraction is available in English translation: see Sims-Williams 1985.

[2] As noticed by Jane Ryan (1993, 85–7), white or pale-coloured horses are the most common in the corpus. Other contemporary sources, such as the *Chansons de geste* where *liard* ('silver grey') and *baucens* ('skewbald') are the most popular colours (Davis 1989, 59), suggest that these horses were much sought after: see further the discussion on the Old Irish term *gabor* by P. Kelly, above, p. 52, and the reference to the special white palfrey (see below, p. 126).

Abbreviations

I	Williams *et al.* 1995.
II	Bramley *et al.* 1994.
III	Jones and Parry Owen 1991.
IV	Jones and Parry Owen 1995.
V	Jones 1991.
VI	Bosco *et al.* 1995.
VII	Andrews *et al.* 1996.
DIL	*Dictionary of the Irish Language* (Dublin, Royal Irish Academy, 1913–76).
EWSP	Rowland 1990.
God	Jarman 1988.
GPC	*Geiriadur Prifysgol Cymru: A Dictionary of the Welsh Language* (Cardiff, University of Wales Press, 1950–).
PT	Williams 1975.

References

Alcock, Leslie. 1987. *Economy, Society and Warfare among the Britons and Saxons* (Cardiff, University of Wales Press).

Andrews, Rhian M. *et al.* (eds.). 1996. *Gwaith Bleddyn Fardd ac eraill o feirdd ail hanner y drydedd ganrif ar ddeg* (Cyfres Beirdd y Tywysogion VII; Cardiff, University of Wales Press).

Bartlett, Robert. 1982. *Gerald of Wales 1146–1223* (Oxford Historical Monographs, Oxford University Press).

Bosco, Y Chwaer *et al.* (eds.). 1995. *Gwaith Dafydd Benfras ac eraill o feirdd hanner cyntaf y drydedd ganrif ar ddeg* (Cyfres Beirdd y Tywysogion VI; Cardiff, University of Wales Press).

Bradbury, Jim. 1985. *The Medieval Archer* (Woodbridge, The Boydell Press).

Bramley, Kathleen Anne *et al.* (eds.). 1994. *Gwaith Llywelyn Fardd I ac eraill o feirdd y ddeuddegfed ganrif* (Cyfres Beirdd y Tywysogion II; Cardiff, University of Wales Press).

Bromwich, Rachel. 1986. *Aspects of the Poetry of Dafydd ap Gwilym: Collected Papers* (Cardiff, University of Wales Press).

Childs, Wendy R. 1978. *Anglo-Castilian Trade in the Later Middle Ages* (Manchester University Press).

Davies, R. R. 1987. *Conquest, Coexistence, and Change: Wales 1063–1415* (Oxford University Press).

Davis, R. H. C. 1983. 'The Medieval Warhorse' in *Horses in European Economic History: A Preliminary Canter*, ed. F. M. L. Thompson (Reading, British Agricultural History Society), 4–20.

Davis, R. H. C. 1988. 'The Warhorses of the Normans' in *Anglo-Norman Studies 10*, ed. R. Allen Brown (Oxford, The Boydell Press), 67–81.

Davis, R. H. C. 1989. *The Medieval Warhorse: Origin, Development and Redevelopment* (London, Thames & Hudson).

Foster, Idris Ll. 1965. 'The Emergence of Wales' in *Prehistoric and Early Wales*, ed. Glyn Daniel and I. Ll. Foster (London, Routledge & Kegan Paul), 213–315.

Graham-Campbell, James. 1991. 'Anglo-Scandinavian Equipment in Eleventh-Century England' in *Anglo-Norman Studies 14*, ed. Majorie Chibnall (Oxford, The Boydell Press), 77–89.

Hamp, Eric P. 1995. 'On Slow and Uneven Change' in *Hispano-Gallo-Brittonica*, ed. Joseph F. Eska *et al.* (Cardiff, University of Wales Press).

Haycock, Marged. 1996. 'Medd a Mêl Farddoni' in *Beirdd a Thywysogion: Barddoniaeth Llys yng Nghymru, Iwerddon a'r Alban*, ed. Morfydd E. Owen and Brynley F. Roberts (Aberystwyth and Cardiff, National Library of Wales and University of Wales Press), 39–59.

Higham, N. J. 1991. 'Cavalry in Early Bernicia?', *Northern History*, 27, 236–41.

Hyland, Ann. 1994. *The Medieval Warhorse from Byzantium to the Crusades* (Stroud, Alan Sutton).

Jarman, A. O. H. 1981. *The Cynfeirdd: Early Welsh Poets and Poetry* (Cardiff, University of Wales Press).

Jarman, A. O. H. (ed.). 1988. *Aneirin: Y Gododdin, Britain's Oldest Heroic Poem* (Llandysul, Gomer Press).

Jones, Elin M. (ed.). 1991. *Gwaith Llywarch ap Llywelyn 'Prydydd y Moch'* (Cyfres Beirdd y Tywysogion V; Cardiff, University of Wales Press).

Jones, Glanville R. J. 1969. 'The Defences of Gwynedd in the Thirteenth Century', *Caernarvonshire Historical Society Transactions*, 30, 29–43.

Jones, N. A. 1987–8. 'Discussions on the Work of the Gogynfeirdd: A Bibliography', *Studia Celtica*, 22–3, 42–7.

Jones, Nerys Ann and Parry Owen, Ann (eds.). 1991. *Gwaith Cynddelw Brydydd Mawr I* (Cyfres Beirdd y Tywysogion III; Cardiff, University of Wales Press).

Jones, Nerys Ann and Parry Owen, Ann (eds.). 1995. *Gwaith Cynddelw Brydydd Mawr II* (Cyfres Beirdd y Tywysogion IV; Cardiff, University of Wales Press).

Koch, John. 1988. 'The Cynfeirdd Poetry and the Language of the Sixth Century' in *Early Welsh Poetry: Studies in the Book of Aneirin*, ed. Brynley F. Roberts (Aberystwyth, National Library of Wales).

Lewis, Ceri W. 1992. 'The Court Poets: Their Function, Status and Craft' in *A Guide to Welsh Literature*, i, ed. A. O. H. Jarman and G. R. Hughes, rev. edn. (Cardiff, University of Wales Press), 123–56.

Lloyd, D. Myrddin. 1992. 'The Poets of the Princes' in *A Guide to Welsh Literature*, i, ed. A. O. H. Jarman and G. R. Hughes, rev. edn. (Cardiff, University of Wales Press), 157–88.

Lloyd, J. E. 1939. *A History of Wales from the Earliest Times to the Edwardian Conquest*, 3rd edn., 2 vols. (London, New York and Toronto, Longmans, Green & Co.).

Lloyd-Jones, John. 1948. 'The Court Poets of the Welsh Princes' (Sir John Rhŷs Memorial Lecture), *Proceedings of the British Academy*, 34, 167–97.

Marchant, E. C. (tr.). 1925. *Xenophon: Scripta Minora* (London, William Heinemann).

McKenna, Catherine A. 1991. *The Medieval Welsh Religious Lyric: Poems of the Gogynfeirdd, 1137–1282* (Belmont, Mass., Ford & Bailie).

O'Rahilly, Cecile. 1960. 'A Welsh Treatise on Horses', *Celtica*, 5, 145–60.

Owen, Morfydd E. 1992. *The Medieval Welsh Poet's Vision of Society: 'A Window on the Iron Age'*, Hallstatt Lecture (Machynlleth, Tabernacl Trust).

Owen-Crocker, Gale R. 1991. 'Hawks and Horse Trappings: The Insignia of Rank' in *The Battle of Maldon A.D. 991*, ed. Donald Scragg (Oxford, Basil Blackwell), 220–37.

Payne, Ann. 1990. *Medieval Beasts* (London, The British Library).

Richter, Michael. 1972. *Giraldus Cambrensis: The Growth of the Welsh Nation* (Aberystwyth, National Library of Wales).

Rowland, Jenny. 1990. *Early Welsh Saga Poetry: A Study and Edition of the Englynion* (Cambridge, D. S. Brewer).

Rowland, Jenny. 1995. 'Warfare and Horses in the *Gododdin* and the Problem of Catraeth', *Cambrian Medieval Celtic Studies*, 30, 13–40.

Ryan, Jane. 1993. 'A Study of Horses in Early Medieval Welsh Literature *c.* 600–*c.* 1300 A.D.' (University of Wales M.Phil. thesis).

Salisbury, Joyce E. 1994. *The Beast Within: Animals in the Middle Ages* (London, Routledge).

Shippey, T. A. 1976. *Poems of Wisdom and Learning in Old English* (Cambridge and Totowa, J. S. Brewer and Rowman & Littlefield).

Sims-Williams, Patrick. 1985. 'Cyfieithiadau o Waith y Gogynfeirdd: Llyfryddiaeth Fer' in *Ysgrifau Beirniadol*, 13, ed. J. E. Caerwyn Williams (Denbigh, Gwasg Gee), 39–47.

Suppe, F. C. 1994. *Military Institutions on the Welsh Marches: Shropshire A.D. 1066–1300* (Woodbridge, Boydell & Brewer).

Thorpe, Lewis (tr.). 1978. *Gerald of Wales: The Journey through Wales and The Description of Wales* (Harmondsworth, Penguin Books).

Williams, Ifor (ed.). 1961. *Canu Aneirin*, 2nd edn. (Cardiff, University of Wales Press).

Williams, Ifor (ed.). 1975. *The Poems of Taliesin*, English version by J. E. Caerwyn Williams (Dublin Institute for Advanced Studies).

Williams, J. E. Caerwyn. 1994. *The Poets of the Welsh Princes*, rev. edn. (Cardiff, University of Wales Press).

Williams, J. E. Caerwyn *et al.* (eds.). 1994. *Gwaith Meilyr Brydydd a'i ddis-gynyddion* (Cyfres Beirdd y Tywysogion I; Cardiff, University of Wales Press).

Williams-Jones, Keith. 1976. *The Meirioneth Lay Subsidy Roll 1292–3* (Cardiff, University of Wales Press).

6

The Triads of the Horses

Rachel Bromwich

Trioedd y Meirch ('The Triads of the Horses') represents a distinctive group of 'Triads' (i.e. triple groupings) within the larger collection known as *Trioedd Ynys Prydain* ('The Triads of the Island of Britain'). A number of collections of these triple groupings of the names of early Welsh heroes are found in manuscripts which date from the thirteenth and following centuries, and the earliest of these is quite probably the fragment of 'The Triads of the Horses' found in the Black Book of Carmarthen, which is translated below. A more extensive collection is to be found in Peniarth MS 16 in the National Library of Wales, and a yet fuller and later collection is preserved in the Red Book of Hergest in the Bodleian Library, Oxford. There is also a partial redaction of the same series in the White Book of Rhydderch (NLW Peniarth MS 4).

The fondness for triadic groupings listing all kinds of names, facts, and precepts is a characteristic indigenous feature of the early Celtic tradition: it is amply demonstrated in the earliest literature of both Wales and Ireland. 'The Triads of the Island of Britain' are believed to have originated as a mnemonic device employed by professional poets in order to systematize, preserve and transmit all branches of their traditional learning. Triads are found in a wide range of early Welsh sources including legal and medical texts, the rules for poetic composition, and collections of proverbial material. The Triads provide an index to a mass of early Welsh traditional narrative: part of it familiar from other sources, but for the most part unknown, because the Triads refer to traditions which were for a long time not committed to writing, but were preserved entirely by word of mouth, and were handed down by professional poets and storytellers.

In the oldest of the Triads, the names of traditional Welsh heroes are grouped together under a single inclusive epithet which asserts their possession of some common characteristic, usually expressed by an archaic or unusual epithet, generally complimentary and yet intentionally vague and imprecise, and one which has no reference to any specific story. Examples are 'Three Bull-Chieftains of the Island of Britain', 'Three Red-Speared Bards', 'Three Horses of Plunder' and 'Three Sprightly Steeds'. The extended Triads, such as the 'Three Horses who carried the Three Horse-Burdens', which include details which refer to specific stories, are probably a later development. But the high status accorded generally to the war-horses of the traditional heroes is recognized and enhanced by the inclusion of the horses' individual or 'personal' names, alongside the names of their owners, in the special subsection which is devoted to 'The Triads of the Horses' in the canonical compendium of 'The Triads of the Island of Britain'.

Occasional citations of Triads are found in the earliest Welsh poetry or *Hengerdd*. But as a whole, the earliest records of the names of the early heroes, and of the Triads in which these are preserved, are found in the poems of the *Gogynfeirdd,* where they are attested from the twelfth century onwards. It is probable that it was about the middle of the twelfth century that the original collections of 'The Triads of the Island of Britain' were first brought together by professional poets, as a convenient means of instructing their pupils in the inheritance of national historical and legendary tradition with which it was their duty to become familiar, to cite in their poetry, and, in their turn, to pass on to their successors. No less than ten of 'The Triads of the Island of Britain' are quoted in 'The Four Branches of the *Mabinogi*' (Williams 1930, xxv), the earliest tales which have come down to us in the *Mabinogion* collection – a further indication of their established traditional status (Bromwich 1996).

The sequence of poems in the mid-thirteenth-century Black Book of Carmarthen (NLW Peniarth MS 1) is briefly interrupted on folio 14 by a short prose fragment of *Trioedd y Meirch*. At this point the last folio of the quire ends, causing the third name of the fourth triad to be lost, together with whatever may have followed it (Evans 1898, 297–8; Jarman 1982, xviii–xix; Williams 1946–7, 42). I append a translation of 'The Triads of the Horses' from the Black Book, since it preserves what may well be the oldest surviving text, even though it is incomplete. (It must be remembered that variant interpretations are possible for several of the horses' names):

Three Horses of Plunder/Plundering Horses (*anreithmarch*) of the Island of Britain: *Carnawlauc* ('Cloven-Hoof'), horse of Owain son of Urien, and *Bucheslum Seri* (?Bucephalos), horse of Gwgawn Gleddyfrudd ('Red Sword'), and *Tauautir Breichir* ('Long Tongue Long Foreleg(s)'), horse of Cadwallon son of Cadfan;

Three Steeds of Burden/Draft Horses (*tom etystir*) of the Island of Britain: *Arwul Melin* ('?Huge Yellow'), horse of Pasgen son of Urien, and *Du Hir Terwenhit* ('Tall Fierce Black'), horse of Selyf son of Cynan Garwyn, and *Drudluid* ('Spirited Grey'), horse of Rhydderch Hael ('the Generous');

Three Sprightly Steeds (*gohoev etystir*) of the Island of Britain: *Gwynev Godvff Hir* ('Long-Necked Chestnut'), horse of Cai, and *Ruthir Ehon Tuth Bleit* ('Fearless Attack[er with] Wolf's Tread'), horse of Gilbert (?son of) Cadgyffro ('Battle-Inciter'), and *Keincaled* ('Fair Hardy'), horse of Gwalchmai;

Three Jaunty Steeds (*hoev etistir*) of the Island of Britain: *Llvagor* ('Host-Splitter'), horse of Caradawg Freichfras, and *Melynlas* ('Pale-Grey'), horse of Caswallawn son of Beli . . .

A fuller, and broadly corresponding version of seven *Trioedd y Meirch* (with the addition of two triads celebrating famous oxen and famous cows) is found in NLW Peniarth MS 16, part iv, which dates from the latter half of the thirteenth century. This version appears to be a copy from an earlier lost manuscript (*TYP* xviii), and its series of Triads of the Horses contains the following (overlapping) additions to the triads in the Black Book (*TYP* nos. 39, 41, 44):

Three Chief Steeds (*pryf edystir*) of the Island of Britain: *Du Hir Tynnedic* ('Tall Fierce Black'), horse of Cynan Garwyn, *Awydavc Breichir* ('Eager Long Foreleg(s)'), horse of Cyhored son of Cynan, and *Rudvreon Tuthvleid* ('Fearless attack[er with] Wolf's Tread'), horse of Gilbert (?son of) Cadgyffro;

Three Lovers' Horses (*gorderchvarch*) of the Island of Britain: *Ferlas* ('Grey Fetlock/Strong Grey'), horse of Dalldaf son of Cunin Cof, and *Rudurych* ('Dappled Roan'), horse of Rhahawd son of Morgant, and *Guelwgan Gohoewgein* ('Silver-White Proud and Fair'), horse of Morfran son of Tegid;

Three Horses who carried the Three Horse-Burdens (*Meir[ch] a dugant y Tri Marchlwyth*):

Du y Moroed[1] ('Black of the Seas'), horse of Elidir Mwynfawr ('the Wealthy'), who carried on his back seven and a half people from Benllech in the North to Benllech in Anglesey. These were the seven people: Elidir Mwynfawr and Eurgain his wife, daughter of Maelgwn Gwynedd, and Gwyn Da Gyfedd ('Good Companion') and Gwyn Da Reiniad ('Good Distributor'), and Mynach ('?Courteous') Nawmon his counsellor, and Prydelaw Menestr ('Cupbearer') his butler, and Arianfagl ('Silver Staff') his servant, and *Gelbeineuin* (?) his cook – who swam with his two hands on the horse's crupper – and that was the half person.

Cornan ('the ?Horned'), the horse of the sons of Eliffer, bore the second Horse-Burden: he carried on his back Gwrgi and Peredur and Dunawd Fwr ('the Stout') and Cynfelyn Drwsgl ('the Clumsy' or '?Leprous'), to look upon the battle-fog of the host of Gwenddolau at Arfderydd. (And no one overtook him but Dinogad son of Cynan Garwyn, [riding] upon the *Kethin Kyflym* ('Swift Roan'), and he won ?censure and dishonour from that day to this.)

Erch ('Dappled'), the horse of the sons of Gwerthfwl Wledig, bore the third Horse-Burden: he carried Gweir and Gleis and Archenad up the hill of Maelawr in Ceredigion in vengeance for their father.

The middle and late fourteenth-century White Book of Rhydderch (NLW Peniarth MSS 4 and 5) and the Red Book of Hergest (Jesus College MS 111) together offer a closely corresponding text of six of the Triads of the Horses, interpolated into the main series of the Triads of the Island of Britain under the separate caption *Trioedd y Meirch yw y rei hynn* ('These are the Triads of the Horses'). But the group which bears this title lacks the extended triad of the Three Horses who carried the Three Horse-Burdens, since this has already been given on a preceding page amongst the general Triads of the Island of Britain – a page which is lacking from the defective copy of the text in the White Book (*TYP* xxiv–xxv). Later manuscript copies of the Triads of the Horses follow one or other of these two main series, either Peniarth 16 (The 'Early Version') or the version of the White Book/Red Book (WR). On several occasions the latter version gives a better text (see further Bromwich 1996, 212–13).

In spite of the later date of the manuscript, some traces of several of these triads, in what may be an earlier form, are to be found in an obscure poem preserved in the fourteenth-century Book of Taliesin (NLW Peniarth MS 2),[2] and entitled by the editor *Canu y Meirch* ('The

Song of the Horses') (Evans 1910, 48; *TYP* xcviii–cii). It is composed in eight short rhyming couplets. As Sir Ifor Williams pointed out (cf. *TYP* xcix–c), the poem begins with an apparent reference to the training or 'breaking-in' of a young horse, followed by six lines which give the names of horses' owners (though not of the horses themselves). These owners are famous heroes, many of whose names are familiar from a variety of traditional Welsh sources. The remaining lines give horses' names, either alone or with the names of their owners. The final allusion to the 'news' or 'report' brought by a horse named Henwyn from Hiraddug (in Flintshire) receives no explanation. I give a tentative translation of the last part of the poem:

Mayawg's horse, Genethawg's horse,
Caradawg's horse – a strong thoroughbred –
Gwythur's horse and Gwa[w]rddur's horse;
Arthur's horse, fearless to give battle.
Taliesin's horse, the horse of Lleu Lledfegin ('Half-raised') (*or* the half-raised horse of Lleu),
And *Pebyrllei* ('Strong Chestnut') the ?dejected, and *Grei* ('Grey'), the horse of Cunin.
Kornan ('the ?Horned') the ?reliable, *Awyd Awydavc* ('Impetuous Vigour'),
Famous *Du Moroed* ('Black of the Seas'), the horse of Brwyn Bron Bradawg ('Wily Breast')
And the Three *Carnawlauc* ('Cloven-Hoofed Ones') – they do not go on a journey to procreate;
Kethin ('Roan'), the horse of Ceidaw, a ?hard hoof on him,
Yscvydurith Yscodic ('Shying Dappled Shoulder'), the horse of Llemenig (*or* ?a leaping horse),
The horse of Rhydderch *Rydic* ('?the Giver') (*or* ?the very wrathful (*rydic*) horse of Rhydderch'), *Llvyt Lliv Elleic* ('Grey Tawny-Colour'),
And *Llamrei ?Llamm Elwic* ('?Swift-Paced, of Surpassing Leap') and *Ffroenuoll Gvirenhic* ('Lively Full-Nostril'),
Sadyrnin's horse, and Custennin's horse,
And others in battle, before a dispirited (*or* ?a foreign land).
Henwyn ('Old White') who brought news from Hiraddug . . .

Canu y Meirch and *Trioedd y Meirch* are virtually unique in medieval Welsh sources by the fact that they give the horses their individual, or 'personal' names, either with or without the names of their owners. The owners of the horses named in the group of triads in the Black Book include two pre-historic legendary British rulers, Caswallawn son of Beli and Caradawg Freichfras; two Arthurian heroes, Cai and Gwalchmai;

three heroes from the 'Old North', Rhydderch Hael and two sons of the famous Urien Rheged, Owain and Pasgen; Selyf son of Cynan Garwyn, who belongs to the ancient dynasty which ruled Powys; Gwgawn Gleddyfrudd and Gilbert (?son of) Cadgyffro, who were both prominent in the early history of Ceredigion, the first in the ninth century, the second in the twelfth. All in all, the list presents a fair section of figures from the early Welsh 'Establishment', whose lives were dispersed over several centuries of the early Middle Ages (*TYP* 263–523).

The horses' names most frequently give their colours – black, grey, yellow, white, dun, dappled, and their physical appearance – *Gwynev Godvff Hir* ('Long-Necked Chestnut'), *Ferlas* ('Grey Fetlock' or 'Strong Grey'), *Tauautir Breichir* ('Long Tongue Long Foreleg(s)'). Less frequent are epithets which describe the horses' characteristics: *Awyd Awydavc* ('Impetuous Vigour'), and *Ruthir Ehon Tuth Bleit* ('Fearless attack[er with] Wolf's Tread'), are highly suggestive, as also are the names of Arthur's mare *Llamrei* ('Swift-Paced') who is known from *Canu y Meirch* and also from the tale of 'Culhwch and Olwen', and Caradawg's *Llvagor* ('Host-Splitter'), another horse known from an external source, as will be seen below. Some of the horses have fabulous characteristics: they are horned (*Kornan*) or cloven-hoofed (*Carnawlauc*); they also swim and carry superhuman burdens. How far these horses' names are in any sense traditional, rather than the inventions of the makers of the Triads, is a difficult question, in view of the scarcity of references to the horses' names outside the Triads themselves. (Such few further allusions as exist will be considered below.) Sporadic witticisms are obvious among the names given to the horses: *Tauautir Breichir, Du Hir Terwenhit* and *Ruthir Ehon Tuth Bleit* are far too long and involved to be credible as real names actually given to horses, and the key epithet *tom etystir* combines the word for manure or dung with the clearly inappropriate 'eddystr' which in all other instances is used to denote a prestigious war-horse. (*Caseg dom* 'a dung mare' is the term used in the Welsh Laws to denote an agricultural draft-horse (see above, p. 69).) Some, at least, of the horses' names are certainly not traditional, but are jokes invented by the redactors of these Triads. Similar witticisms are also very evident in *Canu y Meirch* and in the Triads as a whole.

Throughout all versions of the Triads of the Horses the usual word for horse, *march,* alternates with the far more unusual *eddystr,* an ancient and rare word (from Brythionic *adastrio-* 'steed, colt', *GPC s.v.*), absent from *Canu y Meirch* (though, as pointed out above, p. 52, the plural *edystrawr* is attested once in the *Gododdin* (Williams 1938, 1. 146) and *eddystr* recurs not infrequently in the poetry of the *Cywyddwyr*). As used in these triads, it is clear that no distinction in meaning can properly be drawn between *march* and *eddystr*, since triads which bear the introductory formula *Tri ... edystyr inis pridein* (i.e. all but the first one in the Black Book) in each case follow this description with three horses' names, and then with *march* and the name of each horse's owner. This suggests further that the epithet used in combination with *march* or *eddystr* to introduce the triad, bears no distinctive meaning in relation to the triple group of horses' names which it introduces, but that these epithets merely belong to the generalized complimentary type, designedly imprecise and uninformative, which represents the most archaic type of formula employed for this purpose in *Trioedd Ynys Prydein*. In my translation I have used the word 'steed' to translate *eddystr*, while *march* is literally 'stallion'.

While the names of the horses and their owners usually remain combined in unaltering pairs throughout the three versions of the triads which I have cited, it is plain that these horse-and-owner combinations can be readily transferred from one triad to another which is introduced by a slightly different epithet, and this further emphasizes the non-committal, ambiguous nature of the epithets which most frequently introduce the triads. But there are a few exceptions to this generalization: *Tri Anreithmarch Inis Pridein* ('Three Horses of Plunder/Plundering Horses of the Island of Britain') which opens the Black Book series, is repeated in identical words, naming the same three horses and their owners, in all three of the main versions of 'The Triads of the Horses'. *Tri Anreithvarch* is also one of a group of four triads in Peniarth 16 (*TYP* nos. 38–41) which are exactly paralleled, name-for-name (other than with slight variations in spelling), in both the White Book and the Red. It would seem that all existing texts of *Trioedd y Meirch* are variants of a single archetype.

In the context of 'The Triads of the Horses' it is tempting to suggest that the old word *eddystr* may have fallen together in meaning with the French word *destrier* 'steed' (from Latin *dextrarius*) which it fairly closely resembles. This could have happened, in spite of the fact that the Welsh term *amws* (from Latin *admissarius* 'stallion') is in the law tracts used as the equivalent of Latin *dextrarius* (> *destrier*), a horse which 'was led by the squire's right hand until the knight mounted it to go into battle' (see above, p. 71). The possibility of French semantic influence on *eddystr* gains some support from the name of the Norman lord Gilbert

(?son of) Cadgyffro[3] who is presented as the proud possessor of one of the *tri gohoev etystir* in the third triad in the Black Book. Though the Triads of the Horses are quite likely to be of ancient and primitive origin, it can hardly be concluded that these triads, as they are preserved in manuscripts of the middle and later thirteenth century, can with any probability be regarded as innocent of all external Norman-French influences (see below on *Llvagor* and *Keincaled*; also cf. Jarman 1982, xxix–xxxiii).

In other respects the key epithets which introduce each of the triple groups of horses and their owners show a general similarity to the usual type of unspecific and uninformative epithet, which is used commonly to introduce the triads throughout the major collections. In contrast to this generalized type of 'primitive' introductory key epithet – and presumably a later development – are the expanded triads such as the *Tri Meirch a dugant y Tri Marchlwyth* ('Three Horses who carried the Three Horse-Burdens'), triads which include brief synposes of the stories attached to the names of the traditional heroes, though in nearly all instances the stories themselves have been irretrievably lost. *Tri Meirch a dugant y Tri Marchlwyth* is the only example of the kind to be found among the Triads of the Horses, and it has frequently been regarded as the most interesting of them all.

In place of the usual formula of name + epithet + name of horse's owner, *Tri Meirch a dugant y Tri Marchlwyth* cites three excerpts from stories which evidently reflect the existence of an extensive background of traditional narrative. In the case of the first episode in the triad, the background is the account given in *Breiniau Gwŷr Arfon* ('The Privileges of the Men of Arfon'), an early text of the Welsh laws (*c.* 1200), about a disastrous expedition to Gwynedd made by a certain Elidir Mwynfawr from the 'Old North' to claim the rule of Gwynedd in succession to the famous Maelgwn Gwynedd, in right of his wife Eurgain, who was Maelgwn's daughter (*TYP* 112–13, 51–2; Rowland 1990, 236–7). Of the four horses named in the triad, three appear also in *Canu y Meirch*: *Du y Moroed* ('Black of the Seas'), horse of Elidir Mwynfawr, *Cornan* ('?The Horned'), who belonged to Gwrgi and Peredur, a pair of northern heroes who are known from other sources, and the *Kethin Kyflym* ('Swift or Fierce Roan'). In the triad *Tri Gwyn Dorllwyth Ynys Brydein* ('Three Fair Womb-Burdens of the Island of Britain') (*TYP* no. 70), the horse *Cornan* is said to have been born in a congenital birth with the heroes Gwrgi and Peredur. Their story is evidently closely connected with a saga about the Battle of Arfderydd, a historical event which is recorded in the

Annales Cambriae as having taken place at Arthuret in Cumbria in the year 573, and which was evidently the subject of an elaborate saga which had many overlapping ramifications (*TYP* note to no. 84). One of these recorded the death in the battle of the northern ruler Gwenddolau ap Ceid(i)aw. *Canu y Meirch* names *Kethin* the horse of Ceidaw, and this gives interest to the concluding lines of the *Tri Meirch a dugant y Tri Marchlwyth*, found only in the Red Book version of the triad, and which names *Kethin Kyflym* ('Swift or Fierce Roan') as a horse which was ridden, not by Gwenddolau, but by a certain Dinogad, son of the Powys ruler Cynan Garwyn, to look upon the *mygedorth* or cloud of vapour which rose from the battlefield where Ceid(i)aw's son, Gwenddolau, was slain. Was it because Dinogad rode on the horse *Kethin Kyflym,* which had once belonged to Gwenddolau's father and so perhaps later to Gwenddolau himself, that the triad awards to Dinogad such obloquy and opprobrium?

Du Moroed enwawg ('famous Black of the Seas') is appropriated in *Canu y Meirch* to a different owner, called Brwyn Bron Bradawg (B. 'Wily Breast'). Evidently this was a horse of resounding fame whose name was *Du* ('Black'), but the epithet or owner's name which goes with *Du* differs considerably between the various allusions which are made to him. In the tale of 'Culhwch and Olwen' *Du,* horse of Moro Aerfeddawg ('Battle Ruler'), is listed among the *anoetheu* or 'difficult things' which must be obtained by the hero, in order that *Du* may be ridden by the mysterious Gwyn ap Nudd, and so take part in the hunt for the monstrous boar Twrch Trwyd, which is the central episode in the story (*CO* ll. 717–18n). Clearly the 'Black of the Seas' was a mythical sea-going horse, who has a striking parallel in an Irish tale, evidently of mythological origin, known as *Toruigheacht in Ghilla Dheacair* ('The Pursuit of the *Gilla Deacair*') (O'Grady 1892, II, 292f.) which tells of a mythical water-horse who carried on his back fourteen of the legendary Fionn mac Cumhaill's companions, who were going on a journey to the Otherworld, plus a fifteenth member of Fionn's band who arrived late and was therefore obliged to hang on by the horse's tail. The fame of the story of the 'Black of the Seas' is confirmed by the allusions later made to it by the fifteenth- and sixteenth-century poets Guto'r Glyn and Tudur Aled, who confirm that the Red Book's *Du y Moroed*, rather than any of the variants which appear in other manuscripts, is the authentic form of this horse's name (*TYP* 112–13, 536–7 and below, p. 148). Evidently the 'Black of the Seas' has deep roots in Celtic mythology, and Elidir Mwynfawr was probably by no means his earliest possessor.

The third episode in the *Tri Meirch a dugant y Tri Marchlwyth* belongs to a story from Ceredigion, where *Allt Vaelor* ('the hill of Maelor') is recorded as an earlier name for Pendinas, a hill to the south of Aberystwyth, and in local folklore Maelor was commemorated as the giant whose home was in the Iron Age hill-fort on its summit (Grooms 1993, 197). The horse's name *Erch* 'Dappled' as given in the Red Book text is preferable to Peniarth 16's corrupt form *Heith*.

I return now to the names of some of the horses given in the Black Book triads. The first triad *Tri Anreithmarch Inis Pridein* ('The Three Horses of Plunder/Plundering Horses of the Island of Britain') is the only triad which is actually found in all of the three main versions of *Trioedd y Meirch* (*TYP* no. 40). The same names for the horses and their owners are given in all versions, except that these names sometimes appear in a different order. The name of the horse *Bucheslum* has been compared to that of Alexander's famous horse Bucephalus. This horse appears in *Historia Gruffud vab Kenan* as *Bucefal, march Alexander amperauder* (Evans 1977, 5.11). The Welsh text belongs to the second half of the thirteenth century, and it is therefore of approximately the same age as the Black Book of Carmarthen, according to the findings of modern scholarship (Huws 1993, 19). If the Welsh horse is really to be equated with Alexander's famous Bucephalus of the fourth century BC, (and I quote a suggestion originally made to me by the late Sir Ifor Williams), then the Black Book's *Bucheslum* is probably a secondary borrowing from the *Historia's Bucefal*, or from its lost Latin source. It is significant that *Bucheslvm/Bucheslom* appears in the one and only triad which is found, without variants, in all versions of 'The Triads of the Horses'. Can it be that the 'personal' name recorded as belonging to the world-famous Alexander's horse became the initial inspiration for coining individual names – which are otherwise extremely rare – for the horses named in the Triads as belonging to famous legendary Welsh heroes? The Black Book version of the triad is the only text which appends to *Bucheslum* the obscure epithet *seri*, perhaps denoting some such meaning as 'of the highway' (Williams 1941, 148; 1962, 82). In the default of any more clear-cut explanation, can the epithet have reference to the fame of Alexander's far-flung travels (on his famous war-horse, perhaps)?[4]

The second of the Black Book triads contains the name of *Arwul Melin* ('?Huge Yellow'), the horse of Pasgen son of Urien among *Tri Thom Etystir Inis Pridein* ('The Three Steeds of Burden of the Island of Britain'). Here again we have a horse who is known from an external source, and this time the source is an early Welsh poem. Sir Ifor Williams drew attention to a dialogue poem in the Llywarch Hen cycle relating to a story in which Owain son of Urien Rheged appears to have played a part (though unfortunately his brother Pasgen does not figure in the poem) (Williams 1935, 181; Rowland 1990, 233, 456, 503). The following line appears to be spoken by one of the characters: *Kin ottei eiry hid in aruul melin* ('though snow should fall to [the cruppers of] Arfwl Felyn'). One may infer that the background to the poem is a wintry foraging expedition on which Owain ab Urien is engaged. This seems to be valid, if not very substantial, evidence for the existence of a genuine narrative background as underlying the identity of *Arwul Melin,* the horse named in *Trioedd y Meirch* as belonging to a little-known son of the famous Urien Rheged, who was himself a central figure in early Welsh saga and legend.

The last triad in the Black Book ends with the name of *Melynlas* ('Pale-Grey'), the horse of Caswallawn son of Beli. The owner, Caswallawn, derives his name from that of *Cassivellaunus,* the historical British king who led a confederation of Belgic tribes against the Romans when Julius Caesar made his second, unsuccessful, attempt to invade Britain in the year 54 BC. Sir Ifor Williams (1946–7, 41–3) conjectured that another triad (*TYP* no. 59), though not actually included among the Triads of the Horses, may have a special relevance to a story concerning the horse who is named both here and in the Black Book triad, and that *Melynlas* and *Meinlas* are variant names for a famous horse:

> Three Unfortunate Counsels (*anuat gyghor*) of the Island of Britain: to allow to Julius Caesar and to the men of Rome place for their horses' fore-feet on the land in exchange for *Meinlas* ('Slender Grey'); the second Unfortunate Counsel: to allow Horsa and Hengist and Rhonwen into this Island; and the third: the three-fold division by Arthur of his men with Medrawd at Camlan.

In the other versions of the Black Book triad, *Meinlas,* horse of Caswallawn son of Beli, is one of the *Tri Rodedicuarch* ('Three Bestowed Horses') (*TYP* no. 38). The slight difference between *Melynlas* and *Meinlas* is typical of the kinds of orthographical variants which occur between the horses' names in the different texts of *Trioedd y Meirch,* perhaps the result of long transmission, either orally or in writing. And *Rodedicuarch* certainly seems to be an appropriate enough epithet for this horse, if Sir Ifor's ingenious conjecture is accepted that a story once existed which told how *Meinlas* was 'bestowed' by the Romans on the Britons – no doubt under considerable pressure – in exchange for the permission given to them to land in Britain. The two accompanying items in the triad of the 'Three Unfortunate Counsels' cite two later misfortunes which were remembered equally well by the descendants of the Britons, the permission given to the Saxons to invade the country, and Arthur's last battle at Camlan – two comparisons which served to emphasize the calamitous nature of the alleged permission to land given earlier to the Romans. Tradition had turned the unfortunate horse *Meinlas* (was he a valuable stud horse?) into an innocent object of barter in order to accomplish this exchange.

Two horses who are named in the last two of the Black Book triads have a particular significance in relation to the more general problem of the genesis of these triads, on which they focus our attention. When and under what circumstances were the Triads of the Horses committed to writing, and is the Black Book text a copy, or a first writing down of traditions hitherto preserved solely by oral means? In the fourth and last triad the name of *Llvagor* ('Host-Splitter'), the horse of Caradawg Freichfras, has been preserved intact, as it has in all the other versions of the *Tri Rodedicuarch* (though in the Black Book the triad is given the variant title of *Tri Hoev Etistir* 'Three Jaunty Steeds'). The name of *Llvagor* is well established in the texts of the three main versions of *Trioedd y Meirch*, though he is known in only one instance outside the Triads, as will appear. The second and most significant horse's name is that of *Keincaled* ('Fair Hardy', or perhaps 'Hard Back') (Williams 1935, 100), or even 'Fair Obstinate' or 'Stubborn' (cf. *GPC s.v. caled*), who is named in the third Black Book triad as belonging to Gwalchmai. *Keincaled* is entirely unknown elsewhere, either in the Triads or in any other Welsh source, until we come to a single allusion in a poem by the fourteenth-century poet Casnodyn in which he sends in imagination a horse as a *llatai* ('love-messenger') in greeting to Gwenllian, wife of Sir Gruffudd Llwyd, 'when her husband was in prison', describing it as 'like *Kein Galet . . .* of the nature of *Bugethal*' (= *Bucheslum, Bucefal;* Evans 1911, col. 1239.16–19; Morris-Jones and Parry-Williams 1933, 326.8–11). By this date it seems certain that the poet was drawing on a written text of the Triads of the Horses, most probably that of the Black Book or its original. And Tudur Aled, two centuries later, in a *cywydd gofyn march*, a poem requesting a horse, could still recall that Gwalchmai's horse was famous for his special excellence: 'He is the best of young leapers: look, is he not Gwalchmai's horse?' (Jones 1926,

428.81–2; *TYP* 106). Like Casnodyn, Tudur Aled was surely calling to mind the name of this horse from 'The Triads of the Horses'.

But in view of the scarcity of such later allusions in Welsh literature to the horses named individually in the triads, it is all the more surprising to find that the names of both *Keincaled* and *Llvagor* are to be found in recognizable forms in French poems attested perhaps as much as a century earlier than the Black Book of Carmarthen, poems in which the names of the horses' owners are also recognisable as corresponding to their Welsh forms: *Gauvain* (Gwalchmai) and *Carados Briebras* (Caradog Freichfras). These poems are the late twelfth-century works of Chrétien de Troyes, and a poem by a slightly later unknown poet who composed the 'First Continuation' to Chrétien's unfinished *Conte del Graal*, known as the *Livre de Carados* (Roach 1952, iii. 162). Both *Llvagor*, its several variant forms, and *Keincaled* are meaningless names in French, though both are intelligible in Welsh. *Keincaled* appears in *Érec et Énide* (*c.* 1170), the earliest of Chrétien's poems, as *le Guingalet* (Foerster 1934, ll. 3957, 3967, 4087), the horse who belongs to *Gauvain* (who is invariably Gwalchmai's equivalent, his French *alter ego*).[5] But *Keincaled* is never named in the corresponding Welsh *Mabinogion* tale, 'Geraint': even on the several occasions when Gwalchmai appears in the tale on horseback, the name of his steed is never given. It is easy to believe that *le Guingalet* could have been a corruption by a French story-teller from an earlier **Gwyn Galet* ('Hardy White') in Welsh. But a transference in the first instance in the converse direction, from French into Welsh, is virtually incredible, unless perhaps the French form came in the first instance through an early Welsh or Breton intermediary. *Llvagor* ('Host-Splitter', 'Host-Opener' or 'Host-Anchor') appears as *Lorzagor* or *Loriagor* in the *Livre de Carados* (with further variants in later French sources) (*TYP* note to no. 38). In the *Livre de Carados, Lorzagor* is born in a congenital birth with his owner *Carados Briebras* and with two additional animal companions. Yet it seems incredible that these two horses' names, both found in the Black Book triads, should have become completely obliterated from Welsh tradition, and yet should have come down in medieval French. Taken together, these two names are powerful evidence that early traditions lay behind some, at least, of the names preserved in 'The Triads of the Horses', and that these were transmitted early from Wales or Brittany to France, where they were adopted, directly or indirectly, by Chrétien de Troyes, and by one or more additional tradition-bearers, whose story has come down in the *Livre de Carados*. Any other explanation of these French cognate forms seems incredible.

But, surprisingly, these horses' names were never, as far as we know, brought back into Wales as part of the narrative matter which was reproduced both by Chrétien de Troyes and by the redactor of the corresponding Welsh tale 'Geraint ab Erbin'. Their appearance in the Black Book Triads of the Horses can only be accounted for as one of the several indications of Norman-French influences on this text (cf. below, p. 118n3 on the name Gilbert (?son of) Cadgyffro).

These French survivals are the more remarkable in contrast to the complete absence from 'The Four Branches of the *Mabinogi*' of any of the horses' names belonging to *Trioedd y Meirch*: they are equally absent from the later Welsh tales such as 'The Dream of Rhonabwy', which has many descriptions of horses. But there is one exception to this. In the tale of 'Culhwch and Olwen' horses, hounds and wild boars are all given their distinguishing and individual names, and some of the horses' names re-echo names in *Trioedd y Meirch*. I have already referred to *Du*, horse of Moro Aerfeddawg, as representing the famous horse *Du y Moroed* ('Black of the Seas') of the triad *Tri Meirch a dugant y Tri Marchlwyth*. This horse is specified among the *anoetheu* ('difficult things') which must be obtained by the hero, in order that he may be ridden, not by his mysterious owner, but by the mythical Gwyn ap Nudd, on the occasion of the hunt for the boar Twrch Trwyd. Other named horses in the tale are *Gwyn Mygdwn* ('White Dark Mane or Hacked Mane', *GPC* 2532), horse of Gweddw, evidently another prestigious animal, since he too was among the stipulated *anoetheu*, and was to be ridden by the semi-divine Mabon fab Modron when engaged on the great boar-hunt (*CO* l. 689). Later, Mabon rides *Gwyn Mygdwn* into the Severn, in hot pursuit of the escaping Twrch Trwyd (*CO* l. 1177). And there is also Arthur's mare *Llamrei* ('Swift-Paced') (*CO* ll. 1016, 1225) who is named in *Canu y Meirch*, though it is surprising to find that the name is not found in any text of the Triads. These three horses all play a significant part in one or other of the two great boar-hunts in the tale (the doublet of the hunt for the Twrch Trwyd being that for Ysgithrwyn Benbaedd), though on neither occasion is the horse ridden by his specified owner. In the final episode of 'Culhwch and Olwen' the mare *Llamrei* performs a feat worthy of *Du y Moroed* himself, when she carrries on her back four of Arthur's men, in panic-stricken rout from before the cave of the 'Very Black Witch' (*CO* ll. 1222–5). And there are other horses also named in 'Culhwch and Olwen': *Hengroen* ('Old Skin'), who belonged to Cynwyl Sant, and who is said to have been ridden by him when he was escaping from the Battle of Camlan (*CO* l. 232). Elsewhere the tale incorporates a triad of three horses named as *Call, Kuall* and *Kauall* ('Sharp, Speedy and Horse') (*CO* ll. 336–7, 709). The name Cafall ('Horse'), from Latin *caballus*, is in the story also, inappropriately, bestowed upon Arthur's hound (*CO* pp. 153–4).

One would like to believe that genuine traditional stories lie behind all the names of the horses in *Trioedd y Meirch*, and so it is disappointing to find that so very few of these names have been perpetuated in literary sources, even in contexts where their masters act a part, and where we should most expect to find them named. I have already referred to Casnodyn's citations of the names of *Kein Galed* and *Bugethal*; his younger contemporary Gruffudd ap Maredudd also gives the names of several of these horses, *Kethin Kyflym, Karnaflaw[c], Fferlas* and *Rudvreon Duth Vleid*, in a poem addressed to Gwenhwyfar of Anglesey (Evans 1911, col. 1329.5–10), and Iorwerth Fychan also makes an apparent allusion to this last horse as *Ruth(r)eon* (Andrews *et al.* 1996, 30.26). These are all late thirteenth-century and fourteenth-century references, and all come from *llatai* or love-messenger poems, and I would think that by this date there is little doubt that the poets are quoting the names directly from the Triads of the Horses. An earlier and more problematic allusion is made in an *englyn* which is attributed to Gwilym Rhyfel (*c.* 1170–1220) in a late copy of the version of the Bardic Grammar attributed to Dafydd Ddu of Hiraddug. The text may be translated here from J. E. Caerwyn Williams's edition of the poet's work (Bramley *et al.* 1994, no. 30):

> When you see the brightness of the lady's face, it is rare[ly]
> That you put foot on the ground:
> Lad of the lance, prop of spears,
> Great slender *Gwelwgann Gohoywgein* ('Silver-White Proud
>   and Fair').

This *englyn*, like the poems referred to above, looks as though it is an extract from a *cerdd llatai* in which a horse-messenger is addressed, and we can hardly fail to identify *Gwelwgann Gohoywgein* with the horse of this name in the triad of the *Tri Gorderchvarch* ('Three Lovers' Horses'), not least because it would be difficult to find this identical combination of epithets anywhere else – though this could be merely because our range of reference is limited to the poetry which has fortuitously survived. The point is that the epithets here are used by themselves to denote the horse, without *march, cadfarch, amws, eddystr, gorwydd*, or any noun to complete their meaning. This is entirely in accord with the practice of the *Gogynfeirdd* (see Jones 1915, 20; above, p. 87), and it is exemplified in a significant way in Cynddelw's *llatai* poem to Efa daughter of Madog ap Maredudd, with its repeated greeting to the horse-messenger, beginning *Goruynawc drythyll* ('Eager, spirited [steed]') through successive stanzas (Jones and Parry Owen 1991, no. 5). The origins of this convention are indeed much older, for the use of self-standing epithets denoting the colour and vigour, speed, etc., of horses goes back to the earliest recorded Welsh poetry, being found in the *Gododdin* and elsewhere. As is well recognized, self-standing epithets of this kind for horses, such as *gwelw* ('pale'), *gwineu* ('chestnut'), *llwyd* ('grey'), *melyn* ('yellow'), *llei* ('grey'), *erch* ('dappled'), *myngvras* ('thick-mane') etc., recur several times in the work of the *Gogynfeirdd*, particularly Gwalchmai (Williams *et al.* 1994, 7.125–34), and Hywel ab Owain Gwynedd (Bramley *et al.* 1994, 6.23, 36), and occasionally in that of Llywarch ap Llywelyn (Jones 1991, 24.43), and others. The late G. J. Williams proposed that a knowledge of the contents of the Triads of the Island of Britain formed an essential aid to bardic instruction (Williams and Jones 1934, lxxxviii). This would explain such common linguistic usages as are found alike in the language of the poets and in the Triads of the Horses. The same and similar epithets to these appear in the *Mabinogion* tales (Davies 1995, 140–1), but always preceded by *march*, *cadfarch*, or some other word for horse, thus making a clear distinction between the language proper to prose and to verse (see below, p. 125).

Repeated evocations of the names of heroes from the country's past remained a constant feature of Welsh bardic poetry throughout its long history. Such allusions to early heroes were conveniently supplied for the poets by 'The Triads of the Island of Britain', and the subtitle 'These are the Triads of the Horses' introduces this subsection of *Trioedd Ynys Prydein* in the Red Book of Hergest and in certain later manuscripts. The prestige given by this title to the horses of the famous traditional heroes presents the horses as of status equivalent to that of their masters, and recalls the honourable and important role played by the horse in all aspects of medieval life: for hunting, for message-bearing, for carrying warriors to battle – sometimes, perhaps, even fighting themselves, as is indicated by the description of Arthur's horse Llamrei in *Canu y Meirch* as *ehofyn rodi cur* ('fearless to give battle') (cf. Rowland 1995, 15–18) – as well as for acting in the humbler role of beasts of burden.

Abbreviations

CO   Bromwich and Evans 1992.

GPC   *Geiriadur Prifysgol Cymru: A Dictionary of the Welsh Language* (Cardiff, University of Wales Press, 1950–).

NLW   National Library of Wales manuscript.

TYP   Bromwich 1978.

Notes

[1] This form of the name from the Red Book of Hergest (see below) is substituted for Peniarth 16's *Du Moro*: see further *TYP* 113, 536–7. The sentence in brackets at the end of the triad's second item is supplied by the Red Book (see *TYP* 110), and in the final item, the name *Erch* supplied by the Red Book is preferable to Peniarth 16's corrupt form *Heith* (*TYP* no. 44).

[2] I am indebted to Marged Haycock for allowing me to consult her doctoral thesis (1983) which contains an edition of the poem. I have adopted several of her suggestions for new interpretations of the horses' names in the poem, in place of those proposed previously in *TYP* c–ci.

[3] *Cadgyffro* ('Battle Inciter', cf. Williams *et al.* 1994, 3.23n) in this name seems more likely to be an epithet than a genuine patronymic, as is suggested by the absence of *mab* from the Red Book's text of Triad 24, 'Three Chopping Blocks of Slaughter', another triad which includes *Gilbert (mab) Catgyffro.* Cf. *Englynion y Clyweit* (Haycock, 1994, 331), where *Cadgyffro Hen* ('C. the Old') is named. On Gilbert fitz Richard (Gilbert de Clare, d. 1114), see Lloyd 1937, 426–7; Walker 1990, 38–40 and Griffiths 1994, 322–7. Gilbert was a Norman lord from Clare in Suffolk who was granted the rule of the Marcher lordship of Ceredigion by King Henry I. In 1110 he started to build two castles, one on the site of the later Cardigan, and the other near the mouth of the Ystwyth river. Gilbert's reputation for savagery is reflected by his epithet, as well as by his inclusion in the triad of the three 'Chopping-Blocks'. There is, however, a possibility of confusion between Gilbert's name and that of his son, another Gilbert, who was the father of Richard 'Strongbow', and who died in 1147–8. See *TYP* 360–1.

[4] Evidence for a knowledge of Alexander's story in medieval Wales comes from a poem in the Book of Taliesin and from allusions by the twelfth-century poets Cynddelw Brydydd Mawr and Llywarch ap Llywelyn. On the whole subject, see Haycock 1987.

[5] The use of the French definite article with this name interestingly parallels the Welsh, cf. *y Kethin Kyflym* (*TYP* no. 44). The wide distribution of the variant adapted forms of the name of Gauvain's horse, which are found in a number

of medieval romances in different languages, are outlined in Loomis 1949, 156–9. These include the English fourteenth-century poem *Sir Gawain and the Green Knight*.

References

Andrews, Rhian M. *et al.* (eds.). 1996. *Gwaith Bleddyn Fardd ac eraill o feirdd ail hanner y drydedd ganrif ar ddeg* (Cardiff, University of Wales Press).

Bramley, Kathleen Anne *et al.* (eds.). 1994. *Gwaith Llywelyn Fardd I ac eraill o feirdd y ddeuddegfed ganrif* (Cardiff, University of Wales Press).

Bromwich, Rachel (ed.). 1978. *Trioedd Ynys Prydein: The Welsh Triads,* 2nd edn. (Cardiff, University of Wales Press).

Bromwich, Rachel. 1996. 'Cyfeiriadau Traddodiadol a Chwedlonol y Gogynfeirdd' in *Beirdd a Thywysogion: Barddoniaeth Llys yng Nghymru, Iwerddon a'r Alban,* ed. M. E. Owen and B. F. Roberts (Cardiff and Aberystwyth, University of Wales Press and National Library of Wales), 202–18.

Bromwich, Rachel and Evans, D. Simon (eds.). 1992. *Culhwch and Olwen* (Cardiff, University of Wales Press).

Davies, Sioned. 1995. *Crefft y Cyfarwydd: Astudiaeth o dechnegau naratif yn Y Mabinogion* (Cardiff, University of Wales Press).

Evans, D. Simon (ed.). 1977. *Historia Gruffud vab Kenan* (Cardiff, University of Wales Press).

Evans, J. Gwenogvryn. 1898. *Report on Manuscripts in the Welsh Language,* 2 vols. (London, Historical Manuscripts Commission, 1898–1910).

Evans, J. Gwenogvryn (ed.). 1910. *The Book of Taliesin* (Llanbedrog, J. G. Evans).

Evans, J. Gwenogvryn (ed.). 1911. *The Poetry in the Red Book of Hergest* (Llanbedrog, J. G. Evans).

Foerster, Wendelin. 1934. *Kristian von Troyes: Érec et Énide* (Halle, Max Niemeyer).

Griffiths, R. A. 1994. *Conquerors and Conquered* (Stroud, Alan Sutton)

Grooms, Chris. 1993. *The Giants of Wales: Cewri Cymru* (Lampeter, Lewiston and Queenston, Edwin Mellen Press).

Haycock, Marged. 1983. 'Llyfr Taliesin: astudiaethau ar rai agweddau' (University of Wales Ph.D. thesis).

Haycock, Marged. 1987. '"Some Talk of Alexander and Some of Hercules": Three Early Medieval Poems from the Book of Taliesin', *Cambridge Medieval Celtic Studies,* 13, 8–38.

Haycock, Marged (ed.). 1994. *Blodeugerdd Barddas o Ganu Crefyddol Cynnar* (Cyhoeddiadau Barddas).

Huws, Daniel. 1993. 'Llyfrau Cymraeg 1250–1400', *National Library of Wales Journal,* 28, 1–21.

Jarman, A. O. H. (ed.). 1982. *Llyfr Du Caerfyrddin* (Cardiff, University of Wales Press).

Jones, Elin. M. (ed.). 1991. *Gwaith Llywarch ap Llywelyn 'Prydydd y Moch'* (Cardiff, University of Wales Press).

Jones, Nerys and Parry Owen, Ann (eds.). 1991. *Gwaith Cynddelw Brydydd Mawr I* (Cardiff, University of Wales Press).

Jones, T. Gwynn. 1915. *Rhieingerddi'r Gogynfeirdd* (Denbigh, Gee & Son).

Jones, T. Gwynn (ed.). 1926. *Gwaith Tudur Aled*, 2 vols. (Cardiff, University of Wales Press).

Lloyd, J. E. 1937. *The Story of Ceredigion* (Cardiff, University of Wales Press).

Loomis, R. S. 1949. *Arthurian Tradition and Chrétien de Troyes* (New York, Columbia University Press).

Morris-Jones, John and Parry Williams, T. H. (eds.). 1933. *Llawysgrif Hendregadredd* (Cardiff, University of Wales Press).

O'Grady, Standish Hayes. 1892. *Silva Gadelica I–II* (London, Williams & Norgate).

Roach, W. F. (ed.). 1952. *First Continuation of the Old French Perceval* (Philadelphia, American Philosophical Society).

Rowland, Jenny (ed.). 1990. *Early Welsh Saga Poetry: A Study and Edition of the Englynion* (Cambridge, D. S. Brewer).

Rowland, Jenny. 1995. 'Warfare and Horses in the *Gododdin* and the Problem of Catraeth', *Cambrian Medieval Studies*, 30, 13–40.

Walker, David. 1990. *Medieval Wales* (Cambridge University Press).

Williams, G. J. and Jones, E. J. (eds.). 1934. *Gramadegau'r Penceirddiaid* (Cardiff, University of Wales Press).

Williams, Ifor (ed.). 1930. *Pedeir Keinc y Mabinogi* (Cardiff, University of Wales Press).

Williams, Ifor (ed.). 1935. *Canu Llywarch Hen* (Cardiff, University of Wales Press).

Williams, Ifor (ed.). 1938. *Canu Aneirin*, 2nd edn. (Cardiff, University of Wales Press).

Williams, Ifor. 1941. 'Seri', *Bulletin of the Board of Celtic Studies*, 11, 148–9.

Williams, Ifor. 1946–7. 'Hen Chwedlau', *Transactions of the Honourable Society of Cymmrodorion*, 28–58.

Williams, Ifor. 1962. *Enwau Lleoedd* (Cardiff, University of Wales Press).

Williams, J. E. Caerwyn *et al.* (eds.). 1994. *Gwaith Meilyr Brydydd a'i Ddisgynyddion* (Cardiff, University of Wales Press).

7

Horses in the *Mabinogion*[1]

Sioned Davies

Formal descriptions of the ideal horse have existed since classical times, as reflected in the work of authors such as Varro, Virgil and Palladius. Xenophon's treatise, *Hippike* ('On Horsemanship'), is the most renowned in this context, and is probably the work which has had the greatest influence on European attitudes to horses (Marchant 1934). Xenophon gives advice, among other things, on 'how best to avoid being cheated in buying a horse' (Marchant 1934, 297), and proceeds to list the good (and bad) points of the animal, beginning with the hoofs and working upwards towards the head, a pattern reversed by all later writers. The Welsh, too, had their treatise, the *Llyfr Marchwriaeth* ('Book of Horsemanship') (O'Rahilly 1960), which appears in a sixteenth-century manuscript, NLW Peniarth 86, and seems to be translated in part from *The First (Second, Third) Booke of Cattell* by Leonard Mascall (1587). Here again, the good points of a horse are listed (see below, p. 148), although unlike Xenophon's treatise, no explanation is offered as to why these were considered virtues. This treatise is later than the data under discussion at present, yet it serves to show that the essential features of a good horse remained fairly stable through the centuries.

This chapter offers a survey of the horses in the eleven medieval Welsh prose tales known collectively as the *Mabinogion*. The main focus will be on the descriptions of the horses, although some reference will be made to type and function within the narrative. It must be stressed at the outset that the term *Mabinogion* is almost certainly a scribal error. Nevertheless, due to Lady Charlotte Guest's English translation of the tales in the nineteenth century, it has become a convenient label to describe this corpus of medieval tales, although they should not be perceived as a unified collection of any kind – they all vary in date, authorship, sources, background and content. The eleven tales survive in the Red Book of Hergest (Jesus College MS 111) (*c.* 1400), while ten (some incomplete) are to be found in the White Book of Rhydderch (NLW Peniarth MSS 4 and 5) (*c.* 1350). Fragments also occur in manuscripts earlier by a hundred years or so. The chronology and dating of the tales is problematic, although it is probably safe to assume that they were written down sometime between the end of the eleventh and the beginning of the fourteenth centuries, against a background of vast change in the history of Wales. During this period the Welsh struggled to retain their independence in the face of the Anglo-Norman conquest which ultimately transformed the society, economy and church of Wales (Davies 1987; Walker 1990). As regards content, the tales vary greatly (Mac Cana 1992). Resonances of Celtic mythology are found in 'The Four Branches of the *Mabinogi*', as the author uses traditional material to reinforce his own views regarding proper social conduct. 'Culhwch and Olwen''s dovetailing of two well-known international themes, the Giant's Daughter and the Jealous Stepmother, serves as a framework for a series of independent Arthurian tales in which Arthur, together with warriors such as Cai and Bedwyr, helps Culhwch win his bride. The relationship between 'Owain', 'Peredur' and 'Geraint' (known collectively as 'The Three Romances') and the corresponding metrical romances of Chrétien de Troyes has been a source of much controversy. The Welsh Romances certainly betray foreign influences, yet remain structurally and stylistically within the Welsh narrative tradition. 'The Encounter of Lludd and Llefelys' first appears, in an abbreviated form, in a thirteenth-century translation of Geoffrey of Monmouth's *Historia Regum Britanniae*. The story relates how Lludd overcomes three oppressions that came to Britain, and draws on the same pseudo-historical background as 'The Dream of Maxen'. In his dream, the Roman emperor Maxen (Magnus Maximus) meets a maiden whom he eventually marries, and this is followed by a collection of onomastic tales and an account of the founding of Brittany. A second dream, 'The Dream of Rhonabwy', presents a satirical view of the Arthurian past, and is an extremely sophisticated piece of writing and probably the latest tale of the corpus.

In spite of the differences between these tales, it is fairly certain that, to varying degrees, the authors were drawing on the world of oral story-telling for their narrative techniques as well as for their subject-matter (Davies 1995; forthcoming). However, those stylistic and structural traits that are usually described as 'oral' should not merely be regarded as a residue of the oral past, but as functional within a literate context, for the majority of medieval written texts were composed for *oral* delivery. It could be argued, therefore, that the authors chose to include traditional formulae in their written narratives, they made use of tripartism, of chronological, episodic structure, of verbal repetition, of conjunctive cohesion, not only because they had inherited these techniques from oral tradition, but also because they viewed their texts as performances for a hearing public. It is within such a context that the descriptions of horses should be examined initially, for they are highly formulaic and suggest that we are dealing with an acquired technique. Formulae such as these are an integral part of oral prose narrative, and their presence in medieval written prose texts implies, as with medieval poetry, that formulae 'facilitated the retention, and therefore the reception, of the read or heard written text' (Bäuml 1984, 39). In the *Mabinogion* tales, formulae are used, for example, to open and close tales, to describe physical appearance, fighting, the passing of time, feasting, the approach to a building (Davies 1995, 104–88). Although the descriptions of horses are not numerous, the correspondences between them suggest that the authors were drawing on a well-established narrative technique which could be elaborated or modified to suit particular circumstances.

In some cases, there is a high degree of verbal correspondence between formulae, for example in greetings and oaths. In other cases, identity is established by similar structural patterns and the repetition of key words. Although the data is limited – there are about thirty-six descriptions of horses in the corpus – a basic pattern is discernible:

i.   *ef a welei/nachaf* ('he saw', 'he could see'/'behold');
ii.   personal name/type of character: e.g. Peredur/a rider/woman/ young lad;
iii. *(y) ar* ('on');
iv.   type of horse: e.g. palfrey, war-horse, steed;
v.   adjectives (mainly compound) referring to colour and size/other physical features/pace/spirit.

The following examples reflect this basic pattern:

ef a welei uarchauc . . . y ar uarch erchlas mawr (*PKM* 2)
    ('he could see a horseman . . . on a big dapple-grey steed') (*Mab* 3);

wynt a welynt gwreic ar uarch canwelw mawr aruchel (*PKM* 9)
  ('they could see a lady on a big fine pale white horse') (*Mab* 9);

nachaf varchawc ar varch purdu (*Ow* 9)
  ('lo, a knight on a pure black horse') (*Mab* 161).

There are also two examples of the use of *dan* ('under'), with the focus on the horse, rather than on the rider, which is the construction favoured by the *Cynfeirdd*, for example:

> Meirch mwth myngfras
> O dan forddwyd mygrwas

('Swift long-maned steeds/under the thigh of a handsome youth') (Jarman 1988, 2–3),

and one example of *ar geffyn* ('on the back of'):

ef a welei gwr ar geffyn march coch (*Per* 49)
  ('he could see a man on [the back of] a red horse') (*Mab* 212).

In general, the horse is described as he is seen (*gweld*) by the main protagonist(s), a similar technique to that of describing people, and approaching a court or castle (Davies 1995, 144–58, 176–82). Indeed, this is found to be a common device among oral tellers, and may well be linked to memory processes (Bruford 1981).

The types of horses are varied:

Type (see above, pp. 43–63)	*Tales*						
amws ('steed, war-horse')	PKM	CO					
caduarch ('war-horse, charger')	Ger						
caseg ('mare')	PKM	CO					
ceffyl ('horse')	Per						
ebawl ('foal')	PKM						
ebawluarch ('colt, young horse')	Ger						
gorwydd ('steed, horse')	CO						
gwascwyn ('Gascon horse')	Ow						
palfrei ('palfrey')	Ow	Per	BM				
march ('horse, steed, stallion')	PKM	CO	Ow	Per	Ger	BM	BR

The most common term by far is *march*, of which there are numerous examples in each tale, apart from 'The Encounter of Lludd and Llefelys' which does not contain a single reference to a horse. Although other terms are used, as noted above, the number of examples are very few. The composite form *caduarch* occurs only in 'Geraint', as does the composite *ebawluarch* of which there is only one example. There are Celtic names to the basic biological trio: *march, caseg* and *ebol*. However, it seems that the Welsh began to differentiate between the various types at a later date (Lloyd and Owen 1986, 153–4), and under foreign influence as attested in the borrowings *palfrei* (four examples in all) – 'a fashion word, testifying to the existence of horses serving the purposes of leisure' (Surridge 1984, 249) – and *gwascwyn* (one example), both occurring in the Three Romances. The common Modern Welsh noun for horse, *ceffyl*, is used only in 'Peredur', and clearly does not refer to a quality horse for it is the animal that carries firewood, and brings 'meat and drink from inhabited parts to the desert' (*Mab* 184). The female characters, like many of their male counterparts, ride the *march* and the *palfrei*, so that no horse term is gender-specific, although in 'Geraint' Gwenhwyfar does request 'horses suitable for women to ride' (*Mab* 231).

Whenever horses are described in the tales, then a colour term follows almost without fail. Further adjectives describe the size of the horse, other physical features, pace and finally spirit. This is the formula in its most elaborate form, as reflected best in 'Geraint' (see below, pp. 127–8). Although these further adjectives are not present in every description, nevertheless the general order is usually apparent, while a striking and consistent feature is the use of composite adjectives. The data reveal that, unlike the medieval poets, the prose writers never omit the noun for 'horse' (see above, p. 87). Colour, the most striking and obvious characteristic, is given priority, compare the descriptions of people in the *Mabinogion*, where the type (man, youth, maiden) is invariably followed by hair colour which is often used to identify the character ('the hoary-headed man', 'the yellow-haired youth') rather than a proper name (Davies 1995, 144–58). Indeed, colour is the most consistent feature of the descriptions of horses in the poetry and the triads too, while proper names of horses, as shown by Dr Bromwich (above, p. 107), often consist of a colour epithet. In this the Welsh literary evidence resembles the historical evidence as reflected in the horse rolls and inventories of the medieval period (Davis 1989, 137–8; Ayton 1994, 62). The horse colours themselves are often ambiguous, and must be interpreted with care, as cautioned by Wood (1991) and Geutz who, in his discussion of nomenclature of coat colour, emphasizes that 'words used to describe colour reflect a differing view of the external world from speakers of one language to those of another, even among contemporaries and much more so historically' (1977, 22; see also Bruford 1984). Bearing this in mind, the following references to coat colours are found in the *Mabinogion*:

Simple adjectives	Compound adjectives
du ('black')	*gwineudu* ('dark bay/tawny black')
coch ('reddish-brown, sorrel')	*brychwelw* ('piebald/dapple-grey')
melyn ('light bay')	*canwelw* ('pale white')
gwineu ('bay/chestnut')	*erchlas* ('dapple-grey')
glas ('grey')	*helyglei* ('willow-grey')

Shades of colour are suggested by prefixing *pur* ('pure/bright'), or *gloyw* ('shiny') as in *purdu, purvelyn, purwynn* and *gloywdu*. It could be argued that the uncommon colours – white and black – imply prestige and status for they are unusual and therefore highly sought after – compare twelfth-century England where a palfrey cost between 20*s.* and 30*s.*, 'though a special white palfrey for the papal legate in 1177 cost 33*s.*' (Davis 1989, 83). In some cases the colour may well have a symbolic significance, too, for example the 'pale white horse' of Rhiannon (*Mab* 9). White is often linked with the supernatural in the Four Branches (compare the white boar in the Third Branch, and the white dogs of the king of the Otherworld in the first), while 'fairies riding white horses' is an international motif (Thompson 1932, F241.1.1.1). The colour of Rhiannon's horse may, therefore, have been an indication to a medieval audience of her Otherworld status. (For the possible links between Rhiannon and the horse-goddess Epona, see below, pp. 168–73.)

The second most important characteristic, as reflected in the data, seems to be the size and build of the horse. This is particularly true of the romance horses, reflecting the need for larger, stronger horses to carry armoured knights. There are, of course, practical and psychological reasons why a horse should be *uchel* ('high') and *mawr* ('large'). As emphasized by Jane Ryan (1993, 155), a taller horse is often a faster horse, since he has longer legs while, at the same time, his rider will be looking down on his opponent, thus giving him a psychological advantage. Speed is essential to Pwyll's horse, in the First Branch of the *Mabinogi*, as he tries to overtake Rhiannon (*Mab* 9–11). However, it would seem that in the Romances staying power has become increasingly important, together with an unfaltering, even-paced gait. Some specific gaits are mentioned, middle gaits such as ambling and cantering. The former is a gait which must usually be taught to a horse, and instructions are given in the sixteenth-century Welsh 'Book of Horsemanship' mentioned earlier (O'Rahilly 1960, 149). Spirit seems essential in a horse, and is often conveyed by the movement of the animal, which in turn reflects the hero's own temperament. Pwyll's horse, for example, is described as *drythyll llamsachus* ('mettled and prancing') as he pursues Rhiannon (*Mab* 11), while the adjective *balch* ('proud') often forms part of a compound in the Romance descriptions.

Sometimes specific physical features are emphasized, such as manes of horses in 'Owain':

yd oed balffrei gwineudu a mygen burgoch idaw kyngochet a'r kenn yn barawt gwedy y ystarnu un gyweir. (*Ow* 9)

('there was a tawny-black palfrey with a bright red mane on him, as red as lichen, all saddled ready.') (*Mab* 161)

nachaf vorwyn yn dyfot ar varch gwineu myngrych a'e vwg a gaffei y llawr. (*Ow* 21)

('lo, a maiden coming on a crisp-maned bay horse, and its mane reached to the ground.') (*Mab* 173)

The author of 'Geraint', in particular, stands out in that he uses very elaborate descriptions, based in the main on a long string of compound adjectives, yet adhering to the basic pattern. The examples are worth quoting in full:

ac vynt a welynt uarchawc ar ebawluarch helyglei athrugar y ueint . . . A cherdet yn uchelualch drybelidfraeth gyssonuyr a wnai y march. (*WM* col. 389)

('and they could see a horseman on a young willow-grey charger of immense size. . . . And the horse stepped out high-mettled, brisk and lively, with short even tread.') (*Mab* 231)

Ac vynt a welynt corr yn marchogaeth march ucheldew froynuoll maswehyn cadarndrut . . . Ac yn agos yr corr y gwelynt wreic y ar uarch canwelw telediw a phedestric wastadualch ganthaw . . . Ac yn agos iti hitheu marchawc y ar caduarch mawr tomlyd. Ac arueu trwm gloyw ymdanaw ac am y uarch. (*WM* col. 390) ('and they could see a dwarf riding a big sturdy horse, wide-nostrilled, ground-devouring, strong mettled . . . and near the dwarf they could see a lady on a handsome pale white horse, of proud even pace . . . and near to her a knight on a great mud-stained charger, and heavy shining armour on him and his horse.') (*Mab* 232)

vynt a welynt pymp marchawc awydrut cadarnfer y ar cadueirch cadarndeu eskyrnbraf meswehyn froenuolldrud a dgynder o arueu am y gwyr ac am y meirch. (*WM* cols. 422–3)

('they beheld five knights, impetuous, headstrong and powerful, on chargers strong, thickset, big-boned, ground-devouring, wide-nostrilled and mettled; and armour a-plenty upon the men and upon their horses.') (*Mab* 254–5)

ef a welei vr . . . y ar uarch mawr uchel ymdeithwastat hywedualch. (*WM* col. 433)

('he saw a man . . . on a huge tall even-paced horse, mettled but tractable.') (*Mab* 261)

ef a welei uarchawc . . . y ar catuarch cadarndew kerdetdrut llydangarn bron ehang . . . a dogynder o arueu ymdanaw ac am y uarch. (*WM* col. 434)

('he could see a knight . . . on a powerful stout charger, strong-paced, wide-hoofed and broad-chested . . . and armour a-plenty upon him and his horse.') (*Mab* 262)

ac ef a welei uarchawc allan ar gaduarch froenuoll drud awyduawr eskyrnbraf a chwnsallt deuhanner ymdanaw ac am y uarch. a dgynder o arueu y dan hynny. (*WM* col. 450)

('and he saw a knight outside on a wide-nostrilled, mettled, high-spirited, strong-boned charger, and a cloak in two halves about him and his horse, and armour enough thereunder.') (*Mab* 272)

The attributes conform to the points of a good horse. *Ffroenuoll* ('wide-nostrilled') (Williams 1922) is certainly a virtue; compare Xenophon: 'And wide nostrils afford room for freer breathing than close ones, and at the same time make the horse look fiercer, for when ever a horse is angry with another or gets excited under his rider, he dilates his nostrils' (Marchant 1934, 303). This feature is put to satirical use in the description of the ugly maiden in 'Peredur', who is described as having 'a stub wide-nostrilled nose' (*Mab* 217) rather than the delicate small noses usually attributed to women in literature of the period! The author of 'The Dream of Rhonabwy' perhaps also plays on this particular feature: 'And when the horse breathed forth his breath the men grew distant from him, and when he drew it in they were drawn near to him, right to the horse's chest' (*Mab* 139). In this particular case it is also an international motif, B181.5 (Thompson 1932; Cross 1952), used commonly in the contexts of giants. The detail in 'Geraint' implies that the author had a personal interest in horses, for example, *eskyrnbraf* ('big-boned') – 'The bones of the shanks should be thick, since these are the pillars of the body . . . The arms below the shoulders, as in man, are stronger and better looking if they are thick' (Marchant 1934, 299, 301); *bronehang* ('broad-chested') – 'A chest of some width is better formed both for appearance and for strength, and for carrying the legs well apart without crossing' (Marchant 1934, 301). It should be noted that an additional clause is added to the pattern in 'Geraint', namely a reference to horse-armour. Three of the four references in the above examples use the same verbal combination – *dogynder o arueu ymdanaw ac am y uarch* ('armour a-plenty upon him and his horse'), which is echoed again in 'Owain':

A dyfot a wnaethpwyt a gwascwyn du telediw, a chyfrwy fawyd arnaw, ac a dogyn o arueu gwr a march. (*Ow* 23)

('And a handsome black gascon was brought, with a beechen saddle on him, and arms ample for man and horse.') (*Mab* 176)

'Culhwch and Olwen' has two references to horses that are of particular interest. Arthur's horse, according to this tale, is a *caseg* ('mare'), while the medieval war-horse of the West was almost always a stallion (Davis 1989, 18, 37). Mares were obviously highly valuable for breeding purposes. Does this imply that Arthur was such an excellent warrior that he dared ride a mare into battle? On the other hand, perhaps one should bear in mind the fact that sovereignty among the Celts was often perceived as both equine and feminine, compare Gerald of Wales's report in 1185 where the king of Ulster appears to mate with a 'white mare' (O'Meara 1982, 110). The personal name of Arthur's horse is mentioned – *Llamrei* ('Swift-Paced'). 'Culhwch and Olwen' is the only tale in the corpus to refer to horses' names (see above, pp. 115–16), which is surprising, bearing in mind the evidence in 'The Triads of the Horses' and the poem *Canu y Meirch* ('The Song of the Horses'). The second reference in 'Culhwch and Olwen' is the description of Culhwch and his horse, a passage which functions as 'both a rhetorical digression and as a structural marker' (Roberts 1992, 87):

> Mynet a oruc y mab ar orwyd penlluchlwyt pedwar gayaf gauylgygwng carngragen, a frwyn eur kymibiawc yn y penn. Ac ystrodur eur anllawd y danaw . . . Pedeir tywarchen a ladei pedwar carn y gorwyd, mal pedeir gwennawl yn yr awyr uch y benn, gweitheu uchtaw, gveitheu istaw . . . Gwerth trychan mu o eur gwerthuawr a oed yn y archenat a'e warthafleu (sangharwy), o benn y glun hyt ym blayn y uys. Ni chwyuei ulaen blewyn arnaw rac yscawnhet tuth y gorwyd y danaw yn kyrchu porth llys Arthur. (*CO* 3–4)

> ('Off went the boy on a steed with light-grey head, four winters old, with well-knit fork, shell-hoofed, and a gold tubular bridle-bit in its mouth. And under him a precious gold saddle . . . Four clods the four hoofs of his steed would cut, like four swallows in the air over his head, now before him, now behind him . . . The worth of three hundred kine in precious gold was there in his foot gear and his stirrups, from the top of his thigh to the tip of his toe. Never a hair-tip stirred upon him, so exceeding light his steed's canter under him on his way to the gate of Arthur's court.') (*Mab* 97)

Culhwch's horse is the only animal in the *Mabinogion* referred to as a *gorwydd*, a term rare in medieval Welsh prose, but common in the poetry of the same period (see above, pp. 50–1). Culhwch does not dismount before entering Arthur's court; rather, he makes a violent entry into the hall, as do Cú Chulainn and also his father in Irish literature (*CO* 62). Indeed, Peredur's entry into Arthur's hall *ar geffyl brychwelw yscyrnic* ('on a wan, piebald, bony nag') (*Mab* 186), may be intended as a parody of the scene in 'Culhwch and Olwen', where 'the author's main purpose is to show the boy's ignorance and ingenuity, and to amuse his audience, whereas the author of *Kulhwch* creates an impression of youth, strength, and beauty' (Goetinck 1975, 21–2). The description of Culhwch's horse forms part of a longer description of the archetypal young hero. No details are given regarding Culhwch's own physical appearance – everything is implied through his trappings, his weapons, his dogs, and of course his horse. The horse is young – four winters old – reflecting the hero's own youth and freshness – compare the First Branch of the *Mabinogi*, where Teyrnon breaks in the colt for the youth Pryderi before the end of its fourth year (*Mab* 21). Moreover, Culhwch's horse has strongly jointed hind legs – *gaflgygwng* – and is *carngragen* ('shell-hoofed'), a word not attested anywhere else in Middle Welsh, but found in some later sources, although *carngrwn* ('round-hoofed') occurs in a dialogue poem in the Black Book of Carmarthen (Jarman 1982, 71), and *llydangarn* ('wide-hoofed') in 'Geraint', while the 'Book of Horsemanship' includes 'broad-hollow' hoofs among the traits of an ideal horse. The description ends by emphasizing how light the *gorwydd* is on his feet, an important feature, related to the position of the hoofs, as explained by Xenophon:

> Next you must not fail to notice whether the hoofs are high both in front and behind, or low. For high hoofs have the frog, as it is called, well off the ground; but flat hoofs tread with the strongest and weakest part of the foot simultaneously, like a bow-legged man. (Marchant 1934, 299)

The 'frog' is the soft part in the middle of the horse's hoof, otherwise known as the 'swallow' (*gwennol* in Welsh). This leads one to question the actual meaning of *gwennol* in the comparison: 'Four clods the four hoofs of his steed would cut, like four swallows in the air over his head, now before him, now behind him.' The two greyhounds running alongside Culhwch have already been compared to 'two sea-swallows sporting around him', and it is probably safe to assume that the 'swallows' of the second comparison also refer to the birds. However, is the author playing on the meaning of *gwennol,* or did the swallow in the hoof perhaps encourage him´ to think of the comparison? Yet, the association does occur elsewhere (Cross 1952, K 1872.5.1), for example, in an imaginative treatment of the watchman device in the *Táin*:

> The flock of varied, wonderful, numerous birds which he saw there was the dust of the ground and the surface of the earth which the horses flung up from their feet and their hooves and which rose above them with the driving of the wind. (Sims-Williams, 1977, 93)

It occurs also closer to home, namely in the works of the *Gogynfeirdd* and the *Cywyddwyr* (see above, p. 84, and below, p. 149).

Hitherto, the emphasis in the discussion has been on the verbal and structural parallels between the various descriptions of horses. However, Brynley F. Roberts has argued convincingly that there is a particular rhetorical pattern underlying the description of Culhwch and his horse, a pattern that is also discernible in other prose tales:

gorwydd 'steed', has four compound adjectives, each with the same rhythm of a central stressed syllable flanked by unstressed syllables, *pennllùchlwyt, pedwargàyaf, gauylgy̆gwng, carngràgen.* This oral stylistic device is used throughout the Middle Welsh narrative tradition, not in extended paragraphs as in *Culhwch and Olwen*, but as isolated descriptive phrases where a noun may be accompanied by two or more compound adjectives (or a verb by like adverbs) made up of a monosyllabic and a disyllabic (or even trisyllabic) word which has the same rhythm as the Culhwch passage . . . Under what circumstances an author may decide to use a flourish of adjectives with a single noun is not so obvious, but they occur in *Peredur* and *Geraint* to denote energetic, highly charged movement and emotion, especially therefore with reference to horses, knights, squires, in descriptions of combats, physical or verbal. (1992, 87)

The examples from 'Geraint', quoted above, reflect this stylistic device, as do the following from 'Peredur':

llyma Peredur yn dyuot y'r neuad y mywn ar geffyl brychwelw yscyrnic (*Per* 12)

('lo Peredur coming into the hall on a wan, piebald, bony nag') (*Mab* 186)

Ac ef a welei varchawc yn dyfot y'r porth allan y hela, y ar palfrei gloywdu, ffroenuoll, ymdeithic, a rygig wastatualch, escutlym, ditramgwyd ganthaw. (*Per* 59)

('And he could see a knight coming out to the gate to hunt, on a gleaming-black, wide-nostrilled, easy-paced palfrey, of proud and even tread, fast-stepping and unfaltering.') (*Mab* 219).

Bromwich and Evans argue that 'this rhetorical style bears some resemblance to the elaborate diction of the *Gogynfeirdd*, the court poets of medieval Wales' (*CO* lxxiii). Such a rhetorical prose style reaches its zenith in the *Areithiau Pros* ('The Prose Rhetorics') found in manuscripts from the sixteenth century (Jones 1934; *CO* lxxiii–lxxiv). Indeed, *Araith Wgon* (Jones 1934, 10) contains a direct parody of the description of Culhwch's horse as found in the medieval tale, although Joan Radner would claim that the original is in itself 'a triumph of literary irony' (1988, 49).

Parody and satire are certainly an integral part of 'The Dream of Rhonabwy', probably the only *Mabinogion* tale composed as a written text, and that by a single author from Powys (Lloyd-Morgan 1991; Slotkin 1989). Powys, of course, was famous for its horse-breeding in the Middle Ages, as witnessed, for example, by Gerald of Wales, who emphasizes the 'majestic proportions' and 'incomparable speed' of Powys horses (Thorpe 1978, 201).The descriptions of horses in the tale are unusual, and problematic, for it is uncertain whether they should be taken at face value – one must remember that this is, after all, a dream. Rhonabwy is transported from the twelfth-century Powys of Madog ap Maredudd into the Arthurian world, where the horses are of the strangest colours. Very little attention is devoted to the pace, spirit and physical features of the animals. Rather, the emphasis throughout is on colour. Some colours have a symbolic significance, such as the white and black armies of the men of *Llychlyn* (Scandinavia) and *Denmarc* (Denmark) respectively (*BR* 47). Elsewhere, the interpretation is less straightforward, for example:

Sef y gwelei gwraenc penngrych melyn . . . y ar varch melyn. Ac o penn y dwygoes a thal y deulin y waeret yn las. A pheis o bali melyn am y marchawc, wedy ry wniaw ac adaued glas . . . ac a oed las o wisc y marchawc a'e uarch a oed kyn lasset a deil y ffenitwyd, ac a oed velyn ohonei a oed kyn uelynet a blodeu y banadyl. (*BR* 4)

('He could see a youth with yellow curly hair . . . upon a yellow horse, and from the top of his two legs and the caps of his knees downwards green. And a tunic of yellow brocaded silk about the rider, sewn with green thread . . . And what was green of the rider's and his horse's apparel [or 'of the rider's apparel and his horse'] was as green as the fronds of the fir trees, and what was yellow of it was yellow as the flowers of the broom.') (*Mab* 139)

Ambiguity arises as to whether the colours refer to the horse itself or to its apparel. In each case the horse is closely integrated with his rider, with several references to the *cwnsallt* ('mantle, surcoat, cloak'), often fringed and of two or more colours. Indeed, Mary Giffin (1958) argues that these descriptions have a firm base in reality, and attempts to link them with thirteenth-century heraldry, by placing them beside the roll of horse drawn up for Edward I at the Battle of Falkirk, and the poem the 'Siege of Carlaverock'. On the other hand, as suggested by J. K. Bollard (1980, 159), the precise colour choice or detail might not be of vital importance – this is all part of the author's attempt to parody 'the dramatic, descriptive set-pieces of traditional narrative' (Mac Cana, 1992, 90). This is especially true of the lavish descriptions in the *gwyddbwyll* episode which 'seem to be there for rhetorical display, a display of narrating skill and performance-orientated bravura' (Slotkin 1989, 108). Three descriptions in this section refer to horses, and although they seem complex, they can be seen to follow a definite pattern, echoing the previous descriptions of horses in the tale (Bollard 1980; Davies 1995, 153–6). The first in the trio is described as follows:

A phan edrychant y klywynt marchawc ar varch erchlas yn dyuot attunt. Lliw enryued a oed ar y uarch, yn erchlas, a'r vreich deheu idaw yn purgoch, ac o penn y goesseu hyt y mynwes y garn yn puruelyn idaw. Y marchawc yn gyweir a'e varch o arueu trymyon estronawl. Cwnsallt y varch o'r gorof vlaen idaw y vynyd yn syndal purgoch, ac o'r gorof y waeret yn syndal puruelyn. (*BR* 15)

('And as they looked they could hear a rider coming towards them upon a dapple-grey horse. An exceeding strange colour was upon his horse, dapple-grey and his right leg bright red, and from the top of his legs to the middle of his hoof-horn bright yellow; the rider and his horse arrayed in heavy foreign armour. The housing [surcoat] of his horse from his front saddlebow upwards pure red sendal, and from the saddlebow downwards pure yellow sendal.') (*Mab* 148)

Note the authorial comment in the second sentence, implying that the colours refer to the horse itself and not to apparel. The other two descriptions (*Mab* 149–50) are a variation on this pattern, namely a reference to (a) the main colour of the horse, (b) the colour of the legs, (c) armour, (d) surcoat. The author is not adhering to the pattern found in the other tales but creating his own, based on a traditional system. Such patterned descriptions would be a mnemonic aid in an oral telling of the tale – compare the other variable formulae in the tales (Davies 1995, 143–82). As argued by Ceridwen Lloyd-Morgan (1991, 188), this lends further irony to the colophon which claims that neither bard nor story-teller knew the dream without a book – 'by reason of the number of colours that were on the horses, and all that variety of rare colours both on the arms and their trappings, and on the precious mantles, and the magic stones' (*Mab* 152).

It is apparent, from the discussion hitherto, that armour and accoutrements sometimes form part of the general description of the horse in the *Mabinogion* tales. References include *auwyneu* ('reins'), *cegleu* ('girths'), *coryf* ('saddle-bow, pommel'), *cyfrwy* and *ystrodyr* ('saddle'), *cyfrwy fawyd* ('a beechen saddle'), *ffrwyn* ('bridle'), *pardwgyl* ('hind bow, cantle'), *ystarn* ('harness'), *troelleu yr ysparduneu* ('the rowels of the spurs'). One interesting reference in 'Geraint' differentiates between 'two horses, the one with a man's saddle and the other with a woman's saddle upon it' (*Mab* 266–7). As suggested by Ryan (1993, 165), 'the difference would probably have been in the height of the bows, a man's saddle having high bows to provide security of seat in combat.' The only reference to stirrups (*gwarthafleu* and *sangharwy*) is in 'Culhwch and Olwen' (*CO* 54; Jones 1948), while one example of horse-mail (*lluruc*) occurs in 'The Dream of Rhonabwy', 'and its rings as white as the whitest water-lily, and its rivets red as the reddest blood' (*Mab* 144). Otherwise, the references to horse-armour are non-specific. The care of horses is obviously important. There are several allusions to grooms (*guastrodyon* and *gweisson y meirch*), who are sometimes portrayed as travelling with their lords, as in the Second Branch and 'Owain'. There are also several references to the stabling of horses and to feeding with, for example, *grawn* ('grain') and *yt* ('corn').

The main focus in this chapter has been on the descriptions of the horses in the *Mabinogion* corpus. However, before concluding, some reference should be made to the roles ascribed to horses in the tales. As in the poetry of the period, the horse reflects the dual qualities of the hero himself – both his prowess and his generosity. Horses are often bestowed as a gift or payment, and, of course, the better the horse, the more generous the action. For example, in the First Branch of the *Mabinogi*, horses are exchanged between Pwyll, prince of Dyfed, and Arawn, the king of the Otherworld, as a token of friendship, while in the Romances horses are often given as payment for food and lodging. In the Fourth Branch, horses are exchanged for Pryderi's swine; however, this is a deceptive exchange, for the horses, together with their saddles and bridles, have been made by magic out of toadstools by the magician Gwydion, a common international motif (Thompson 1932, K139.1). An incident central to the Second Branch is the mutilation of the king of Ireland's horses, which leads to Welsh horses being offered as compensation:

> And thereupon he set upon the horses and cut off their lips to the teeth, and their ears to their heads, and their tails to their backs, and wherever he could clutch their eyelids he cut them to the very bone. And he maimed the horses thus till there was no use could be made of the horses. (*Mab* 27)

As suggested by Ryan (1993, 187–8), this episode may well reflect the trade in horses between Wales and Ireland. Matholwch brings horses with him to Wales, supposedly by ship (for discussions of horse transport by ship, see Pryor 1982; Davis 1989, 85). Horse-trade between Wales and Ireland in the Middle Ages is well attested, and British horses are mentioned in Irish accounts of royal wages and tribute lists (Ó Corráin 1972, 58). According to Ó Corráin, British horses were imported to Ireland for breeding before the Norman invasion, and sources show clearly 'that British horses were considered superior and were highly prized'. The mutilation of horses, whereby tails are cut off and manes torn off with the skin in order to humiliate the owner, is found in other cultures too (Thompson 1932, S175); compare, for example, the mutilation of Hrolf's Danish horses by a trouble-maker among the Swedes (Jones 1972, 144). The practice is also attested in the Welsh laws (see above, pp. 73–6), as well as in the late eleventh-century 'Life of St Cadoc' by Lifris of Llancarfan (Wade-Evans 1944, 58). Cadog returns to his monastery one day to find Sawyl Benuchel and his men feasting on his food and drink. He waits until they fall asleep and instructs his monks to 'shave off with the sharpest razors the half part of their beards and hair as an eternal disgrace against them, and also cut off the lips of their horses and their ears as well' (Wade-Evans 1944, 59). As compensation for the mutilation in the Second Branch, the king of Ireland is paid 'a sound horse for each one of those spoiled' (*Mab* 28). These are 'made over to him as long as tamed horses lasted. And then they journeyed with him into another commote, and colts were made over to him until his tally was completed' (*Mab* 29), presumably unbroken colts. As a result of this, the commote was given the name *Talebolion*, interpreted (incorrectly) by the author as meaning 'the payment of the colts' (Mac Cana 1958, 156–8), thus involving horses in an onomastic tale.

Horses are sometimes used in hunting, as in the Romances and 'Culhwch and Olwen', where Ysbaddaden the giant demands specific horses of Culhwch for the hunting of Twrch Trwyth (the wild boar). They are commonly used for transport, and also, of course, for combat. It is outside the scope of this essay to analyse military tactics in the *Mabinogion*. However, some brief comments can be made. There are no references to large-scale mounted battles in the tales, although this may be implied in 'The Dream of Rhonabwy' where there are four references to *bydin* ('troops') carrying standards. Mounted combat between Pwyll and Hafgan occurs in the First Branch of the *Mabinogi*, where Hafgan's shield and armour are broken and he goes 'his spear's length over his horse's crupper to the ground' (*Mab* 6). This passage has implications for the dating of the tale, for some scholars have argued that it implies mounted shock combat which, according to popular view, originated with the Normans. (See Hooker 1995, 89–97 for a detailed analysis of the passage, together with a review of the debate.) In the Three Romances, Anglo-Norman influence is apparent in the references to tournaments and large, strong, armoured horses. Fighting takes the form of single combat between mounted knights, expressed by means of the same formula as in the First Branch (Davies 1995, 159–66; Middleton 1991, 153–5). It is debatable to what extent this was a true reflection of contemporary Welsh fighting techniques – compare the references to warfare in the poetry of the period (above, pp. 88–9). However, the Welsh authors have taken this foreign practice and integrated it into their tales by means of a traditional narrative technique – the formula.

This chapter has focused on the descriptions of horses as a stylistic element within the *Mabinogion* corpus. It has been argued that the Welsh prose writers have an established technique for describing horses – the animal is always closely integrated with his rider, he is identified mainly by colour, while further allusions may refer to size, pace, spirit, and finally armour. Moreover, a combination of compound adjectives is favoured by some authors, resulting in a rhythmic pattern which in itself echoes the movement of the animal. Stylistic and linguistic concerns have obviously been at the core of the discussion. Yet, it is evident that doors have also been opened to wider issues such as the relationship between poets and story-tellers, and the development of military techniques in Wales, reflecting the invaluable contribution of narrative literature to any study of medieval life and society.

Note

[1] My initial reflections on these issues were presented at the Eighth International Congress of Celtic Studies (Swansea, 1987). My latest thinking has benefited from research undertaken by Jane Ryan, under my supervision, and I should like to acknowledge my debt to her.

Abbreviations

BM   Williams 1908.
BR   Richards 1945.
CO   Bromwich and Evans 1992.

Ger	Evans 1973, cols. 385–451.
Mab	Jones and Jones 1949.
Ow	Thomson 1968.
Per	Goetinck 1976.
PKM	Williams 1930.
WM	Evans 1973.

References

Ayton, Andrew. 1994. *Knights and Warhorses: Military Service and the English Aristocracy under Edward III* (Woodbridge, Boydell Press).

Bäuml, F. H. 1984. 'Medieval Texts and the Two Theories of Oral-Formulaic Composition: A Proposal for a Third Theory', *New Literary History*, 16, 31–49.

Bollard, J. K. 1980. 'Traddodiad a Dychan yn *Breuddwyd Rhonabwy*', *Llên Cymru*, 13 (1980–1), 155–63.

Bromwich, Rachel and Evans, D. Simon (eds.). 1992. *Culhwch and Olwen* (Cardiff, University of Wales Press).

Bruford, Alan. 1981. 'Memory, Performance and Structure in Traditional Tale', *ARV: Scandinavian Yearbook of Folklore*, 37, 103–9.

Bruford, Alan. 1984. 'Colour Epithets for Gaelic Chiefs', *Shadow: Journal of the Traditional Cosmology Society*, 1, 14–23.

Cross, T. P. 1952. *Motif-Index of Early Irish Literature* (Bloomington, Indiana University Press).

Davies, R. R. 1987. *Conquest, Coexistence, and Change: Wales 1063–1415* (Oxford University Press).

Davies, Sioned. 1995. *Crefft y Cyfarwydd: Astudiaeth o dechnegau naratif yn Y Mabinogion* (Cardiff, University of Wales Press).

Davies, Sioned. Forthcoming. 'Written Text as Performance: The Implications for Middle Welsh Prose Narratives' in *Literacy in Medieval Celtic Societies*, ed. Huw Pryce (Cambridge University Press).

Davis, R. H. C. 1989. *The Medieval Warhorse. Origin, Development and Redevelopment* (London, Thames & Hudson).

Evans, J. Gwenogvryn (ed.). 1973. *Llyfr Gwyn Rhydderch: y chwedlau a'r rhamantau*, 2nd edn. (Cardiff, University of Wales Press).

Geutz, R. 1977. *Hair Colour in the Horse*, tr. Anthony Dent (London, J. A. Allen).

Giffin, Mary. 1958. 'The Date of the *Dream of Rhonabwy*', *Transactions of the Honourable Society of Cymmrodorion*, 33–40.

Goetinck, Glenys. 1975. *Peredur. A Study of Welsh Tradition in the Grail Legends* (Cardiff, University of Wales Press).

Goetinck, Glenys (ed.). 1976. *Historia Peredur vab Efrawc* (Cardiff, University of Wales Press).

Hooker, Jessica. 1995. 'A Textual Commentary on the First Branch of the Mabinogi' (University of Cambridge Ph.D. thesis).

Jarman, A. O. H. (ed.). 1982. *Llyfr Du Caerfyrddin* (Cardiff, University of Wales Press).

Jarman, A. O. H. (ed.). 1988. *Aneirin: Y Gododdin, Britain's Oldest Heroic Poem* (Llandysul, Gomer Press).

Jones, D. Gwenallt. 1934. *Yr Areithiau Pros* (Cardiff, University of Wales Press).

Jones, Gwyn. 1972. *Kings, Beasts and Heroes* (Oxford University Press).

Jones, Gwyn and Jones, Thomas (trs.). 1949. *The Mabinogion* (London, Dent).

Jones, Thomas. 1948. 'Nodiadau Cymysg: *sangharwy*', *Bulletin of the Board of Celtic Studies* 13 (1948–50), 17–19.

Lloyd, Nesta and Owen, Morfydd E. (eds.). 1986. *Drych yr Oesoedd Canol* (Cardiff, University of Wales Press).

Lloyd-Morgan, Ceridwen. 1991. 'Breuddwyd Rhonabwy and Later Arthurian Literature', in *The Arthur of the Welsh*, ed. Rachel Bromwich *et al.* (Cardiff, University of Wales Press), 183–208.

Mac Cana, P. 1958. *Branwen Daughter of Llŷr* (Cardiff, University of Wales Press).

Mac Cana, P. 1992. *The Mabinogi,* 2nd edn. (Cardiff, University of Wales Press).

Marchant, C. E. (ed. and tr.). 1934. *Xenophon,* 7 vols., Loeb Classical Library (Cambridge, Mass., Harvard University Press, and London, William Heinemann).

Mascall, Leonard. 1587. *The First (Second, Third) Booke of Cattell* (London).

Middleton, Roger. 1991. 'Chwedl Geraint ab Erbin' in *The Arthur of the Welsh*, ed. Rachel Bromwich *et al.* (Cardiff, University of Wales Press), 147–57.

Ó Corráin, Donncha. 1972. *Ireland before the Normans* (Dublin, Gill & Macmillan).

O'Meara, John (tr.). 1982. *The History and Topography of Ireland*, 2nd edn. (Harmondsworth, Penguin Books).

O'Rahilly, Cecile. 1960. 'A Welsh Treatise on Horses', *Celtica*, 5, 145–60.

Pryor, John H. 1982. 'Transportation of Horses by Sea during the Era of the Crusades: 8th C. to 1288 A.D.', *The Mariner's Mirror*, 68, 9–28.

Radner, Joan. 1988. 'Interpreting Irony in Medieval Celtic Narrative: The Case of *Culhwch ac Olwen*', *Cambridge Medieval Celtic Studies*, 16, 41–59.

Richards, Melville (ed.). 1945. *Breuddwyd Rhonabwy* (Cardiff, University of Wales Press).

Roberts, B. F. 1992. *Studies on Middle Welsh Literature* (Lewiston, Queenston and Lampeter, Edwin Mellen).

Ryan, Jane. 1993. 'A Study of Horses in Early and Medieval Welsh Literature, c. 600–c. 1300 A.D.' (University of Wales M.Phil. thesis).

Sims-Williams, Patrick. 1977. 'Riddling Treatment of the "Watchman Device" in *Branwen* and *Togail Bruidne Da Derga*', *Studia Celtica*, 12/13 (1977–8), 83–117.

Slotkin, Edgar. 1989. 'The Fabula, Story, and Text of Breuddwyd Rhonabwy', *Cambridge Medieval Celtic Studies*, 18, 89–111.

Surridge, Marie. 1984. 'Words of Romance Origin in the Four Branches of the Mabinogi and Native Tales', *Études Celtiques*, 21, 239–55.

Thompson, Stith. 1932. *Motif-Index of Folk Literature,* 6 vols. (Bloomington, Indiana University Press, 1932–6).

Thomson, R. L. (ed.). 1968. *Owein or Chwedyl Iarlles y Ffynnawn* (Dublin Institute for Advanced Studies).

Thorpe, Lewis (tr.). 1978. *Gerald of Wales: The Journey through Wales and The Description of Wales* (Harmondsworth, Penguin Books).

Wade-Evans, A. W. (ed. and tr.). 1944. *Vitae Sanctorum Britanniae* (Cardiff, University of Wales Press).

Walker, David. 1990. *Medieval Wales* (Cambridge University Press).

Williams, Ifor (ed.). 1908. *Breuddwyd Maxen* (Bangor, Jarvis & Foster).

Williams, Ifor. 1922. 'Froenuoll', *Bulletin of the Board of Celtic Studies*, 1 (1922–3), 225–7.

Williams, Ifor (ed.). 1930. *Pedeir Keinc y Mabinogi* (Cardiff, University of Wales Press).

Wood, Juliette. 1991. 'Colour in the Mabinogion Tales' in *Colour and Appearance in Folklore*, ed. John Hutchings and Juliette Wood (London, The Folklore Society), 16–21.

8

'Praise lasts longer than a horse': Poems of Request and Thanks for Horses

Bleddyn Owen Huws

Poems by medieval Welsh *cywydd* poets requesting specific gifts (*cywyddau gofyn*) or giving thanks for them (*cywyddau diolch*), form a class of verse which deserves systematic study. In a recent survey of 650 such poems composed between *c.* 1350 and *c.* 1630, I found that 170 poems, over a quarter, were composed to ask for or to give thanks for mares, colts or stallions. The present chapter attempts to describe this substantial body of poems and to draw attention to the more significant and interesting aspects.

This custom of asking and thanking in verse appears to be more developed in Wales than in the other Celtic countries: a larger corpus of poems has survived, and, moreover, the Welsh poets, unlike their counterparts in Ireland and Scotland, offered their services to their patrons, asking and thanking for gifts on their behalf. In the earliest examples of the genre, the poets request gifts for themselves, but from the mid-fifteenth century onwards there is a marked increase in the poems composed on behalf of patrons, reflecting the custom whereby the nobility exchanged gifts, either with their own relatives or with close friends, and commissioned poets to mark the event. Such ritual exchanges strengthened and extended the bonds of family and friendship, and benefited the poets too, enabling them to secure a double measure of patronage by taking a single poem to two noble houses.

The fifteenth century, when the *cywydd gofyn* reached its zenith, was a period of considerable poetic activity. Many poems describe in great detail the noble houses, the buildings themselves and the largesse on offer, especially the delicacies served at feasts. It was this concern with consumer goods of all kinds, manifested most overtly in the asking poems, which Saunders Lewis had in mind when he drew attention to the materialistic ethos of the fifteenth century (Lewis 1932, 119).

By the second half of the century, the structure of the *cywydd gofyn* was comparatively fixed, although the poems were by no means uniform. The *cywydd* would begin by greeting and praising the donor and tracing his noble ancestry before introducing the suppliant, either the poet himself, or the nobleman who had commissioned the request. The gift would then be named and described before concluding with one of a number of standard motifs – usually a promise that the gift would be reciprocated, or else an exhortation to the donor to request a gift in return. The chief literary interest of the poems lies in their descriptions of the gift itself, and the evidence suggests that it was the quality of the description which determined the reception of poems throughout the centuries, and the worth which they were accorded.

In describing material objects of all kinds, the *Cywyddwyr* regularly used the particularly apt technique of *dyfalu* which enabled them to give a very detailed and graphic picture of the gift in question. A typical passage of *dyfalu* would consist of a swift barrage of similes and metaphors, each one following hard on the heels of the other, thereby building up a composite, mosaic-like picture of the object. This prodigal imagery is the distinguishing feature of the *dyfalu* of the early *Cywyddwyr*, but by the end of the fifteenth century the technique is rather more controlled and ordered.

According to Dr Rachel Bromwich, *dyfalu* has its origins in the colourful metaphorical style of invective poetry (Bromwich 1986, 156). Such descriptive rhetoric was exploited brilliantly by Dafydd ap Gwilym to curse various objects which impeded him on his journeys in search of love. Particularly good examples are the *cywyddau* entitled 'The Mist' and 'The Frost' (Parry 1952, nos. 68 and 91), where the images rain down on the objects which are so hateful to the poet. Dr Bromwich notes further (1982, xix) that *dyfalu* is most often used by the early *Cywyddwyr* in vituperative description. It appears that there is only a thin line between negative satirical description and positive praise. The satirical portrait presented by Madog Dwygraig, one of the Later *Gogynfeirdd,* of the disappointing calf he had been given suggests that the same metaphorical skills would be required both for invective and for the type of praise of objects seen in the asking poems (Evans 1911, col. 1278).

From early times, horses had been highly prized by the Welsh. Their importance in society is reflected both by 'The Triads of the Horses' and by 'The Song of the Horses' discussed above by Rachel Bromwich.

Horses could be used in harness for a number of tasks on the land, such as drawing carts, traps and sledges, and they were also ridden for warfare and hunting; but their main use was for transport. Of the *cywyddau* asking for horses studied, just under a quarter were sung by poets requesting a horse for their own use, and this is hardly surprising. A professional poet needed to be mobile in order to make his living; there was not much of a future for a poet who did not have a reliable mount to take him from court to court. NLW Llanstephan MS 188 preserves an interesting story about the fifteenth-century poet, Dafydd Epynt, going on foot on a poetic circuit to Rhwng Gwy a Hafren in mid-Wales. Dafydd ap Hywel, the court poet of Watgyn Fychan of Hergest, took pity on his fellow-poet and gave him not only a horse, but a bridle, spurs and buskins too. Dafydd Epynt in turn sang a *cywydd* thanking him for his generosity (Bowen 1951, 274).

According to one of the recensions of the Welsh Laws, a horse was one of the gifts which a medieval *bardd teulu* ('poet of the retinue') could expect from the king; another was a heavy woollen garment (Wiliam 1960, 10). This accords with the evidence of the requesting and thanking poems: horses and clothes (cloaks or gowns) were the most common items to be bestowed on the poets both in the late Middle Ages and in the early modern period.

In the earliest *cywydd gofyn* extant, Iolo Goch (*c.* 1320–1400), in a poem composed at Easter, asked his friend and chief patron, Ithel ap Robert of Coedymynydd near Caerwys, for a horse to replace his former mount which had died of the staggers (Johnston 1993, no. 12). Interestingly enough, a poem giving thanks for the new horse is also preserved, and it takes the form of a dialogue between the horse and Iolo (Johnston 1993, no. 13). It may well be that Iolo Goch set a new fashion in this poem, for there are at least two later *cywyddau gofyn* composed in the form of a colloquy. This common literary device is apposite in this context: by personifying the horse and giving it the ability to speak, the poet was able to convey the close relationship between man and beast, as well as stressing man's dependence on the horse. In one *cywydd*, Tudur Penllyn (*c.* 1420–85), a poet and nobleman from Llanuwchllyn, tells his horse, *Gwyn Moel* ('Bare White'), that he is planning a poetic circuit to Anglesey and that he wishes to be carried there. But the horse complains that it is lame and half-starved, and that it cannot hope to last the journey. It advises its owner to approach Deio ap Dafydd Goch from Penanlliw in the parish of Llanuwchllyn, where a radiant black horse can be his in exchange for a eulogy (Roberts 1958, no. 17). This entertaining poem was presumably declaimed before an audience at the house of Deio ap Dafydd who then, indeed, rewarded the poet. We see the same framework in a *cywydd* by Siôn Tudur of Dyffryn Clwyd (*c.* 1522–1602) asking Morys Wynn of Gwedir, Llanrwst, for a horse (Roberts 1980, no. 29). The poet orders his horse to carry him to Bishop Richard Davies's palace at Abergwili near Carmarthen, but the horse baulks at the mere thought of the journey, and tells the poet to ask Morys Wynn for a better mount. The proposed trip from north to south Wales is described in more detail (with valuable information on the bardic itinerary through mid-Wales in the sixteenth century) in another *cywydd* by Siôn Tudur which asks in a half-joking, half-mocking way for Sir Thomas Goch's horse (Roberts 1980, no. 124).

Central to the *cywyddau gofyn* is the idea that a praise poem to a patron is equal in value, if not more valuable, than the horse being requested. This point is made in a couplet by Iolo Goch in which he echoes the proverb *Hwy pery clod na golud* ('Fame lasts longer than wealth'):

> Hwy y pery na haearn
> Gwawd na march, gwydn yw fy marn.

('Praise lasts longer than a horse, / [or even] than iron, firm is my judgement.') (Johnston 1993, 12.15–16)

The poem was a commodity which could be traded, and there are plenty of references showing that a poem for a horse was regarded as a fair exchange. Iolo Goch says of Ithel ap Robert's generosity:

> Ardreth dichwith gan Ithael
> Y sydd yn gyflym i'w gael,
> Pensiwn balch, gwalch gwehelyth,
> Diwallu cleirch ar feirch fyth,
> A chael ar bob uchelwyl
> Anrheg a gwahawdd, hawdd hwyl.
> Teilyngorff tawel angerdd,
> Talm a'i gyr, da y tâl am gerdd,
> Rhoddai arian a rhuddaur,
> Marchog wyf, a meirch ac aur.

('Easy profit from Ithel / is readily obtainable for me, / a splendid tribute, hawk of a kindred, / supplying an old man with horses forever, / and getting

144

on every high festival / a gift and an invitation, easy course. / Worthy body
of quiet strength, / many know it, well does he pay for song; / he gave silver
and burnished gold, / I am a horseman, and horses and gold'.) (Johnston
1993, 13.91–100)

By the fourteenth and fifteenth centuries, the relationship between
poet and patron had become closer than ever before, and this intimacy is
evident in the work of poets such as Lewys Glyn Cothi (*c.* 1420–89).
There are three *cywyddau* extant in which he asks various patrons for a
horse for himself, as well as an *awdl* of thanks. *Gorwydd gwâr am gerdd a
gaf* ('I'll get a gentle horse in return for a poem'), says Lewys in a *cywydd*
to one of these patrons before inveighing against lesser itinerants, low-
grade poets who would speed past him on their hackneys and reach the
wedding-feasts while he was obliged to toil along on foot (Johnston
1995, no. 70). It should also be mentioned that there are at least four
cywyddau extant that specifically request riding gear, two of them by
Lewys Glyn Cothi. In one he asks for a saddle and its trappings from
two patrons from Dyffryn Gwy to harness his white horse (Johnston
1995, no. 154), and in the other he asks for a shining new saddle from a
patron from the cantref of Buellt, comparing it to an empty spoon
(Johnston 1995, no. 40). Another prominent fifteenth-century poet,
Dafydd Llwyd of Mathafarn, addressed a *cywydd* to Wiliam ap
Gruffudd ap Robin of Cochwillan near Bangor to thank him for a horse
that he had given him. By composing a poem and sending a servant to
fetch the horse, Dafydd Llwyd shrewdly encourages the donor to saddle
the horse so that his journey would be comfortable:

> Gwell ym Grog y marchogwn
> O rhoi di gyfrwy ar hwn.
> (Richards 1964, 51.53–4)

('I would get a better ride, by the Cross, / if you will put a saddle on its
back.')[1]

Particularly interesting are the reasons given for requesting horses.
Allusions to needing a new one because of theft suggest that horse-
thieves were common in the fifteenth century. Gruffudd ap Llywelyn
Fychan sent a *cywydd* by messenger to his cousin, Tudur ab Ieuan,
asking for a horse and complaining of the 'way horse-thieves abroad at
night stole my three horses' (*y modd yr aeth lladron meirch / yn tramwy*

nos a'm trimeirch) (NLW Mostyn MS 146, 343). And Guto'r Glyn (*c.* 1435–*c.* 1493), one of the most notable fifteenth-century poets, was obliged to compose a plea on behalf of one of his patrons for a new colt to replace the roan which had been seized by a thief. He expresses indignation on behalf of the suppliant: 'I should like to see a noose round the neck of the thieving cur who impoverished me' (*Gwden am ei ben, o'm bodd, / i'r ci lleidr a'm colledodd*) (Williams and Williams 1939, XXII.25–6). It was also common to refer to horses falling ill or dying. Huw Pennant (*fl.* 1565–1619) asked for a horse on behalf of his patron because his had gone blind (NLW MS 832, 29); and Dafydd Benwyn, a Glamorganshire poet active in the second half of the sixteenth century, asked whether he could have one of his patron's nine mountain colts in place of his horse which had died:

> 'Y ngheffyl, myn vy nghyffes,
> oll oedd yn gwnaythyr vy lles:
> mawr yw'n y ol, marw a wnaeth,
> yma herwydd ym hiraeth.
> (Evans 1981, XXXII.47–50)

('My horse, by my troth, / always did its best for me, / great is my grief – he died, / hereafter he has gone.')

One can infer from the references to husbandry in poems requesting mares and stallions that horse-breeding was highly regarded by certain of the nobility. Some poems asking for brood mares promise that the gift will be repaid once the mares have foaled. One of the patrons famed as a horse-breeder was Dafydd ab Owain, abbot of the Cistercian houses of Strata Florida, Ystrad Marchell and Aberconwy, who became bishop of St Asaph in 1503. Five different poets addressed a total of eight poems asking him for a horse, and in a eulogy sung while Dafydd was abbot of Ystrad Marchell, Guto'r Glyn refers to the corn which was grown there for the foddering of the horses (Williams and Williams 1939, CXX.14–15).

Various kinds of horses were requested, as the following list of terms collected from the poems illustrates: *amler* ('ambler'); *caseg* ('mare'); *ceffyl* ('horse'); *cwrser* ('courser or war-horse'); *cwrtal* ('a docked mare'); *ebol* ('colt'); *eddystr* ('pack-horse'); *ffolwer* (a 'follower' or young war-horse); *gelding*; *gorwydd* ('stallion'); *gwasgŵyn* ('a horse or mare from Gascony'); *gwilff* ('a mare or filly'); *gwilog* ('mare'); *hacnai* ('hackney'); *hobi* ('a reasonably sized riding-horse'); *march* ('horse/stallion'); *nag* ('a small horse or pony'); *rownsi* ('pack-horse'); *ystalwyn* ('stallion'). The term *gwasgŵyn* shows that horses were imported from France; and there is an unedited sixteenth-century *cywydd* which asks for a 'hobby from Ireland' (*hobi Iwerddon*) (NLW Peniarth MS 112, 555).

The historical evidence found in these poems more than justifies their study, but we should also acknowledge that they were polished literary productions which demanded of the poet great skill and craft. During the golden age of the *cywydd*, between *c.* 1450 and *c.* 1525, the description of the horse formed the heart of the poem. In a fairly extended passage the poet would paint as detailed a picture as possible, exploiting simile and metaphor in imaginative and often fanciful ways. The technique of *dyfalu*, frequently lively and restless, was well-suited to the describing of an animal as spirited as the horse. The *Cywyddwyr* managed to convey the same delight that modern breeders must feel when they admire the graceful movement of a horse. This visual element is a further distinguishing feature of the Welsh poems of request; it seems that in the poetry of no other Celtic country was there such a detailed picture of the horse. For example, only one short eight-line stanza is given over to the description of the animal in an Irish poem asking Niall Mág Shamhradháin (d. 1363) for a mare, in which the poet is offered a choice of horses from his patron's stud (McKenna 1947, XV.1755–62). And although a poem preserved in the Book of the Dean of Lismore, by the Gaelic poet, Fionnlagh an Bard Ruadh, brings to mind the descriptions of the *Cywyddwyr*, it has little of the figurative language which is the hallmark of *dyfalu* (Watson 1978, XVII).

Medieval Welsh descriptive poetry tended to deal in ideals; in praising an object, it was those features which belonged to the perfect prototype which would be emphasized. There was a core of characteristics regarded as a *sine qua non* in a good horse, and these are listed in the illustration of the *cywydd deuair hirion* in the bardic Grammar attributed to Einion Offeiriad (*c.* 1330) (Williams and Jones 1934); the quotation by an anonymous poet is thought to be drawn from a poem of request or thanks, or possibly from a messenger poem (*cerdd latai*), for it was customary for poets to describe the animal or object which carried the love-message in the fourteenth century:

> Breichfyrf, archgrwnn, byrr y vlew,
> Llyfn, llygatrwth, pedreindew,
> Kyflwyd, kofleit, kyrch amkaff,
> Kyflym, kefnfyrf, karn geugraff,

Kyflawn o galonn a chic,
Kyfliw blodeu'r banadlvric.
(Williams and Jones 1934, 52.16–21)

('Strong of foreleg, round-chested, short-haired, / sleek, keen-eyed, thick-haunched, / victorious darling, greedy for oats, / swift, short-backed, firm and hollow-hoofed, / fulfilled in spirit and in flesh, / one hue with the flower-tips of the broom.') (Bromwich 1986, 152)

The characteristics of the ideal horse as found in the Grammar match those listed in the 'Book of Horsemanship' (*Llyfr Marchwriaeth*) in NLW Peniarth MS 86; according to Cecile O'Rahilly, this text is in part a translation from an English book written by Leonard Mascall and published in London in 1591 (O'Rahilly 1960). The tractate contains much advice on the treatment of various equine complaints as well as on the choice of a horse and its training. Among the characteristics noted are:

i dyraed ol yn wyn, a ffen bychan, kylvsdiav bychain, ffyroenav mawr llydain, llygaid mawr, tal llydan, mwnwgyl addyfain, mw[n]g tenef, dwyfyron lydan laes, gylyniav kvlion, koes lydan, giav tenav mawr ... kefyn byr, asenav hirion . . . llwynav byrion yn ol rrawn hir, keill[i]av bychain, ssafiad ar bedwar karyn pob vn y[n]ghifair i gilvdd. (O'Rahilly 1960, 146)

('His hind-feet white, a small head and ears, large flaring nostrils, big eyes, a broad forehead, a narrow neck, a fine mane, a wide, low chest, narrow shanks, wide in the leg, thin long tendons . . . a short back, long ribs, short loins, long tail, small testicles, standing on four hoofs, each opposite the other.')

The evidence of the *cywyddau gofyn* is further confirmation that these features marked out the perfect horse.

Although the poets tended to portray an ideal, that did not prevent them from specifying the kind of beast they wished for, of a certain colour or temperament or pedigree. Guto'r Glyn, in the poem already mentioned, made an eloquent request for a colt with a known pedigree: *Ucha march ei achau'm Môn* ('The horse with the best pedigree in Anglesey') (Williams and Williams 1939, XXII.51). The poet believed that the colt was descended from the stock of Du'r Moroedd, one of the horses named in 'The Triads of the Horses' (see above, p. 110).

It becomes apparent on reading the poems that the descriptions of horses have recurring features. This is largely to be expected, given the conservative nature of the poetic tradition and the dependence of the poets on available models, and, of course, the fact that they were all describing the same animal. Horses had been portrayed by Welsh poets long before the *Cywyddwyr*, particularly by the *Gogynfeirdd* (1100–1370) in their praise poems, but their descriptions are limited to generalities in comparison with those of their successors. The *Gogynfeirdd* were content to refer briefly to three main qualities – strength, spiritedness and speed (see above, pp. 84–5). Occasionally, they might mention the colour of the horse or pause to dwell on its nostrils, its mane or its ability to jump. Nevertheless, it is possible to see in the *Gogynfeirdd* poems some of the themes which appear in a more developed form in the works of the *Cywyddwyr*, for example, the idea of sods of earth being thrown up by horses' hoofs. Llywarch ap Llywelyn 'Prydydd y Moch' referred to 'Swift horses, the fury of flying sods' (*Mythion feirch, ffwyr tyweirch fforddawl*) (Jones 1991, 1.150), and a similar description occurs in the tale of 'Culhwch and Olwen', where Culhwch's horse threw up four sods 'like four swallows' on the way to Arthur's court (Bromwich and Evans 1992, 3.74–5, and see above, pp. 130–1). The poems of the *Gogynfeirdd* also contain certain adjectives and figures of speech which are regularly used by the *Cywyddwyr*. The *Cywyddwyr*'s most common comparison for horses is with birds; and the stag or hind, also lively and spirited, provides the most frequently used metaphor.

The fifteenth-century poet Owain ap Llywelyn ab y Moel, in one of his *cywyddau* of request for a horse, seems to express an intention to eschew convention:

> ni ddyfalwn hwn yn hydd
> ond yn wennol dan winwydd.
> (Rolant 1984, 5.51–52)

('I would not liken this one to a deer, / but rather to a swallow beneath the vine.')

It is significant that the poet is searching for some latitude within his given framework, but as we see, he is still unable to come up with a very new image. This illustrates the dilemma of a poet working within the confines of a classical tradition and yet striving to introduce a measure of originality. Another feature of these descriptions of horses, which continued down to the sixteenth century, is the constant use as touchstones of the horses ridden by legendary and semi-historical figures, such as Arthur, Oliver, Sir Guy of Warwick and Fulk fitz Warin. The system of *cynghanedd*, with its alliteration and rhyme, led to certain collocations being used over and over again; and further similarities between the work of poets were due to their dependence on a stock of traditional vocabulary which every trained poet would be expected to master. These common adjectives included *braisg* ('stout'), *byrflew* ('smooth-coated'), *cefnfyr* ('short-backed'), *dihafarch* ('brave'), *drythyll* ('spirited'), *llygadrwth* ('gazing'), *pedreindew* ('broad-quartered'), *rhawnllaes* ('long-tailed') and *rhygyngog* ('ambling').

Relevant in this context is the question of whether rhetorical theory influenced the poets' descriptions of horses. Research during the last twenty years has suggested that imported rhetorical techniques had some influence on the *Cywyddwyr*, especially in their descriptions of feminine beauty: Dr Ann Matonis, in particular, has pointed out the correspondences between descriptions in the work of Iolo Goch and Gruffudd Gryg and the topos of the *descriptio pulchritudinis* whereby a set pattern was followed, starting with the head and working down to the feet (Matonis 1976, 108–21). But Welsh scholars have been rather reluctant to accept that the native poets were consciously adhering to detailed rhetorical models. Eurys Rowlands, for example, in his discussion of Iolo Goch's *cywydd*, *I Ferch* ('To a Girl'), thought otherwise:

> Fy marn i yw nad canlyniad uniongyrchol i astudiaeth o rethreg sy'n cyfri am drefn y disgrifio yng nghywydd Iolo Goch, ond mai mater oedd o ymgydnabyddiaeth â syniad llenyddol cyffredinol – fel y gellir heddiw wybod yn amlinellol gyffredinol am syniadau gwyddonol heb astudio'r pynciau fel y cyfryw. (Rowlands 1984, 42–3)

> ('I do not believe that the order of the description in Iolo Goch's *cywydd* derives from the study of rhetoric, but rather that it stemmed from a familiarity with a general literary idea – just as today one can be familiar with the outline of scientific ideas without having actually studied the subjects themselves.')

Although Saunders Lewis stated categorically that rhetoric never formed part of the Welsh poets' curriculum (Lewis 1967, 7), it is difficult to dismiss the possibility that rhetorical handbooks, such as Mathew of Vendôme's *Ars Versificatoria* (*c.* 1175), and Geoffrey of Vinsauf's *Poetria Nova* (*c.* 1210), may have been a source of inspiration, if only because these works had such an influence on medieval descriptive literature in general: as mentioned above, some of the *cywyddau* which describe the beauty of the female body appear to reflect the models contained in these works. The Bardic Grammar acknowledged that animals could feature in poetry, citing amongst other things 'a corporeal living being, such as a man or a creature or a place' (Williams and Jones 1934, 131.16–17); but it did not offer detailed instructions as to the characteristics to be treated, as it did in the case of the nobleman or noblewoman in the section entitled 'How to praise each thing' (Williams and Jones 1934, 132–3). It seems, then, that the poets continued to follow the pattern set by their predecessors; an apprentice would learn from his poetic mentor how to shape a description. This practice would go a long way to explain the similarity found in the poetry between descriptions of the same object. Another consideration which should not be dismissed entirely is that the poets may have appreciated being able to turn to a familiar model because they did not know when they might be commissioned to compose a *cywydd* requesting a horse.

As long ago as 1922, W. J. Gruffydd argued that the *cywydd march* followed a rigid and predetermined pattern. He based his argument on the parallels he saw between descriptions of horses by Gutun Owain (*fl.* 1450–98) and Tudur Aled (*c.* 1465–*c.* 1525):

> Y mae ei ddyfaliad o'r march mor debig [*sic*] i gywydd Tudur Aled ar yr un testun ag i beri inni dybied bod rheolau caethion i 'gywydd march', a bod rhaid disgrifio rhannau arbennig o'r anifail hwnnw mewn ffordd arbennig. (Gruffydd 1922, 62)

> ('His description of the horse is so similar to that in Tudur Aled's *cywydd* that we are led to believe that there were strict rules for the composition of the *cywydd march*, and that one had to describe certain parts of the animal in a certain way.')

In order to reveal the supposed pattern, Gruffydd compared the two descriptions, and indeed a rough pattern can be seen, starting with the horse's head, and moving on to the nostrils, the eyes and the hoofs. But some reorganization of Tudur Aled's couplets was necessary to make them correspond to Gutun Owain's *cywydd*, and therefore it would be misleading to assert that there was a fixed order, or 'strict rules', to use Gruffydd's phrase, to the *cywydd march*. I certainly have found no evidence of it in the *cywyddau* studied. If such rules were laid down, we would expect a poet such as Tudur Aled to adhere to them and to compose every *cywydd* to the same pattern. But he has a poem which begins by describing the tail and mane, without referring at all to the head and nostrils; and another which begins with a description of the hoofs before moving on to the head and the nostrils (Jones 1926, CI, CVII). Both poems are far from uniform in content. When common patterns emerge in the *cywyddau march* they are due to the nature of the animal itself, and the limited number of characteristics which can be mentioned. And when those patterns are ordered in similar ways, this can be attributed to the poets' recourse to reason and instinct.

There is every justification for regarding Tudur Aled as the master and supreme exponent of the *cywydd march*. Twelve of his *cywyddau* of request for horses have survived (one is also attributed to Lewys Môn), together with two poems of thanks, and in these poems the description of the horse is at its finest. He was able to convey its prancing spiritedness in spite of the requirements of metre and *cynghanedd* and the trammels imposed by tradition. One fine *cywydd* requesting a horse on behalf of Llywelyn ap Madog of Llaneurgain from Abbot Dafydd ab Owain incorporates all the familiar motifs and stock descriptions; the high number of copies of this inspired piece (it appears in seventy-six manuscripts) testifies not only to its popularity with copyists but also to its frequent performance. Here follows an extract from that *cywydd* and a translation by Joseph Clancy:

> Hyder Lewis amhadawg –
> Erchi a rhoi march y rhawg;
> A'i ddewis erbyn mis Mai –
> Merch deg a march a'i dygai.
>
> Trem hydd am gywydd a gais,
> Trwynbant, yn troi i'w unbais;
> Ffriw yn dal ffrwyn o daliwn,
> Ffroen y sy gau fal Ffrawns gwn;
> Ffroen arth a chyffro'n ei ên,
> Ffrwyn a ddeil ei ffriw'n ddolen.
> Llygaid fal dwy ellygen
> Llymion byw'n llamu'n ei ben.
> Dwyglust feinion aflonydd,
> Dail saets wrth ei dâl y sydd.

Trwsio fal goleuo glain
Y bu wydrwr ei bedrain.
Ei flew fal sidan newydd,
A'i rawn o liw gwawn y gwŷdd.
Sidan ym mhais ehedydd,
Siamled yn hws am lwdn hydd.

Ail y carw, olwg gorwyllt,
A'i draed yn gwau drwy dân gwyllt.
Dylifo heb ddwylo 'dd oedd,
Neu wau sidan, nes ydoedd.
Ysturio cwrs y daran,
A thuthio pan fynno'n fân;
A bwrw naid i'r wybr a wnâi
Ar hyder yr ehedai.
Cnyw praff yn cnöi priffordd,
Cloch y ffair, ciliwch o'i ffordd!
Sêr neu fellt o'r sarn a fydd
Ar godiad yr egwydydd.
Drythyll ar bedair wyth-hoel,
Gwreichionen yw pen pob hoel.
Dirynnwr fry draw'n y fron,
Deil i'r haul dalau'r hoelion.
Gwreichion a gaid ohonun',
Gwnïwyd wyth bwyth ymhob un.
Ei arial a ddyfalwn
I elain coch ymlaen cŵn.
Yn ei fryd nofio'r ydoedd,
Nwyfol iawn anifail oedd.
O gyrrir draw i'r gweirwellt,
Ni thyr â'i garn wyth o'r gwellt.

Neidiwr dros afon ydoedd,
Naid yr iwrch rhag y neidr oedd.
Wynebai a fynnai fo,
Pe'r trawst, ef a'i praw trosto.
Nid rhaid, er peri neidio,
Dur fyth wrth ei dor efô.
Dan farchog bywiog, di-bŵl,
Ef a wyddiad ei feddwl.

153

Draw os gyrrir dros gaered,
Gorwydd yr arglwydd a red.
Llamwr drud lle mwya'r drain
Llawn ergyd yn Llaneurgain.
(Parry 1983, no. 90, pp. 172–4)

Lewis ap Madog's trustful,
Steed begged and bestowed for long,
Choosing by the month of May
Fair girl and steed to bear her.
A stag's form, for a cywydd,
Dimple-nosed, loose in his skin,
Nose that will hold my bridle,
Wide muzzle like a French gun,
Bear's muzzle, jaw in motion,
Bridle's loop holding his nose.
Keen eyes that are like two pears
In his head lively leaping,
Two slender and twitching ears,
Sage leaves beside his forehead.
A glazier's glossed his crupper
As if he polished a gem,
His skin like silk new-woven,
Hair the hue of gossamer,
Silken robe of a skylark,
Camlet upon a young stag.

Like the deer, his eye frenzied,
His feet weaving through wild fire,
He was spinning without hands,
Weaving of silk, moved nearer.
Pursuing the thunder's path
And trotting when he chooses
He loosed a leap at heaven,
Sure of his power to fly.
Stout colt chewing the highway,
A fair-bell, flee from his path!
Stars from the road or lightning
Whenever his fetlocks lift,
Frisky on thirty-two nails,
Sparks they are, every nailhead,
A spinner on a hilltop,

Holds the nailheads to the sun,
Sparks flash from each one of them,
Each hoof sewn with eight stitches.
His vigour I'd compare to
A red hind before the hounds:
His mind was fixed on floating,
A most lively beast he was;
If driven to the hayfield,
His hoof will not break eight stalks.

He was a river-leaper,
A roebuck's leap from a snake;
He'd face whatever he wished:
If rafter, try to clear it;
There's no need, to make him leap,
For steel against his belly.
With a keen horseman, no clod,
He would know his intention.
If he's sent over a fence,
He will run, the lord's stallion,
Bold jumper where thorns grow thick,
Full of spikes, in Llaneurgain.
(Clancy 1965, 244–5)

Here the descriptions are not piled up at random as in the work of the early *Cywyddwyr*. There appears to be a more ordered movement from one characteristic to the next with the emphasis on a complete picture. The poet deals with each part in turn: nostrils, ears, eyes, coat, tail, legs, hoofs and fetlocks. Note how he makes clear that the feet are 'weaving' before extending the metaphor of 'weaving silk'. The fine detail and the appeal to the senses are what mark out these poems, and by appealing to the literary tastes of the patrons in this way, the poets were able to secure the attractiveness and popularity of the genre.

Later poets mention Tudur Aled's famous *cywydd march* with admiration; he was clearly acknowledged as a master. Richard Cynwal (d. 1634), for example, in requesting a horse from four cousins on behalf of Thomas Johns, states:

Ni chae Aled ni choeliwn
Am i holl wawd mo well hwn.
(BL Add 14979, 199ᵛ)

('I don't believe that Aled would be able to get / a better horse in return for all his verse.')

The many echoes of Tudur Aled's poem in sixteenth-century poems show that it was regarded as a model for the *cywydd march*. It was not his poetic skill alone which enabled him to describe the horse with such mastery. He evidently took a great interest in horses, as is testified by two of the elegies sung to him. According to Huw ap Llywelyn ap Madog, 'he loved horses, he was a friend of the horseman' (*Carai feirch, câr i farchawg*) (Jones 1926, 728.19). This is confirmed by Morys Gethin:

> Canu mwsg fawl ebawlfeirch,
> Cwyraidd ei fodd, carodd feirch.

('Singing the musky praise of colt-horses, / polished in style, he loved horses.') (Jones 1926, 741.17–18)

Consider, too, the poet's own words in thanking Gruffudd Llwyd ab Elisau from Rhagad near Corwen for a gift of a horse:

> Nodais ef, naw deisyfiad,
> Wrth droell ym mherthyd yr iâd;
> Wrth ei lun, wrth ei laned,
> Wrth ei rym, ei werth a red;
> Cnyw o fis cynhaeaf fu,
> Carw o anian yn crynu;
> Cefais ei ddal, cof sydd well,
> Cyn erchi, cenau iyrchell;
> Cei urddas fwy, cerdd sy fau,
> Dra ganwyf draw â genau.
> (Jones 1926, CX.41–50)

('I noticed him, nine desires, / by the curl on his forehead; / by his shape, by his fairness / by his strength, his virtue is his ability to run; / a young animal born at harvest time, / [with] the nature of a spirited stag; / I was allowed to break him in, the best record of all, / before making a request, a young roe-deer; / you will have a greater honour – I have a poem / while a song comes past my lips.')

Cefais ei ddal here shows that Tudur Aled was singing about something which he had experienced for himself. His knowledgeable comments suggest that he had an eye for a horse.

It is apparent that the description of the horse, now well established, was at its most developed in the poetry of the first quarter of the sixteenth century, and just as the Welsh descriptive tradition in general tended to self-parody, so the traditional *cywydd march* itself became an object of parody. This tendency, whereby an idealized and ordered description was parodied by an anti-ideal, is best exemplified by the prose-tale 'The Dream of Rhonabwy', in which Heilyn Goch's house, in all its sorry state, is the antithesis of Arthur's ordered court in the tale 'Culhwch and Olwen' (Richards 1945, 2–3; Bromwich and Evans 1992, 4–5).

Parody can be regarded as a symptom of decay in a literary genre: descriptions become clichéd, and conventions become tired and worn. This is how D. Gwenallt Jones viewed the parodies in the *Areithiau Pros* ('The Prose Rhetorics'): 'Parody arises when a movement goes into decline, when over-familiarity turns to the seeds of decay' (Jones 1934, xiv). Certainly, many of the metaphorical descriptions in the *cywyddau meirch* were old and tired by the sixteenth century; perhaps the description of the horse in poems such as Tudur Aled's was so accomplished that it could not easily be bettered. But it does not follow that parodies of the *cywydd march* necessarily denote the decline of the genre; it may be that some poets were better able to be original in describing the most unpromising beast.

When poets requested horses for their own use, they usually asked for a tame animal which was not too spirited. The aged Lewys Glyn Cothi asked for a slow horse:

> Yn llew main oll y'i mynnwn,
> Yn gawr cryf, neu yn garw crwn,
> Mor deg â'r march mawr ei dad,
> Mor ddof ymy â'r ddafad.
> (Johnston 1995, 143.13–16)

('A slim lion I'd like it to be, / a strong giant, or a rounded stag, / as fair as a horse with a noble sire, / as tame as a sheep for me.')

But the horses in the parodies are far inferior to such tame or slow beasts. At least a dozen true parodies survive. The master of this sub-genre was undoubtedly Robin Clidro (*fl.* 1545–80) of Dyffryn Clwyd, who was harshly criticized by his fellow-poets for his alleged incompetence. Occasional references to him in the manuscripts show that the scribes regarded him as a joke: his description of a horse is unfavourably compared by them with the famous piece by Tudur Aled (Davies 1964, xvii). Robin Clidro created an anti-ideal by turning the usual conventions on their head. He described a limping, pestilential old nag with a thousand and more faults:

> Rhai a ofyn, yn rhyfedd,
> March gwych i ddwyn merch a'i gwedd.
> Minne a 'fynna' it, f'annwyl,
> Farch hen fal biach dan hwyl.
> Ni châr na ffrwyn na chyfrwy,
> Nid â i'r maes i daro mwy;
> A'r erthyl ar ei drithroed,
> Crymanaidd lun, canmlwydd oed;
> Ysgerbwd hen was gargam
> A llun ei goes oll yn gam;
> A'i glustie yn llarpie ar lled,
> À llewygu mae'r llyged.
> . . . Os rhedeg a ddymunwn
> Yn fflwch, cynt yw'r hwch no hwn;
> Od arwain dyn dros y bryn draw,
> Gwae'r ysgwydd fâi'n ei lusgaw;
> Bwch neddog, bychan, eiddil,
> Nid oes le i gath is ei gil.
> Oediog, pryfedog ydyw,
> Cnyw nedd a chwys, afiach yw;
> Tabler brain y tir obry,
> Bwrdd tâl y piod a'u tŷ;
> A chefngribin gethingoch,
> Drewi mae mewn tyrfau moch;
> Ysgwydd bwdwr ac asgwrn
> Glain cefn yn bedere cŵn.
> (Davies 1964, IX.21–32, 45–58)

('Some [people] ask, quite strangely, / for a fine horse suitable to carry a girl. / [But] I ask you, my friend, / for an old horse like a snipe under sail. / It likes neither bridle nor saddle, / it does not go to run in a field any more; / a cripple on his three feet, / the shape of a sickle, a hundred years old; / skeleton of an old hunchbacked servant / and the shape of its leg all bent; / its ears are torn and flat; / and his eyes are drooping. / . . . If I would wish to gallop / swiftly, [I would find] that a sow is faster than this one; / if a man leads [the horse] over the yonder hill, / his shoulder will suffer from having to drag it; / a small, feeble buck with lice, / there isn't room for a cat on its back. / Sluggish and verminous is he, / sweaty with nits – an unhealthy beast; / a tabler for crows on the ground, / a feeding-table and a roost for magpies; / a back like a rake, sore and bruised, / it stinks in the midst of pigs; / a rotten shoulder and bone; / a knobbly back is a rosary for dogs.')

The same inventiveness of imagery and metaphor links the parodies and the non-parodies. Note the apposite description of a reluctant animal, all skin and bone:

> Aradr o Fôn ydyw 'fô,
> Weithie mae'n rhaid ei wthio.
> (Davies 1964, IX.89–90)

('He's a plough from Anglesey, / sometimes you have to push him.')

Why did Robin Clidro take such delight in caricaturing such horses? He can hardly have wanted a scabby beast himself! He is surely sending up the poets' idealized descriptions of horses, but as suggested above, this does not necessarily mean that the genre was in decline. Indeed there is evidence to suggest that the *cywydd march* continued to be a popular genre until the later seventeenth century when patronage dwindled away, and with it many varieties of praise poetry which had been nurtured by the nobility and practised with such skill by generations of professional poets.

Note

[1] Unless otherwise stated, the quotations have been translated by the author.

Abbreviation

NLW   National Library of Wales manuscript

References

Bowen, D. J. 1951. 'Two *Cwrs Clera* Poems', *National Library of Wales Journal*, 6, 274–6.

Bromwich, Rachel (ed.). 1982. *Dafydd ap Gwilym: Poems* (Llandysul, Gomer Press).

Bromwich, Rachel. 1986. *Aspects of the Poetry of Dafydd ap Gwilym: Collected Papers* (Cardiff, University of Wales Press).

Bromwich, Rachel and Evans, D. Simon (eds.). 1992. *Culhwch and Olwen* (Cardiff, University of Wales Press).

Clancy, Joseph P. 1965. *Medieval Welsh Lyrics* (New York, Macmillan).

Davies, Cennard. 1964. 'Robin Clidro a'i ganlynwyr' (University of Wales MA thesis).

Evans, Dafydd H. 1981. 'The Life and Work of Dafydd Benwyn' (University of Oxford D.Phil. thesis).

Evans, J. Gwenogvryn (ed.). 1911. *The Poetry in the Red Book of Hergest* (Llanbedrog, J. G. Evans).

Gruffydd, W. J. 1922. *Llenyddiaeth Cymru, 1450–1600* (Liverpool, Hugh Evans a'i Feibion).

Johnston, Dafydd (ed.). 1993. *Iolo Goch: Poems* (Llandysul, Gomer Press).

Johnston, Dafydd (ed.). 1995. *Gwaith Lewys Glyn Cothi* (Cardiff, University of Wales Press).

Jones, D. Gwenallt. 1934. *Yr Areithiau Pros* (Cardiff, University of Wales Press).

Jones, Elin M. (ed.). 1991. *Gwaith Llywarch ap Llywelyn 'Prydydd y Moch'* (Cardiff, University of Wales Press).

Jones, T. Gwynn (ed.). 1926. *Gwaith Tudur Aled*, 2 vols. (Cardiff, University of Wales Press).

Lewis, Saunders. 1932. *Braslun o Hanes Llenyddiaeth Gymraeg* (Cardiff, University of Wales Press).

Lewis, Saunders. 1967. *Gramadegau'r Penceirddiaid* (Cardiff, University of Wales Press).

Matonis, A. T. E. 1976. 'Medieval Topics and Rhetoric in the Works of the Cywyddwyr' (University of Edinburgh Ph.D. thesis).

McKenna, Lambert (ed.). 1947. *The Book of Magauran* (Dublin Institute for Advanced Studies).

O'Rahilly, Cecile. 1960. 'A Welsh Treatise on Horses', *Celtica*, 5, 145–60.

Parry, Thomas (ed.). 1952. *Gwaith Dafydd ap Gwilym* (Cardiff, University of Wales Press).

Parry, Thomas (ed.). 1983. *The Oxford Book of Welsh Verse*, 6th edn. (Oxford University Press).

Richards, Leslie (ed.). 1964. *Gwaith Dafydd Llwyd o Fathafarn* (Cardiff, University of Wales Press).

Richards, Melville (ed.). 1945. *Breuddwyd Rhonabwy* (Cardiff, University of Wales Press).

Roberts, Enid P. (ed.). 1980. *Gwaith Siôn Tudur*, 2 vols. (Cardiff, University of Wales Press).

Roberts, Thomas (ed.). 1958. *Gwaith Tudur Penllyn ac Ieuan ap Tudur Penllyn* (Cardiff, University of Wales Press).

Rolant, Eurys (ed.). 1984. *Gwaith Owain ap Llywelyn ab y Moel* (Cardiff, University of Wales Press).

Rowlands, Eurys. 1984. 'Canu Serch 1450–1525', *Bulletin of the Board of Celtic Studies*, 31, 31–47.

Watson, W. J. (ed.). 1978. *The Verse from the Book of the Dean of Lismore*, 2nd edn. (Edinburgh, Scottish Academic Press).

Wiliam, A. Rhys (ed.). 1960. *Llyfr Iorwerth* (Cardiff, University of Wales Press).

Williams, G. J. and Jones, E. J. (eds.). 1934. *Gramadegau'r Penceirddiaid* (Cardiff, University of Wales Press).

Williams, J. Llywelyn and Williams, Ifor (eds.). 1939. *Gwaith Guto'r Glyn* (Cardiff, University of Wales Press).

9

The Horse in Welsh Folklore: A Boundary Image in Custom and Narrative

Juliette Wood

Background

A folklorist setting out to study the horse in Welsh folklore might consider Wirt Sikes's economical entry in his *British Goblins: Welsh Folk-lore, Fairy Mythology, Legends and Traditions,* which includes general comment, a reference to the Mari Lwyd and sightings of fairy horses (Sikes 1880, 107). Its very shortcomings illustrate the problems inherent in the topic. The range of material, as to both period and genre, makes it difficult to establish cultural links and meaningful interpretations, particularly when these links are sought in distant cultural origins. So prevalent is the assumption that recent folk traditions and narratives can be traced back to Celtic mythology and social practice that scholars are apt to overlook the relative modernity of this theoretical approach. Interest in links between ancient and modern Celts, at least in relation to their folklore, developed in parallel with more generalized concepts of cultural evolution and universal pre-rational consciousness which were fundamental to the theories of the great cultural synthesists such as James G. Frazer and E. B. Tylor. The ebb and flow of these ideas in the history of anthropological and folklore theory has been well documented (Harris 1968, 142–216; Bennett 1994; Dorson 1968; Bronner 1984). These synthesists saw primitive myth and ritual as essentially a form of sympathetic magic, implying a literal relationship between primitive man and the natural world which this magic was intended to control. Folklore consisted of fragments or survivals of these ancient beliefs and customs found among uneducated or semi-educated subgroups living in modern and, by definition, civilized societies (Spence 1921, 11–13).

The Mari Lwyd in Llangynwyd, c. 1910 (Museum of Welsh Life).

Although this rather naïve cultural evolutionism is still current among popular writers (Hutton 1991), the nature of the connection between the Celtic past and the traditional literature and folklore of modern Celtic cultures, has been reassessed in mythological criticism (Rees and Rees 1961), and more recent archaeological research (Ross 1967). The links between Celtic antiquity and modern Celtic cultures are now usually expressed as continuity of structure and symbolic meaning (Hutton 1991). A feature common to these approaches is the assumption that correlations between past and present are the result of cultural continuity.

In studies of horse traditions in Welsh folklore, models of cultural survival have greatly influenced the analysis of the Mari Lwyd custom and the explanation of the origin of the figure of Rhiannon in 'The Four Branches of the *Mabinogi*'. The Mari Lwyd is the most common name for a dramatic winter custom in which a horse skull draped in a sheet is carried from house to house accompanied by a group of men, one of whom operates the horse. At each house there is a competitive interchange of sung verses between those outside and those inside. The Mari Lwyd's entrance is followed by wassailing, dancing, broad humorous interchanges and sometimes mumming. The figure of Rhiannon appears in two of the Four Branches. Initially Rhiannon is accused of infanticide and forced to sit near a horse-block and offer to carry visitors to court. Later Rhiannon is lured into the Otherworld and forced to wear horse-collars. These associations have suggested to many scholars a link between Rhiannon and a Celtic goddess, Epona.

The intention here is to discuss two examples, one social, the other a narrative tradition, where the model of cultural survival has influenced the analysis of the tradition. The performance of customs and the telling of narratives present complex metaphorical structures which are not easily reduced to one set of meanings. However, the over-emphasis on origins has resulted in perhaps too little balance in understanding these complexities. The primary concern, however, is less with the theoretical difficulties of the established position than with extending our understanding of these traditions and of others in which the horse plays a significant role.

The Mari Lwyd: Custom as Temporal and Social Boundary

The Mari Lwyd custom was well attested throughout south Wales from the eighteenth to the early twentieth centuries and has been recently revived.[1] The dominant academic view suggested that this, as with other mumming customs, originated in a pre-Christian fertility ritual which survived as a folk custom. As such it supposedly retained enough of its earlier function and symbolism for it to be attacked and suppressed by Christian culture (Ifans 1983, 15–30). This essentially nineteenth-century view of cultural development, which views primitive cultural understanding of phenomena as magical rather than rational and necessitates rituals of sympathetic magic rather than complex symbolic systems, has been questioned by scholars in several fields (Vickery 1973; Fontenrose, 1966, 34–5, 50–60; Hutton 1991). Criticism has focused on the assumption that official disapproval of a custom indicates the disquiet of a Christian mentality in the face of a pagan one (Hutton 1991; Newall 1974; Cressy 1989), on the concept of primitive culture (Tambiah 1990), and on interpretation of supposed evidence which forms the basis for linking pre-Christian and modern periods (Cawte 1993).

The Mari Lwyd custom is associated with the Christmas season, in particular Twelfth Night, although there are accounts of it both before and after. This link with a seasonal transition, together with other aspects of practice, suggests that it might be possible to see the custom not as a survival depending on tenuous correlations with antiquity, but as a ritual associated with a liminal period which is fully functional in a more modern context. The complex associations of cultural boundaries have already been identified as important in Celtic cultures (Rees and Rees 1961, 83–94; Gose 1985, 99–104). Anthropology has had a long-standing interest in the ways in which cultures mark change, and the term 'rite of passage' has become common parlance. Interest has focused on the mechanism and attendant symbols by which passage rites are accomplished, especially the period after separation from an old identity and before incorporation into a new one. The anthropologist Victor Turner uses the term 'liminal period' to describe this in-between state which, as a time of maximum vulnerability, is accompanied by rich and varied symbolic behaviour (Turner 1967, 93–111).

Wassailing and even wren-hunting accompany the Mari Lwyd (Owen 1959, 63–9). The provision of food and drink is an important aspect of such customs, especially in rural societies in which food surpluses were not plentiful. Economic and social contexts can be important factors in understanding these customs (Owen 1959, 69). Where, for example, there are reports of Mari Lwyd performances after Christmas, it would be interesting to know if there was a corresponding economic crisis. Unfortunately the search for primitive origins tends to exclude the contemporary context, and this information, where it exists, is frequently omitted.

Iorwerth Peate considered possible origins for the custom, leaning towards a combination of pre-Christian ritual and Marian celebration (Hoggan 1893, 122; Jones 1888), but widened the argument with the inclusion of detailed Welsh material. He focused on the procession elements, on the drinking and on the meaning of Mari Lwyd as 'Grey Mary' (Peate 1943). Procession and drinking are features of celebration too general to convince on their own, and the Mari Lwyd is not associated with times that marked Marian celebrations other than

February. Nor does Peate address the problem of how a pre-Christian horse cult, whose symbolism is more usually masculine, became fused with the Virgin Mary. Peate dismisses the idea that the phrase is actually 'Merry ludus', a solution just as convincing linguistically, and one which does not involve the convolutions needed to create Marian links. Indeed, the links between late medieval social practices, of which the interlude was one, and modern folk customs appear to be very strong (Hutton 1994), while the Mari Lwyd is primarily a Candlemas custom, not associated with other former Marian feasts. Essentially the same argument is presented in a full-length study of wassailing songs (Ifans 1983). The lack of evidence over long periods of time (in this case, centuries between pre-Christian Wales and the earliest notice of the Mari Lwyd at the end of the seventeenth century) has to be accounted for by something more specific than folk memory. The history of certain May customs applies equally to the Mari Lwyd. There is little hard evidence before the end of the eighteenth century, yet only a century later, these customs had been transformed into a threatened heritage, the remnants of pagan custom hundreds of years old (Cawte 1993, 39).

While correlation between early and later customs should not be dismissed entirely, these survivalist models present continuity as basically a linear process with emphasis on the origin point. Evidence for antiquity is often sought in the negative attitudes of churchmen and other officials to the allegedly 'pagan' nature of the rites. Despite the terminology, however, this rhetoric may be directed against potential social unrest rather than pagan survival (Cressy 1989), while contemporary interest in the 'pagan' can be tinged with a disaffection for present cultural circumstances. The introduction to a classic romantic study of Celtic religion describes the Mari Lwyd as the survival of an ancient horse cult. The focus is less on historical circumstances than on a romantic and revivalist view that 'the oral tradition of unlettered country people has preserved elements of the [ancient] religion' whose recovery is important 'when the bankruptcy of popular materialism is becoming apparent' (Raine 1977, xii). The horse is a prominent feature of the custom, and the name Mari Lwyd is usually rendered as 'Grey Mare'. As a recent study of folk revivals points out, these models prioritize certain types of information. The performers are assumed not to understand what they perform, whereas comments from churchmen and public officials are taken at face value (Boyes 1988).

In her analysis of a satirical Christmas carol, 'The Grey Mare', by the Scots poet Dunbar, Priscilla Bawcutt draws attention to similarities with

'Old Horse' folksongs containing humorous allusions to broken-down and useless animals. She compares the poet's use of the horse image as a means to petition his patron in the context of Christmas with the Mari Lwyd as a Christmas custom with a petitioning function (Bawcutt 1986, 388–9). The analysis is both elegant and persuasive, and establishes links in terms of the demands of ceremony rather than ancient ritual. The late Theo Brown put forward the suggestion that Tom Pearce's Grey Mare which becomes a ghost at the end of the famous West Country folksong 'Widdicombe Fair', can be viewed as a boundary image. Brown focused on the horse and its grey colour as having affinities with the Otherworld. Although the article ranges rather too widely in looking at analogues in other cultures, what is interesting is that it retains both the comic and contemporary aspects of the song. She hints that the song may be a comic version, rather than a direct survival, of the Wild Hunt without suggesting ancient rituals, either Christianized or corrupted by time (Brown 1993).

Boundary imagery provides an important nexus for the Mari Lwyd custom. It is associated with an interstitial period: Christmas, Twelfth Night and Candlemas. The aim of the poetic interchange is 'getting across a threshold'. The agonistic nature of the singing, a challenge and response between those inside and those outside, produces a rhetorical tension and creates a verbal boundary which dissolves with the resolution of the rhyme. Hugh Hughes described a nineteenth-century hybrid between wassail and Mari Lwyd which took place on Twelfth Night at the house of a newly married couple or a family which had recently moved (Owen 1959, 58–9). While this may not have been general practice, it illustrates that the custom could provide a traditional context for the integration of outsiders or for reaffirmation of the status of insiders within fixed parameters.

Instances like this suggest that the Mari Lwyd may possess qualities of passage rites as defined by anthropologists (Turner 1967, 93–8). Typically this kind of ritual first articulates the existence of a boundary, thereby marking the difference between those within the group and 'others'. The outsiders are initially caught in a liminal state. As transitional beings they often exhibit specific behaviours or are marked by special symbols. In the Mari Lwyd, conventional names mask the revellers' identities, while the white/grey colour spectrum indicates the supernatural. Crossing the boundary is marked by celebration, the entrance of the Mari Lwyd is followed by feasting, drinking and clowning. This paradoxically reaffirms the integrity of the boundary and the safety of the group shielded by it. The horse appears to be the agent which can cross the interstice. It gives its name to the custom in parts of Wales, for example: *Pen Ceffyl* ('Horse's Head') in Gower and *Y March* ('The Horse') or *Y Gynfasfarch* ('The Canvas Horse') in Pembrokeshire (Owen 1959, 49), and, as the draped horse's skull, is the most recognizable sign of the custom.[2]

Rhiannon and Epona

The concept of liminality can add a dimension to understanding Rhiannon's function in the medieval prose tales, 'The Four Branches of the *Mabinogi*'. Her punishment for alleged infanticide is to tell her story at a horse-block and offer to carry visitors to the hall. The son is raised by the man who rescues him when a supernatural being attempts to steal his foal. In the Third Branch, mother and son are trapped in the Otherworld. Rhiannon is condemned to wear horse-collars, and her son blacksmith's hammers. This material is usually seen in the context of surviving Celtic myth about a horse goddess, Epona, although nothing is known directly of such a myth. Equine associations apart, the accusations of infanticide and persecution parallel the dilemma of the Calumniated Wife in folk-tales where the heroine's status as queen, wife and mother is jeopardized and she becomes marginalized. The supernatural being who punishes Rhiannon implies that his antagonism stems from actions prior to her first marriage. His role parallels some of the Calumniated Wife tales in which a supernatural antagonist torments the heroine.

The Calumniated Wife episode occurs in a number of tale-types;[3] however, the existence of a persecuted-heroine sub-genre of Märchen tales has been suggested (Jones 1993, 13–14 n. 1), one whose main theme concerns the maturation of a female protagonist. The coincidence in the way that the acts and episodes of the tales use symbols can reveal their thematic preoccupation, here maturation (Jones 1993, 23). The parameters in the sub-genre are broader than the Calumniated Wife episode on its own, taking in events which drive the girl from home, surround her marriage and beset her as wife and mother. This presents the Calumniated Wife material as more than a series of motifs. It sets out structural and thematic patterns found in a number of tales and opens the way to answering questions of meaning and motivation which identifying myth as source leaves unanswered.

In his study of the socio-cultural aspects of ritual, Victor Turner characterized the liminal period as a special structure within the interrelating positions which constitute a society. It functions as a microcosm of the larger social order in which relationships can be mixed and rematched because ritual's function is the reintegration of social structure. Ritual passage affects society as a whole, not just one person. The individual adjusts to a new identity and society accommodates this new role through the internally timeless, but externally defined, period which is the ritual (Turner 1967, 7, 27–9, 93–5). Both narrative and ritual share apparently conflicting qualities of timelessness and definition. On a narrative level, Rhiannon is caught between her position as supernatural maiden/earthly wife and wife/mother, a situation initiated by the accusation of barrenness, brought to a crisis with the implication of infanticide and resolved with the restoration of her son. Later, her wifely role, heeding her husband's warning, conflicts with her motherly impulse to protect her son. Morfydd E. Owen highlights the vulnerability of a woman's legal position in marriage where she risks being caught between her own family and her husband's kin (Owen 1980). Recent criticism of the persecuted heroine sub-genre also focuses on maturation as an important theme (Bacchilega 1993, 9–10; Jones 1993; Nicolaisen 1993, 61–7; Perco 1993).

Earlier criticism of 'The Four Branches of the *Mabinogi*' suggested a heroic context in which the original narratives were Welsh versions of *compert* stories about a young male hero. The key to understanding these tales was the character of the hero and an idea of myth in decline which characterized so much romantic theorizing. W. J. Gruffydd suggested that Rhiannon was a reflex of the horse goddess Epona, whose myth (freely reconstructed by him) became corrupted into a late folk-tale (Gruffydd 1953, 103–10). Although the reconstruction has been questioned, the link between Rhiannon and Epona continues to be accepted on linguistic grounds, backed up by archaeology (Mac Cana 1970, 55, 83; Ross 1967, 227, 267–8, 326–7). Kenneth Jackson had reservations about the horse-goddess link (1961, 92 n. 77). His work on the folk-tale genre in early Welsh narrative suggested new interpretations to replace Gruffydd's romantic speculations through the use of then current theories of tale-analysis.

Work by Rachel Bromwich (1961), Marie-Louise Sjoestedt (1949) and Roberta Valente (1988) shifts the focus to the female characters. This can, however, lead back to a concept of myth in decline, with a goddess rather than a hero providing a focal point (Gimbutas 1982). While this produces interesting metaphorical readings of the text as a cognitive description of culture, it retains many of the problems of earlier evolutionary models (Wood 1992). Some of the middle ground opened up by Jackson, however, enables us to see the female figures, not as the accoutrements of a heroic world or as the focus of a lost goddess culture, but as figures carrying layers of meaning whose functions within the narrative structures carry a significance comprehensible to audiences contemporary with the tales and to those of today. Interest in folk-tales with female protagonists has demonstrated the complexity of the 'Innocent Persecuted Heroine Folktale' (Jason 1982; Dan 1977; Bacchilega and Jones 1993), and its ability to reflect conflicting social norms about gender roles within the framework of the social order (Bacchilega 1993, 7–8; Nicolaisen 1993, 68–9)

Riding a mysterious white horse, Rhiannon approaches Pwyll and declares her love. He defeats a rival and they marry, but she fails to produce children. Pwyll's loyalty, against the advice of his courtiers, appears justified when Rhiannon has a son. The child disappears and the mother is forced to sit near the horse-block and offer to carry visitors to court. Pwyll's actions towards his wife remain courteous (Owen 1980), the missing son, Pryderi, returns and her status is restored. After the widowed Rhiannon remarries, Pryderi is lured into the Otherworld and his mother impulsively rushes after him. Her new husband secures their release and is told by their captor that as a punishment Rhiannon wore horse-collars and Pryderi hammers. Indeed, it is from this that the story takes its name *Mabinogi Mynweir a Mynordd*.

Rhiannon's name is derived from *Rigantona*, meaning 'Great Queen'. The suffix indicates a deity. Epona contains the same deity element plus the word for horse. The connection between the two has been made so often that it has become perhaps too readily accepted. This may be due in part to a perceived relationship between myth and folk-tale. Kenneth Jackson cautioned against applying the term 'myth' to material which could also be found in international narrative (Jackson 1961, 47–51). The term 'myth' carries a positive emotional impact in Celtic studies, but its use can be imprecise and even misleading. Scholars continue to debate the relationship between the genres of myth and Märchen. If myth is viewed essentially as a sacred narrative, primary in time to folk-tales, then it is easy to see tales such as the Four Branches as de-sacralized narratives which still convey some of the symbolic force of myth. This was the view of Mircea Eliade, who has been an important influence on critics working with literary folk-tales such as are found in the

Mabinogion (Zipes 1994, 1–16). However, other scholars have presented analyses in which folk narrative represents a continuum of material in which myth, wonder tale and legend all draw on the same set of themes and motifs, and boundaries between genres are not quite so clear-cut (Röhrich 1991; Jason 1982, 1–2).

Epona is known only from iconography and inscriptions. Her cult was popular in Britain, although she is not a universal Celtic figure by any means (see above, pp. 11–14). The iconography is consistent in depicting her as a mature woman seated on the back of a horse or with a horse nearby. She rides sideways without tackle, is often accompanied by a foal, and frequently feeds the animal from a dish or cornucopia. The overall iconographic impression is serene. The circumstances which link Rhiannon and horses are quite different: the horse is associated with punishment both in the court and in the Otherworld.

The divine associations in the Four Branches derive from her name and those of several characters associated with her: Teyrnon (*Tigernonos,* 'Great or Divine Lord') and Manawydan, the Welsh cognate of the sea-god *Mannánan mac Lir* (Mac Cana 1970, 79–83). The close pairing of mother and son suggests a possible relationship with *Maponos,* the great son of the great mother whose cult was particularly strong in northern Britain (Ross 1967, 368). Two figures, Mabon and Modron, appear briefly in another medieval Welsh tale, 'Culhwch and Olwen'. These names suggest links with deities, but not specifically with a horse goddess. Those associations depend on narrative elements in both the First and Third Branches of the *Mabinogi,* specifically the punishment meted out to Rhiannon for supposed infanticide, the congenital pairing of the rescued child and a horse, and the humiliation endured by Rhiannon and her son.

How exactly do the elements of the tale correspond to what is known of Epona? The archaeological material does not associate the goddess with a child, and when she appears with a male, there is no indication whether he is consort or son. Elements attached to Rhiannon in the Welsh narratives are consistent with international folk-tale motifs found in a series of tales or tale episodes in which a wife is estranged from her husband because of a false accusation of infanticide (Wood 1985; 1992, 126–9; Dan 1977; Jones 1993). The elements appear in a negative context linked to loss of status and punishment. Relevant too is a reference in the Third Branch to Pryderi's punishment of wearing hammers, a detail overlooked in constructing an equine myth. Any suggestion as to mythic origin of the horse elements needs to account for the dissimilarities between the positive iconographical images and the negative overtones of the tales.

One suggestion is that myth has become misunderstood through time, although no satisfactory mechanism for this has been proposed. Rather, it is assumed that the elements which match expectations of Celtic myth are genuine survivals and anything else is a corruption or later intrusion. The equine nature of the punishment is found only in the Welsh tales, but at least one other tale in this sub-genre regularly involves the heroine's magic horse (Jones 1993, 19). Ultimately one can only speculate on how the details of Rhiannon's equine associations approximate a myth about Epona and whether she and Pryderi reflect a mother/son deity pairing. The themes of persecution, humiliation and restoration are consistent with other persecuted-heroine tales, and this suggests that the equine links could as well derive from international tale material adapted to a Welsh context as from myths known to earlier Celtic cultures.

Equally, it is difficult to read the Four Branches in the same way as a traditional tale. The narrative flow is less linear than a folk-tale. Rhiannon is fleeing an unwanted marriage, but the details are never made clear. Llwyd fab Cilcoed's role is not unlike that of the antagonist in 'Our Lady's Child' (Jones 1993, 19–20), but here too this is more by implication than action. Pwyll is more active preceding the marriage than the husband in traditional tales. Only after Rhiannon becomes a mother, which corresponds to the third section in the traditional tale (Jones 1993, 15–17), do the parallels with other persecuted heroines become obvious. Even here, the humiliation is considerably mitigated since the text makes clear that Pwyll does not reject Rhiannon and no one actually accepts her offer of a ride on her back. While Rhiannon's position carries the instability and vulnerability associated with liminality, the course of these narratives charts the process by which the outsider woman is integrated into a group. The Third Branch contrasts her husband's patience and Rhiannon's impulsive attempt to protect her son. Again the role of wife is opposed to that of mother, and again the punishment has equine overtones. The tormentor provides a possible link between the sections. By implication he caused the disappearance of Rhiannon's son and his antagonism is linked to her first marriage.

The story of a woman who becomes estranged from her husband through the machinations of a jealous antagonist is one of the commonest of tales involving a female heroine, a tale in which the female protagonist undergoes trials and endures hostility rather than accomplishing tasks and seeking competition. The change from maiden to wife, and from wife to mother, has implications not only for a woman's status but for those around her. Hence the concern over her failure to produce children, the uncertainty of her position without them and her vulnerability to slanders, such as the implication of cannibalism, which further marginalizes the outsider-wife. Her demotion to the status of beast of burden is unusual in terms of other persecuted-heroine tales and may well echo a mythic theme (Goetinck 1988; Roberts 1970), but the structure of the narrative clearly reflects and refracts the shifting relationships within the social group as marriages are formed and children produced.

Crossing Boundaries: Narratives about Real and Ghostly Horses

The horse as a real or as a ghostly figure is central to a popular supernatural-experience narrative. These narratives are usually short and deal with a supernatural event experienced at first hand or by some known person. Both context and style convey a sense of immediacy and involvement on the part of the narrator. They are set in a relatively recent time-frame and told as actual events, although literal belief is not required from narrator or audience. The supernatural intrudes into the context of the ordinary, everyday world, rather than a distant imagined Otherworld. The following translation of a printed Welsh tale (Davies 1911, 173–4) illustrates common narrative features such as personal tone, familiarity of place, location at geographical boundaries and, most importantly, the link between the horse and the supernatural intrusion.

I was going home one evening from my work from Ros y Wlad, and had to go through Rosmeheirin. That place, you know, is a terrible spot for its ghosts . . . I was near the spot where I had seen the cat, when I heard the sound of a horse coming after me. I jumped one side to make room for him to pass; but when he came opposite me he did not go forward a single pace faster than myself. When I went on slowly, he went slowly; when I went fast, he went fast. 'Good night,' said I at last, but no answer. Then I said it was a very fine night, but the gentleman on horseback did not seem to take any notice of what I said. Then thinking that he might be an Englishman (the man was speaking in Welsh), I said in English 'Good night,' but he took no notice of me still.

   By this time I was beginning to perspire and almost ready to fall down with fright, hoping to get rid of him, as I now perceived that he was the Devil himself appearing in the form of a gentleman. I could think from the sound of the saddle and the shining stirrups that the saddle was a new one. On we went along the dark narrow lane till we came to the turnpike road, when it became a little lighter, which gave me the courage to turn my eyes to see what kind of man he was. The horse looked like a soldier's horse, a splendid one, and his feet like the feet of a calf, without any shoes under them, and the feet of the gentleman in the stirrups were also like the feet of a calf. My courage failed me to look what his head and body were like. On we went till we came to the cross-road. I had heard many a time that a ghost leaves everybody there. Well, to the cross-road we came. But ah! I heard the sound of the ground as if it were going to rend, and the heavens going to fall upon my head; and in this sound I lost sight of him (the Spirit). How he went away I know not, nor the direction he went.

Examples of such tales appear in published collections, and, unlike some of the longer legendary types, are still current in Welsh folk tradition. Several examples listed in the appendix below were collected quite recently in Snowdonia and the former Merionethshire. Many more can be found on tape recordings in the archives of the Museum of Welsh Life at St Fagans. Printed tales seldom include information about the narrators or the circumstances of narration. Tape recordings at the Museum of Welsh Life and field recordings from Snowdonia and the former Merionethshire give fuller details about narrators and locations. None of the sources gives much information on the circumstances which might elicit these tales, and consequently there is no direct information on how, why and when they were told. Nor is there much information on the nature of the belief. Narrative convention presents them as true, but the degree of belief on the part of both narrator and audience can vary. Despite limitations in our knowledge of their context, these narratives share an important constant, namely the horse provides the link to the experience. Sometimes a horse senses the supernatural; sometimes the horse is an apparition. Whether real or ghostly, horses clearly serve as a contact point with the supernatural.

Not surprisingly, ghostly riders and their mounts are common where the horse is an important mode of transport. That an earthly means of transportation should become a means of transport to the Otherworld or afterlife requires no great conceptual leap. The popularity of this narrative is so far undimmed by the transition from horse to motor car. A subset within these narratives involve flesh-and-blood horses, animals on the human side of the boundary who warn of a supernatural intrusion but are not part of it. Typically a horse refuses to move although its rider is unable to see or hear a supernatural presence. Lack of contextual information limits the analysis of this material, but the boundary associations in tales with both real and ghostly horses are reinforced by colour, temporal context and by place names and motifs which locate sightings at crossroads or bridges.

The pale colour is an important feature in narratives in which the horse is part of the ghostly apparition. The white/grey spectrum is itself often associated with liminal and interstitial times and activities. This reinforces the temporal context for those narratives which occur at dusk, a period of transition, or at night. It is hardly surprising that man, a diurnal mammal, should develop symbolic systems which associate the natural with daylight and the supernatural with the dark. However, the system shows specificity as well as generality. Ghostly dogs are as common as ghostly horses, but their colour is usually black. Where the narrative involves a real horse which senses the supernatural, its colour is not a factor, although pregnant mares are both more and less susceptible to supernatural experiences depending on the narrative. When dogs occur in this type of tale, their colour is not mentioned.[4] Spatially and temporally, however, these experiences, like those involving ghostly horses, occur at crossroads, near running water or at dusk or night.

Place names can indicate natural or man-made junctures; gates, crossroads, bridges or water. Without more data about the context, it is impossible to determine whether they also indicate farm or parish boundaries. Their specificity does, however, imply a local and well-defined sense of place. This reinforces the possibility that these tales are an imaginative means of signalling a break in a boundary and a potential danger, namely the intrusion of the supernatural. By doing so, these narratives articulate a converse process which reaffirms the integrity of the boundary and, by extension, the safety of the group within it. A variety of motifs suggest that the horse is the agent which both disrupts and heals the boundary. Ghostly horses and riders warn the living, scare thieves, and allow safe passage over water. The real horse balks in the presence of the supernatural, refusing to cross a bridge or continue on a road, to protect its rider who is unaware of supernatural peril.

While none of these elements on their own would necessarily indicate liminality, the interplay between motif, place, time and context is revealing. In considering the modes by which cultures express liminality, it is perhaps best to think of elements within an inter-connecting network. Turner describes the 'unification of disparate *significantia*' in which things and actions are linked under a single formulation as one of the properties of ritual symbols (Turner 1967, 28). An element such as white colour is not automatically an indication of liminality. In early and medieval Welsh praise poetry, for instance, pale colour in a horse might serve to emphasize the high status of the warriors (Ryan 1993, 85–7). So too in 'The Triads of the Horses', the preternatural and supernatural characteristics of the horses, which come in many colours, provide a conterpoint to their owners.

Conclusion

The suggestions put forward do not preclude the possibility that some of this material may have resonances with earlier Celtic traditions, nor do they overcome the range in genre and time-span. However, identifying some of the formal similarities among traditions about horses in Welsh folklore presents another perspective, one which is compatible with historical analysis but which highlights the complex functions of these traditions and suggests that the formal similarities may indicate similar thematic preoccupations. Narratives about spectral horses and horses which see ghosts are often localized at particular junctures in the physical environment. Some of the customs and the tales are embedded in temporal contexts such as Christmas and dusk, or geographic ones such as the bridge and the crossroads. Significant too is the ease with which pragmatic activities (the horse as an actual means of transport) can take on a metaphysical or metaphorical dimension (a means of transport between natural and supernatural fields of experience). Rhiannon's punishment is associated with her difficulties in maintaining her status as wife and mother at her husband's court. All of them involve temporal, geographical or social transition, in very different contexts of custom, oral narrative and literary tale.

Appendix: Personal Experience Narratives: Ghostly Horse/Horse Sees Ghost

The following list outlines examples of narratives in which horses appear in connection with supernatural events. The motifs follow the standard citations in Stith Thompson's *Motif-Index of Folk-Literature* (1932–6). They provide a summary of the motifs most commonly found in these narratives and are given in order to facilitate comparisons with related traditions.

The examples drawn from printed sources are given a bibliographical reference and a location. Material taken from the archives of the Museum of Welsh Life is referred to by the number of the tape and the location only, although full information about informants is held at the Museum. The examples are listed by pre-1975 county names as this was the method used in the printed sources and in field collecting.

Ghost as man on a white horse

The outcome varies, but the dominant element is the appearance of ghost and pale horse, often at a bridge or crossroads.

Motifs
E423.1.3.4 Revenant as white horse. E581.2 Ghost rides horse. E363 Ghost returns to aid living. E 293.1 Ghost scares thief, prevents theft. E282 Ghost haunts castle. E402.2.3 Hoofbeats of ghost horse. D1786 Magic power at crossroads. E332.1* Ghost appears at bridge.

Sources
Breconshire: Tape 5010 (Llangamarch).
Caernarfonshire: Huws 1976, 281 (Nantlle); Tape 1975 (Llithfaen); Tape 2000 (Aberdaron); Tape 3911 (Capel Curig).
Cardiganshire: Davies 1911, 173–4 (Rhosmeheirin).
Denbighshire: Jones 1930, 47 (Cerrigydrudion) swine appear in this variant; Tape 2310 (Pentrefoelas).
Glamorgan: Trevelyan 1909, 182–3 (Dyffryn Golych).
Merionethshire: Tape 3175 (Llanymawddwy); Tape 3179 (Llanuwchllyn).
Pembrokeshire: Tapes 2904, 4927 (Trefdraeth); Tape 3179 (Cas-mael).

Ghost as horse

The ghostly horse appears on its own in this narrative. Otherwise it is similar to the previous one in that the appearance of the ghost usually acts as warning or protection.

Motifs
E423.1.3 Revenant as horse. E423.6 Revenant as centaur. E423.1.3.4 Revenant as white horse. E423.1.3.2 Revenant as mare. E402.2.3 Hoofbeats of ghost horse.

Sources
Caernarfonshire: Huws 1976, 266, 298 (Nant y Betws), 292 (Nantlle); Tape 3553 (Pen-y-groes); Tape 4363 (Betws Garmon).
Cardiganshire: Tape 2580 (Rhydlewis).

Denbighshire: Tape 2760 (Rhosllannerchrugog) centaur.
Merionethshire: Gwyn 1983, 157 (Cwm Abergeirw); Tape 2452 (Cynllwyd).
Pembrokeshire: Tape 1883 (Cwm Gwaun); Tapes 2883, 2904, 2906 (Trefdraeth).

Animals sense presence of ghost

Like many personal-experience narratives, this does not follow a regular pattern. However, the core is always the same – a situation in which the supernatural presence is perceived by an animal and not by a human being. This relates to a widespread belief that animals are more sensitive to the supernatural (and, in particular, animals such as horses, cats and dogs, which are closest to man). This belief provides a frame situation for such tales.

Motifs
E421.1.1 Ghost visible to one person alone. E421.1.2 Ghost visible to horses alone. E276 Ghost haunts tree. E421.1.7* Mare cannot see ghost. E421.1.2(b)* Horse sees ghost and is unable to proceed on way. E267 Ghost in tree. D1786 Magic power at crossroads. E332.1(a)* Ghost appears at bridge. E422.4.4 Revenant in female dress. D1524.5 River crossed by means of charm.

Sources
Breconshire: Tape 2210 (Penderyn).
Caernarfonshire: Huws 1976, 284 (Nantlle); Tape 1976 (Llithfaen) two examples; Tape 1980 (Nefyn); Tape 1999 (Aberdaron); Tape 3552 (Rhoslan).
Cardiganshire: Jones 1896, 283–4 (Penrhyn-coch); Tape 2580 (Glynarthen); Tape 2918 (Bronnant).
Merionethshire: Gwyn 1983, 140 (Gwerhefin), 164 (Ceunant y Wenallt), 165 (Wenallt-fach Cwm-main); Tape 2447 (Llangywer); Tape 2453 (Llanuwchllyn); Tape 2978 (Y Bala); Tape 3179 (Parc); Tape 3271, 3274 (Cwmtirymynech); Tape 4761 (Aberllefenni); Tape 6466 (Parc).
Montgomeryshire: Davies 1911, 197 (Machynlleth); Tape 3130 (Llangadfan).
Pembrokeshire: Tape 2885, 4927 (Trefdraeth).

Notes

[1] The Mari Lwyd has received comparatively little attention considering the long-standing fascination with mumming activity in Great Britain. Trefor Owen (1959, 48–59) and Iorwerth Peate (1943) have concentrated on the historical and social context of the custom, but there is only one full-length

study of the Mari Lwyd and that within the wider context of wassailing traditions of Wales (Ifans 1983). The form of the Mari Lwyd custom is agonistic with one side trying to best the other in verse, but it lacks the resurrection element which has been the focus of so much mumming criticism.

[2] A number of horse-head burials have been discovered in Wales. Although it is unlikely that they represent a survival from an early period, they do suggest links to boundary and rite-of-passage rituals: see Lloyd 1969, Brown 1966. (On ancient Celtic horse burials, see above, p. 4.)

[3] These tales were originally identified in the Aarne–Thompson Index (1964). The titles given there have been used by subsequent researchers almost as a convention even when the title does not always fit the exact details of the tale. The twenty-two tale-types included in the Innocent Persecuted Heroine sub-genre are listed by Jones (1993, 17–20), who explains their links with type/motif tale analysis and with structural tale analysis.

[4] Horses and dogs are the most common animals who sense supernatural beings and communicate their presence to man, and it is worth noting that these animals are closely associated with man in the performance of many important cultural activities.

References

Aarne/Thompson. 1964. Antti Aarne, *The Types of the Folktale: A Classification and Bibliography*, tr. and enlarged by Stith Thompson, 2nd revision (Helsinki, Folklore Fellows Communications, no. 184).

Bacchilega, Cristina. 1993. 'An Introduction to the "Innocent Persecuted Heroine" Fairy Tale' in Bacchilega and Jones 1993, 1–12.

Bacchilega, Cristina and Jones, Steven Swann (eds.). 1993. *Perspectives on the Innocent Persecuted Heroine in Fairy Tales, Western Folklore*, 52, 1.

Bawcutt, Priscilla. 1986. 'Dunbar's Christmas Carol' in *Proceedings of the Fourth International Conference on Scottish Language and Literature Medieval and Renaissance,* ed. Dietrich Strauss and Horst W. Drescher (Frankfurt am Main, Peter Lang), 381–92.

Bennett, Gillian. 1994. 'Geologists and Folklorists: Cultural Evolution and "The Science of Folklore" ', *Folklore*, 105, 25–38.

Boyes, Georgina. 1988. 'Cultural Survivals Theory and Traditional Customs: An Examination of the Effects of Privileging on the Form and Perception of some English Calendar Customs', *Folklife*, 26, 5–11.

Bromwich, Rachel. 1961. 'Celtic Dynastic Themes and the Breton Lays', *Études Celtiques*, 9, 439–74.

Bronner, Simon J. 1984. 'The Early Movements of Anthropology and their Folkloristic Relationships', *Folklore*, 95, 57–73.

Brown, M. S. 1966. 'Buried Horse Skulls in a Welsh House', *Folklore*, 77, 65–6.

Brown, Theo. 1993. 'Tom Pearce's Grey Mare: A Boundary Image' in *Boundaries and Thresholds: Papers from a Colloquium of The Katharine Briggs Club*, ed. Hilda Ellis Davidson (Stroud, The Thimble Press), 76–83.

Cawte, E. C. 1993. 'It's an Ancient Custom – But How Ancient?' in *Aspects of British Calendar Customs*, ed. Theresa Buckland and Juliette Wood (Sheffield Academic Press), 37–56.

Cressy, David. 1989. *Bonfires and Bells: National Memory and the Protestant Calendar in Elizabethan and Stuart England* (London, Weidenfeld & Nicolson).

Dan, Ilana. 1977. 'The Innocent Persecuted Heroine: An attempt at a Model for the Surface Level of the Narrative Structure of the Female Fairy Tale' in *Patterns in Oral Literature*, ed. Heda Jason and Dimitri Segal (The Hague, Mouton), 13–30.

Davies, J. Ceredig. 1911. *Folk-Lore of West and Mid-Wales* (Aberystwyth; reprint Llanerch Publishers, 1992).

Dorson, Richard M. 1968. *The British Folklorists: A History* (London, Routledge & Kegan Paul).

Fontenrose, Joseph. 1966. *The Ritual Theory of Myth* (Berkeley, University of California Press).

Gimbutas, Marija A. 1982. *The Goddesses and Gods of Old Europe, 6500–3500 BC: Myths and Cult Images* (London, Thames & Hudson).

Goetinck, Glenys. 1988. '*Pedair Cainc y Mabinogi*: Yr Awdur a'i Bwrpas', *Llên Cymru*, 15, 249–69.

Gose, Elliott B. 1985. *The World of the Irish Wondertale: An Introduction to the Study of Fairy Tales* (University of Toronto Press).

Gruffydd, W. J. 1953. *Rhiannon: An Inquiry into the Origins of the First and Third Branches of the Mabinogi* (Cardiff, University of Wales Press).

Gwyn, Rhydian. 1983. 'Chwedlau lleol Penllyn a phlwyf Llanfachreth' (University of Wales MA thesis).

Harris, Marvin. 1968. *The Rise of Anthropological Theory: A History of Theories of Culture* (London, Routledge & Kegan Paul).

Hoggan, Frances. 1893. 'Notes on Welsh Folk-Lore', *Folklore*, 4, 122–3.

Hutton, Ronald. 1991. *The Pagan Religions of the Ancient British Isles* (Oxford, Basil Blackwell).

Hutton, Ronald. 1994. *The Rise and Fall of Merry England: The Ritual Year 1400–1700* (Oxford and New York, Oxford University Press).

Huws, John Owen. 1976. 'Straeon gwerin ardal Eryri' (University of Wales MA thesis).

Ifans, Rhiannon. 1983. *Sêrs a Rybana: Astudiaeth o'r Canu Gwasael* (Llandysul, Gomer Press).

Jackson, Kenneth Hurlstone. 1961. *The International Popular Tale and Early Welsh Tradition* (Cardiff, University of Wales Press).

Jason, Heda. 1982. 'The Fairytale of the Active Heroine: An Outline for

Discussion' in *Le Conte. Pourquoi? Comment? Folktales . . . Why and How?*, ed. G. Claame-Griaule *et al.* (Jerusalem, Israel Ethnographic Society), 1–18.

Jones, David. 1888. 'The Mari Lwyd: A Twelfth Night Custom', *Archaeologia Cambrensis*, 389–94.

Jones, R. Gwmryn. 1896. 'Ofergoelion Tafarn Magl', *Cymru*, 11, 283–5.

Jones, Steven Swann. 1993. 'The Innocent Persecuted Heroine Genre: An Analysis of its Structure and Themes' in Bacchilega and Jones 1993, 13–41.

Jones, T. Gwynn. 1930. *Welsh Folklore and Folk-Custom* (London, Methuen; reprint Cambridge, D. S. Brewer, 1979).

Lloyd, J. D. K. 1969. 'A Discovery of Horses' Skulls at Gunley', *The Montgomershire Collections*, 61, 131–5.

Mac Cana, Proinsias. 1970. *Celtic Mythology* (London, Hamlyn).

Newall, Venetia. 1974. 'The Allendale Fire Festival in Relation to its Contemporary Social Setting', *Folklore*, 85, 93–103.

Nicolaisen, W. F. H. 1993. 'Why Tell Stories about Innocent, Persecuted Heroines?' in Bacchilega and Jones 1993, 61–71.

Owen, Morfydd E. 1980. 'Shame and Reparation: Woman's Place in the Kin' in *The Welsh Law of Women: Studies presented to Professor Daniel A. Binchy on his Eightieth Birthday*, ed. Dafydd Jenkins and Morfydd E. Owen (Cardiff, University of Wales Press), 40–68.

Owen, Trefor M. 1959. *Welsh Folk Customs* (Cardiff, University of Wales Press).

Peate, Iorwerth C. 1943. 'Mari Lwyd: A Suggested Explanation', *Man: A Record of Anthropological Science*, 43, 53–8.

Perco, Daniela. 1993. 'Female Initiation in Northern Italian Versions of "Cinderella" ' in Bacchilega and Jones 1993, 73–84.

Raine, Kathleen. 1977. Foreword to W. Y. Evans Wentz, *The Fairy-Faith in Celtic Countries* (Buckingham, Colin Smythe).

Rees, Alwyn and Rees, Brinley. 1961. *Celtic Heritage: Ancient Tradition in Ireland and Wales* (London, Thames & Hudson).

Roberts, Brynley F. 1970. 'Penyd Rhiannon', *Bulletin of the Board of Celtic Studies*, 23, 325–7.

Röhrich, Lutz. 1991. *Folktales and Reality*, tr. Peter Tokofsky (Bloomington and Indianapolis, Indiana University Press).

Ross, Anne. 1967. *Pagan Celtic Britain: Studies in Iconography and Tradition* (London, Routledge & Kegan Paul).

Ryan, Jane. 1993. 'The Study of Horses in Early and Medieval Welsh Literature, *c.* 600–*c.* 1300 A.D.' (University of Wales M.Phil. thesis).

Sikes, Wirt. 1880. *British Goblins: Welsh Folk-lore, Fairy Mythology, Legends and Traditions* (London).

Sjoestedt, Marie-Louise. 1949. *Gods and Heroes of the Celts*, tr. Myles Dillon (London, Methuen & Co.).

Spence, Lewis. 1921. *An Introduction to Mythology* (London, George G. Harrap; reprint London, Senate, 1994).

Tambiah, Stanley Jeyaraja. 1990. *Magic, Science, Religion, and the Scope of Rationality* (Cambridge University Press).

Thompson, Stith. 1932–6. *Motif-Index of Folk-Literature* (Helsinki, Folklore Fellows Communications), 106–9, 116–17.

Trevelyan, Marie. 1909. *Folk-Lore and Folk-Stories of Wales* (London, Elliott Stock).

Turner, Victor. 1967. *The Forest of Symbols: Aspects of Ndembu Ritual* (Ithaca and London, Cornell University Press).

Valente, Roberta L. 1988. 'Gwydion and Aranrhod: Crossing the Borders of Gender in *Math*', *Bulletin of the Board of Celtic Studies*, 35, 1–9.

Vickery, John B. 1973. *The Literary Impact of 'The Golden Bough'* (Princeton University Press).

Wood, Juliette. 1985. 'The Calumniated Wife in Medieval Welsh Literature', *Cambridge Medieval Celtic Studies*, 10, 25–38.

Wood, Juliette. 1992. 'Celtic Goddesses: Myths and Mythology' in *The Feminist Companion to Mythology*, ed. Carolyne Larrington (London, Pandora) 118–36.

Zipes, Jack. 1994. *Fairy Tale as Myth: Myth as Fairy Tale* (Lexington, University Press of Kentucky).

Index